4

$\mathcal{W}$ORLDWIDE $\mathcal{A}$RCHAEOLOGY $\mathcal{S}$ERIES 4

THEORETICAL ROMAN ARCHAEOLOGY:
FIRST CONFERENCE PROCEEDINGS

$\mathcal{W}$ORLDWIDE $\mathcal{A}$RCHAEOLOGY $\mathcal{S}$ERIES   SERIES EDITOR: ROSS SAMSON

edited by
ELEANOR
SCOTT

THEORETICAL ROMAN ARCHAEOLOGY:
FIRST CONFERENCE PROCEEDINGS

Avebury
Aldershot · Brookfield USA · Hong Kong · Singapore · Sydney

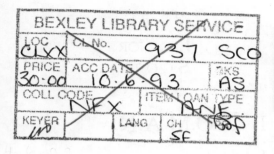
© 1993 Individual authors

Avebury
Ashgate Publishing Ltd
Gower House, Croft Road
Aldershot
Hampshire GU11 3HR
Great Britain

Ashgate Publishing Company
Old Post Road
Brookfield
Vermont 05036
USA

A CIP catalogue record for this book is available from the British Library and the US Library of Congress.

ISBN 1 85628 703 3

Set in New Baskerville by ARCHAEOLOGICAL SERVICES AND PUBLISHING, 197 Great Western Rd, Glasgow G4 9EB, Great Britain

and printed and bound in Great Britain by Athenaeum Press Ltd, Newcastle upon Tyne.

CONTENTS

List of Figures

Cover: impression of the Venus mosaic from Rudston villa, Yorkshire, by Robert Scott

CONTRIBUTORS: SHORT BIOGRAPHIES

SUSAN ALCOCK

Dr Susan Alcock is Assistant Professor in Classical Studies at the University of Michigan, and was previously Lecturer in Archaeology and Classics at the University of Reading. She took her PhD at Cambridge University in 1989 with a thesis examining social and economic change in Greece following the Roman conquest. Her primary research interests include the regional field survey, landscape archaeology and problems of ritual geography, especially in the context of the Hellenistic and Roman East.

SIMON CLARKE

Simon Clarke obtained his first degree from the Department of Archaeological Sciences, the University of Bradford; he is there currently completing his PhD entitled A Regional Archaeological Study of the Severn-Cotswolds Region from the Iron Age to the Early Saxon Periods. He has published articles on Romano-British rural and urban settlement.

KENNETH RAINSBURY DARK

Kenneth Rainsbury Dark is based at Sidney Sussex College, Cambridge and teaches at the University of Cambridge. He is founder and editor of the *Journal of Theoretical Archaeology*, now produced and distributed by Oxbow Books. He is a regular contributor to TAG (the Theoretical Archaeology Group Conference).

PETER VAN DOMMELEN

Peter van Dommelen has studied archaeology and classics at Leiden University (Holland) where he specialised in spatial and landscape archaeology as well as in Italian archaeology. His interest in social and theoretical issues was further developed at the Department of Anthropology at UCL, London. Currently he is involved in a survey project of the Department of Archaeology at Leiden University examining long term developments in socio-political organisation in Sardinia.

KEVIN GREENE

Kevin Greene lectures on the archaeology of the Roman and early medieval periods at the University of Newcastle upon Tyne. His research into ceramics has led to a broader interest in the Roman economy as a whole, and technology in particular.

RICHARD HINGLEY

Dr Richard Hingley is an Inspector of Ancient Monuments for Historic Scotland, Edinburgh. He read archaeology at the University of Durham and undertook research at the University of Southampton. He has published works concerning the social analysis of Iron Age and Romano-British settlements and has an interest in the study of artefacts, ritual, and archaeology.

KURT HUNTER-MANN

Kurt Hunter-Mann is a Field Officer with the York Archaeological Trust. A graduate from the University of Lancaster in 1981, he has worked on excavation and post-excavation projects throughout Britain. He is particularly interested in archaeological theory, and the archaeology of Britain in the first millenium AD. Despite being a 'dirt' archaeologist, he does nevertheless try to put some thought into his work from time to time. . . .

ROB POULTON

Rob Poulton is the manager of the Surrey County Archaeological Unit and has spent most of his archaeological career in Surrey, working on sites of most types and periods as well as carrying out Sites and Monuments Record and related work.

RICHARD REECE

Richard Reece trained as a Biochemist and started teaching Chemistry in 1961. He is still teaching, but now Archaeology, and insists that, unlike other scientists who have become interested in archaeology, he still works scientifically. He amasses facts on Roman coins throughout the Roman Empire and has beautiful thoughts about Roman Britain.

ROBERT RIPPENGAL

Rob Rippengal studied Archaeology & Anthropology at St Catherine's College Cambridge, graduating in 1988. He then took an MA in Archaeology at the Institute of Archaeology, University College London, and returned to Cambridge to take up research towards a PhD on social aspects of life in rural Roman Britain.

ELEANOR SCOTT

Eleanor Scott currently holds a research and teaching post at the University of Leicester. She obtained a BA in Archaeology from the University of Newcastle upon Tyne; her PhD (1988) examined Romano-British villas using traditional and structuralist approaches. Research interests include: villas, farms and farming in the Roman Empire; field survey in the Middle East; and gender theory in archaeology and contemporary society. She has worked for the University of Newcastle upon Tyne and the Royal Commission on the Historical Monuments of England, and she founded the TRAC series and organised the first conference.

SARAH SCOTT

Sarah Scott received her degree in Archaeology from the University of Leicester in 1989. Since this time she has been a research student in the Institute of Social and Cultural Anthropology at the University of Oxford, holding a British Academy Studentship and a Linacre College Research Scholarship. Her thesis is concerned with the social significance of Romano-British villa architecture and mosaics.

PATRICIA SOUTHERN

Patricia Southern BA, MA, MPhil, ALA has worked as a professional librarian for thousands of years before taking her current post in the Department of Archaeology of the University of Newcastle upon Tyne. She has published various papers and is joint author of a book on the Roman Cavalry (1992).

ACKNOWLEDGEMENTS

I would like to thank David Rhodes, Robert Scott, Sandra Hooper, Kevin Greene and Mark Bowden for their help with preparation of this volume. Craig Cessford and Graeme Stobbs were discreet floor managers at the conference, and Aiden Glendinning assisted with registration. The papers of John Casey and Richard Reece were read in absentia by Jon Coulston and Ross Samson, who also chaired sessions. My special thanks go to Ian Hodder for chairing the Saturday afternoon session. For their ideas, support and practical help I would also like to thank John Chapman, Nick Hodgson, Frances Mawer, Pat Southern, Richard Reece and Clive Waddington. For playing host to the conference and reception I thank the Museum of Antiquities of Newcastle upon Tyne and the Department of Archaeology of the University of Newcastle upon Tyne, and I am indebted to the staff of the Computing Department. I am grateful especially to the TRAC 91 delegates, and to those who originally contributed papers: Sue Alcock, Geoff Carter, John Casey, Simon Clarke, Jim Crow, Peter van Dommelen, Kevin Greene, Karen Griffiths, Richard Hingley, Kurt Hunter-Mann, Martin Jones, Rick Jones, Martin Millett, Richard Reece, Rob Rippengal, Sarah Scott, Pat Southern and Greg Woolf. For inspiration and a number of colossal gin and tonics I can only offer my enduring gratitude to Brian Boyd.

BRIDGING THE DIVIDE: A COMMENTARY ON THEORETICAL ROMAN ARCHAEOLOGY

Ian Hodder

Archaeology incorporates and attempts to integrate both sides of the science/humanities, anthropology/history divide. The division is perhaps most clearly expressed in the differences between prehistoric archaeology, which has increasingly attempted to use a philosophy modelled on the natural sciences and to be anthropological, and classical and medieval archaeology which may have embraced scientific techniques but which have been less happy to endorse a natural science epistemology. The division between prehistory and historical archaeology (Renfrew 1980) is also associated with differences in the scale and nature of theoretical debate. The emphasis on theoretical discussion in prehistoric archaeology is only recently becoming evident in historical archaeology.

It is certainly the case that the introduction of theoretical debate in Britain and North America is associated with processual archaeology. In contrast to empiricism according to which it is thought necessary to stay close to the facts, which will 'speak for themselves' if described in adequate detail, the positivism of processual archaeology recognises the theory-laden nature of 'facts', and tries to avoid bias by the separation of theory and data. Theory construction becomes self-conscious. The stage is thus set for theoretical debate in archaeology and for fora such as TAG (the annual Theoretical Archaeology Group conference). But this theoretical debate has been mainly associated with prehistoric archaeology, and not so much with Roman, classical or other branches of historical archaeology.

I would argue that if there is a culprit here it is the one- sided embracing of anthropology and science by Anglo-American archaeology in the 1960s and 1970s. The embrace itself already had a morbid character at its inception, since anthropology and science as perceived by archaeologists were undergoing demise at that time. Archaeologists saw anthropology as generalising, cross-cultural and ahistorical, and they saw science as deductive positivism. But in fact anthropology was increasingly incorporating history (e.g. Said 1978, Sahlins 1981) while the critique of positivism was well underway (e.g. Kuhn 1970, Feyerabend 1975). Archaeology thus assumed an outmoded, law-and-order, non-reflexive, and ahistorical anthropology and adopted a disappearing, objective, universal and neutral science. The form of processual archaeology which resulted was thus difficult to integrate with historical archaeologies, which have always been committed to history and specific interpretation. So while theoretical discussion burgeoned in prehistoric archaeology, it remained slight in historical archaeology.

Processual archaeology of course has had its impact in historical archaeology, but theoretical discussion in historical archaeology has tended to increase only recently (e.g. Smith 1978, Burnham and Johnson 1979, Rahtz 1980, Greene 1986, Reece 1987, Hingley 1989, Millett 1990). This tardiness may be due to more than the ahistorical positivism of processual archaeology. It may also derive from the fact that classical and medieval archaeology are more closely tied to larger disciplinary frameworks (classics and history) than is prehistoric archaeology. The latter has, for institutional reasons, perhaps more room to manoeuvre than the disciplinary giants from which it has largely broken free. The smaller and more independent prehistoric archaeology can perhaps more easily incorporate and discuss new theoretical ideas.

Roman archaeologists may have been starved of substantial theoretical debate, but the papers in this volume show an enormous thirst for new ideas and a delight in the avenues that have recently been discovered. Despite Reece's (chapter 4) caution, most contributors seem to accept the need for theory and to be attracted by the new horizons that theoretical debate opens up in our interpretations of the past. Such debate need not involve moving very far beyond the bounds of classical scholarship as Simon Clarke's (chapter 6) reference to Moses Finley testifies. And very often much can be done by simply taking a fresh and critical look at the stereotypes which we have come to take for granted in our discussions of, for example, Roman technology (as Greene shows in chapter 5). At other times, the excitement and sense of freshness found in these papers derive from the application of theory from outside, as in Hunter-Mann's (chapter

7) use of a Marxist perspective to take a refreshing look at the old chestnut of the end of Roman Britain.

The rise of theoretical debate in historical archaeology, and conferences such as a Roman TAG, often show characteristics which might be termed post-processual (e.g. Carver 1990, Leone and Potter 1989, Johnson 1989). In fact, I would argue (Hodder 1992) that there has been so much movement and accommodation of each other's positions by both processual and post-processual archaeologists that it is no longer helpful to maintain the processual/post-processual distinction. Rather, archaeological theory is incorporating a diversity of debate which mirrors that in social theory more generally. One aspect of that debate which is of relevance for this volume, and for the growth of theory in Roman archaeology, is the distinction between explanation and interpretation. To some degree or other, all the authors in this volume are trying not only to explain but also to interpret.

The term 'explanation' has tended to be used in archaeology with reference to the search for causality. In addition, the causal relationships invoked in any particular case are expected to be instances of more general cross-cultural regularities. The variables leading to a particular outcome are thought to be universally identifiable. Thus, one might argue from this position that the French Revolution or the Roman invasion of Europe north of the Alps are to be explained by reference to cross-cultural knowledge about the factors that lead to revolutions and military invasions in general. The explanatory task is to identify the factors (population increase, economic disarray and so on) in the particular case which can be shown to be causal cross-culturally.

Interpretive positions tend to accept the value of such understanding but only as identifying certain necessary *conditions* for revolution or military invasion. But there are perhaps three further arms to an interpretation. The first is that the emphasis on causal variables is deemed to be inadequate because it does not allow for the intentionality of social agents. Population increase does not lead to the need for invasion on its own - thinking people are involved, monitoring population, determining the wisdom of invasion, competing for power and so on. In other words, variables do not affect variables in simple chains. Rather, the variables are monitored and evaluated by sentient agents. An adequate interpretation needs to take into account intentionality and meaning from the actors' points of view.

The second direction in which interpretation takes us is towards the notion that different people in society perceive and act on the world from different and often conflicting positions. This emphasis on situated multivocality is also extended to archaeology itself. Different people read and write the past differently. Some alternative to an objective past studied by neutral scientists is needed, and various options have been suggested in the recent theoretical debate in archaeology. My own view (Hodder 1992) is that it is necessary to avoid an extreme relativism. The past is objectively patterned and this patterning contributes to our subjectively constituted understanding of it. We may all come to different interpretations, in both the past and the present, but our interpretations are informed and even transformed by the encounter with patterned data.

The third strand of an interpretive approach is that if we expect the first and second points, then there is always some uncertainty in the relationship between actor or analyst and the material world. We can never know with certainty how people will act or write since the act or the writing are themselves interpretations - they involve interpreting the relationship between the general and the particular. Acting or writing involve deciding whether a particular case is an example of a general relationship, deciding whether other people understand the case in similar ways, trying to decode the intention behind the act and so on. There is always a creative and uncertain moment in any act of interpretation, and some degree of judgement is always involved.

Aspects of these three points are evident in all the chapters in this volume, indicating the commitment to interpretation as opposed to explanation, as befits a branch of archaeology closely allied with history. For example, Rippengal (chapter 8) makes use of Bourdieu's theory of action to suggest new ways of looking at villa spatial organisation. He argues that villa space was actively used by social divisions. Alcock (chapter 13) suggests that the geography of cult was actively manipulated in Greece to serve the interests of Roman imperial power. S. Scott (chapter 9) recognises that different people come to different interpretations, and in her consideration of mosaics argues for an approach that includes the viewpoint of the interpreter, situated within an active social context.

If these papers show the need to consider intentional human agents in the past, they also acknowledge that we need to be critical of the way our interpretations are situated in the present. Perhaps particularly in classical scholarship there is a need to battle against certain entrenched images and against the assumptions which underlie them. As Scott implies (chapters 1 and 2) a discourse has grown up about what can be said about Roman archaeology (military campaigns, politics, villas etc.) and what cannot. But now the unspoken, such as issues of gender, resistance and ideology are being increasingly debated. Hingley (chapter 3) argues that we need to criticise the benign 'civilising' view of the Roman empire which itself derives from the model of the British empire. It may even be the case that if we follow the line taken by Hunter-Mann (chapter 7) the very notion of a 'Roman period' in a 'Roman Britain' may come under scrutiny. Perhaps even the appellation 'Roman' is not 'politically correct' and we should more properly focus on the challenges provided to those living in Britain under imperial rule. The term 'Roman' would have had different meanings to different groups involved. The term should not automatically imply subordination to a greater 'civilising' power.

But perhaps the clearest message from the papers in this volume is that we need not fight shy of specific historical interpretation. An adequate account is one that uses generalisation, but creatively in the understanding of a particular case. To use Eleanor Scott's terminology (chapter 2) we should not simply 'download' the general theory of prehistoric archaeology onto Roman archaeology. The papers in this volume show ample evidence of a sensitivity to the specific nature of 'Roman' historical problems. Even van Dommelen (chapter 14) who uses a processualist method to characterise Roman rural settlement in Italy, accepts the need to conduct detailed contextual study in order to understand the specific socio-economic organisation involving slaves and peasants. Clarke (chapter 6) uses general theory about types of of urbanism to make a specific interpretation of the difference between *civitas* capitals and the more commercial walled small towns. Poulton and Scott (chapter 10) use a contextual approach to argue that the specific meanings associated with the use and deposition of pewter were ritual in nature. Dark (chapter 11) attempts to understand Romano-British re-use of prehistoric monuments in specifically Romano-British terms, although he uses general theory well in arguing that the continuity of use does not imply a continuity in religion but rather a superstition linked to burial.

In summary, I would argue that these papers, invigorating in their freshness of approach and in their thirst for new ideas and perspectives, are also mature in that they accept the need to go beyond explanation to interpretation. They are not afraid to link the study of the general to an understanding of the specific. They are not afraid to use the contextual richness and the historical specifity of their data to contribute to wider debates. They accept that material culture is actively and meaningfully constituted and that our interpretations in the present are open for critical evaluation and re-interpretation by different interest groups.

Indeed, a theoretically informed debate in Roman archaeology can only contribute to an understanding of how to interpret in other branches of archaeology, and in particular in prehistoric archaeology. Within anthropological archaeology it became common practice to 'test' theories in ethnographic contexts. Ethnoarchaeology was the handmaiden of processual archaeology. But the timeless 'snap-shot' provided by most ethnography seems less relevant in an archaeology committed to historical and contextual depth. Within the current debate in archaeology it is history and historical archaeology which become more appropriate handmaidens. It is only an historical context which can contribute to prehistoric archaeology's demand for the 'testing' of theories about agency, the negotiation of contested meanings, the relationship between the general and the historically specific.

I have so far painted a rosy picture in which Roman archaeology is opened up by vigorous theoretical discussion and begins to be a source for interpretive solutions for other parts of the discipline which deal with less complete information. As all of archaeology becomes more accepting of history and of the critique of positivism, the divide between prehistoric and historic archaeology can begin to be bridged. The papers in this volume contribute to this bridging process as they debate theory which transcends parochial interests and provides a common currency within archaeological and social theory discussion.

But there may need to be some caution in the slide towards extensive theoretical debate. While theoretical debate may help the bridging of the divide, its very generality takes us away from the data. This is in many ways a productive move, leading to broader perspectives. But there is a danger that so much emphasis is placed on theory, and the theory is so cut free from data, that theory becomes dogma. We would be back then with entrenched and blinkered scholarship tied to a politics of the present. Indeed recent formulations of archaeological theory see the data only as 'networks of resistances' (Shanks and Tilley 1987). The data simply resist while all the action comes from theory. Within this view, archaeological data cannot play an active role in the present. The data simply resist our vested interests and we do not come to a new understanding of ourselves in the interpretation of data.

I would argue, on the other hand, that the objectively patterned archaeological remains, as uncovered by archaeologists, provide an experience of the world from which we can learn and in which we transform our expectations. But this learning process is only possible in the contextualising of theory in data – that is in the process of interpreting the general in relation to the particular. Pure theoretical discussion or the imposition of pre-formed theory on a scarcely resisting data may initially appear to open horizons for Roman archaeology. But in the longer run, theoretical discussion can itself become closed, leading to entrenched positions and narrow vistas. The potential dogmatism of theory needs to be confronted with the experience of other worlds, theory needs to be sensitive to particularity and to practice, explanation needs to be extended to include interpretation, scientific anthropology to be allied with the understanding of history.

Bibliography

Burnham, B. and H. Johnson (eds.) 1979 *Invasion and Response*. Oxford; British Archaeological Reports.

Carver, M. 1990 'Digging for data: archaeological approaches to data definition, acquisition and analysis' In R. Francovich and D. Manacorda (eds.).

Feyerabend, P. 1975 *Against Method*. London; NLB.

Francovich R. and D. Manacorda 1990 (eds) *Lo scavo archeologico: dalla diagnosi all'edizione*. Florence.

Greene, K. 1986 *The Archaeology of the Roman Economy*. London; Batsford.

Hodder, I. 1992 *Theory and Practice in Archaeology*. London; Routledge.

Johnson, M. 1989 'Conceptions of agency in archaeological representation' *Journal of Anthropological Archaeology* 8, 189–212.

Kuhn, T. S. 1970 *The Structure of Scientific Revolutions*. Chicago; University of Chicago Press, (2nd edition).

Leone, M. and P. Potter 1989 *The Recovery of Meaning*. Washington.

Millett, M. 1990 *The Romanisation of Roman Britain*. London.

Rahtz, P. 1980 'The new medieval archaeology' Inaugural lecture, University of York.

Reece, R. 1987 *My Roman Britain*. privately circulated.

Renfrew, C. 1980 'The great tradition versus the great divide: archaeology as anthropology?' *American Journal of Archaeology* 84, 287–98.

Sahlins, M. 1981 *Historical Metaphors and Mythical Realities*. Ann Arbor; University of Michigan Press.

Said, E. 1978 *Orientalism*. Harmondsworth; Penguin Books.

Shanks, M. and C. Tilley 1987 *Reconstructing Archaeology* Cambridge; Cambridge University Press.

Smith, J. T. 1978 'Villas as a key to social structure.' In M. Todd (ed.).

Todd, M. 1978 (ed.) *Studies in the Romano-British Villa*. Leicester; Leicester University Press.

Introduction: TRAC (Theoretical Roman Archaeology Conference) 1991

Eleanor Scott

The objectives and the content of the Theoretical Roman Archaeology Conference 1991 are described, and dissatisfaction is expressed with the rhetoric and storyboard archaeology of Romanists as a means of explaining the past. Some editorial comments on the production of the volume are made.

This volume has its origins in the Theoretical Roman Archaeology Conference (TRAC 91) held in the Department of Archaeology of the University of Newcastle upon Tyne during the weekend 23–24 March 1991.

The aim of this volume is to reproduce and expand upon the issues presented and discussed at the conference. TRAC was designed to be a structured but essentially egalitarian arena for discussion of the introduction and operation of theory in Roman archaeology. It would also be true to say that I organised TRAC because I wanted to attend it. The papers addressed a number of themes and demonstrated inextricable links between them all. The underlying concept of 'Romanisation' was ever-present, and with it was a clear understanding that this is more than just a useful term: it is a process which must be described and defined. There were also discussions of the Roman economy and technology and a heartening number of papers on the social and ideological configurations of space.

Theory and Roman archaeology are not concepts normally found linked together in people's minds, and their protagonists tend to sit in different camps, a situation applauded and promoted by many establishment Romanist figures. The reasons for and implications of this somewhat reactionary stance were explored in a series of research seminars at the University of Newcastle upon Tyne in the mid-1980s, and from early critique grew more developed attempts to incorporate theory into Roman archaeological research. But what is theory? All archaeological methods and perspectives involve theoretical concepts to some degree, but 'theoretical archaeology' seeks to be explicit about these concepts and to turn uncritical assumption into critical analysis.

As an undergraduate I was introduced to legionaries and natives, Caesar and Suetonius, Pompeii and Pliny – a plethora of names to invoke an age of lucubration, action and adventure. Roman archaeology is a prestigious scholarly world of excavations and texts, where pieces of evidence are skilfully manipulated and fitted together to give a full picture of events and even everyday life, which we can all understand. For a while I was hooked. But then, slowly, and I think directly as a result of attending the annual TAG (Theoretical Archaeology Group) conferences, I felt that there were cracks showing. The reasons for the attraction no longer seemed tenable, or even reasonable, and there were clearly dangers in succumbing to rhetoric and storyboard archaeology *as a means of understanding the past*. Traditionalist Roman archaeology is essentially an easy subject and can quickly become intellectually lazy and philosophically bankrupt. That there are a lot of facts to be learnt does not imbue the subject with a special epistemological magnificence.

The actual TRAC plot was hatched in East Jerusalem in the summer of 1990, where many evenings were whiled away with rumblings of discontent about the methodological and ethical iniquities of biblical and classical archaeology in the Near East; some western archaeologists seem to enjoy being an occupying power themselves. They dig in other peoples' countries to find a 'Roman past', but frequently offer little to those whose country it is. I have seen Arab artefacts dumped unrecorded by the skipful in the Middle East and Islamic buildings and cemeteries hacked out of the ground as if a nuisance. At a conceptual level, I am perturbed by Roman archaeology's uncritical fascination with hierarchies and its lack of interest in gender relations and the experience of women. In this latter regard, it is relevant to note that women are still marginalised within the profession of Roman archaeology – statistics show they do the archaeological housework while men have the cream of the university posts. It is still not unusual to attend conferences where every (invited) speaker is male, a situation almost unheard of in other professions, and there are documented cases where women who have spoken at conferences have been excluded from the published proceedings. The presentation of women in the past in many standard Roman archaeology textbooks is also disturbing when one considers that they are designed for mass consumption by students. Are these undergraduates being sold short? I suspect that Roman archaeology will soon begin to find that it cannot compete with the more methodologically rigorous and conceptually honest and exciting disciplines of prehistory and archaeological science. The better undergraduates have simply turned off from comments like 'A recent study of Roman women has compared their status to that of women in Victorian England . . . it was usually her own fault if a woman let herself be repressed' (Dudley 1970, reprinted 1987, 46) as they become more aware not only that this is poor scholarship, but also that this general tendency toward sexism and androcentrism goes unchecked. For those who have remained in Roman archaeology to try and change it, there has so far been little reward: they have received no patronage, but have been merely patronised. TRAC is an attempt to offer an alternative to this depressing orthodoxy and to create a visible network of ideas and new approaches.

Predictably, TRAC has had its detractors, that curious breed of non-attenders whose criticism of the event, apparently the result of an enviable meld of telepathy and staggering insight, reveal more about their concerns with the power politics of the archaeological establishment than with the open exploration of ideas. TRAC 91 was host to about 90 delegates from Britain, Germany, the Netherlands and the USA; the audience heard 18 papers. Many of the delegates attended out of curiosity and in order to keep abreast of potential new developments in Roman archaeology, and this was much to their credit, as they were not especially familiar with or keen on the idea of theory *per se*. Others were feeling a growing concern for the state of the discipline and were anxious to hear from graduate students, academics, field staff and museologists about their published and unpublished work. We all wanted to hear *ideas*; and as an informative gathering, TRAC succeeded. The conference ran again very successfully in March 1992 at the University of Bradford, organised by Pete Rush, where contributors offered a wider range of exciting papers on the themes of ideology, resistance and discourse. TRAC 93 will be held in Scotland, organised by Ross Samson.

This volume is intended to reflect the content of the conference in 1991 and to operate as a discussion document. The different authors involved come from a wide variety of archaeological backgrounds and have chosen to express themselves in quite different ways. This is in itself contextually interesting, and I haven't attempted to enforce a 'house style', as styles of writing can influence expression and content. The volume also avoids taking a 'party line', not only because there isn't one, but also because I have never found a prepared consensus inspiring. Contrary to dark rumour, it is not my intention to force a structuralist 'agenda' on to Roman archaeology. The authors have made use of a wide variety of perspectives, as well as a wide variety of data. In addition, the volume has lost a few of the original papers but has picked up a couple along the way from contributors who were unable to attend the 1991 conference.

Regarding overall layout, the volume has three broad categories: the general papers; Roman Britain; and other provinces of the Empire. Roman Britain is probably over-represented, and I hope that this imbalance might be redressed at future TRACs. There are already plans to invite more contributions from Europe and the USA, as well as the Middle East. The general consensus seems to be that it would not be prudent to include TRAC in TAG, as this would mean TRAC becoming a 'parallel session', possibly competing against an important general theory session, and, more crucially, many delegates would no longer wish to attend. Yet TRAC is certainly a child of TAG, although we would be well advised to be wary of certain TAG 'agendas'; but of course Roman archaeology, coming relatively late to theory, has the precious gift of hindsight.

There is a fierce resistance to the introduction of theory into Roman archaeology. Perhaps Max Planck was right when he pondered that new ideas only become accepted when the old guard die. Yet the concept of a theoretical approach to history is not new and was propounded at length by R. G. Collingwood, the philosopher and Roman archaeologist. 'The gods have commanded us to philosophize' he wrote in 1932 in a letter to J. A. Smith, which forms part of the little used archive kept in Magdalen College, Oxford. Indeed it has been said that Collingwood is our best known 'neglected' British philosopher. His philosophical works have undergone something of a revival in popularity in recent years, but I suspect that some of his ideas of history remain unread by the very Roman archaeologists who claim his fieldwork legacy.

Bibliography
Dudley, D. 1970. *Roman Society*. London; Pelican.

2

WRITING THE ROMAN EMPIRE

Eleanor Scott

The paper offers: a) A critique of traditionalist Roman archaeology, including its lack of contact with such overlapping issues as an archaeology of material culture, gender relations, structuration, the social meanings of power, and human agency. It is suggested that this is linked to the dominant concerns and social strategies of the influential traditionalist Romanist Establishment. b) Some examples of remedial research in the field of villa studies are the Brislington well, the Hambleden infant burials, and the distribution of villas in Britain. c) And, linked to the above, a brief a discussion of the opportunities for theory-building in Roman archaeology.

INTRODUCTION ———

History cannot proceed without philosophical presuppositions of a highly complex character. It deals with evidence, and therefore makes epistemological assumptions as to the value of evidence; it describes the actions of historical characters in terms whose meaning is fixed by ethical thought; it has continually to determine what events are possible and and what are not possible, and this can only be done in virtue of some general metaphysical conclusions. . . . It is equally certain that philosophy is impossible without history; for any theory must be a theory of facts, and if there were no facts there would be no occasion for theory.

– R.G. Collingwood 1916

Reading and Writing the Narratives

The Roman Empire once was. This is what we might call a fact, not a fantasy (although some people have fantasies about it). But the Roman Empire

is not an external entity with one objective, tangible, totally knowable existence. We cannot achieve an impartial complete account of the past events,
structures and contingencies which might be deemed to constitute the
Roman Empire. This is not because we are all mournfully trapped in post-
Derridean post-modernism, although it is perhaps useful to realise that we
create and construct our own perceptions of the human condition. It is
because the Roman Empire had social structures, gender relations,
economic forces, relations of production, and systems of symbolism and
signification, all human structures which we debate and re-invent the meanings of in our own societies. In effect, we write the Roman Empire into
existence.

How might we begin to write our Empire? I believe that we should do
this with boldness and optimism, though Professor Sheppard Frere (1987)
has advised:

> But above all, we need to teach the new generations of archae-
> ologists the virtues of clear selective reporting, and to show them
> that Roman Britain was an outpost of the classical world, where
> anthropological or sociological theories and their accompanying
> jargon, introduced from the shadowy and depersonalised world of
> prehistory, have little place.

I suspect this is a rhetoric with which Collingwood may well have felt un-
comfortable.

The 'theories' and the 'jargon' originate for the most part in the disciplines of philosophy, anthropology and history, and the theories incorporate
vital issues such as epistemology and gender theory. Professor Charles
Thomas too has complained of 'awful jargon', when reviewing Gregson
(1989): 'what . . . does the neologism emic mean?' (Thomas 1990, 184). If I
may be forgiven for smashing back his gentle lob, I know what emic means
because I have read a book on anthropology.

INTERPRETIVE FRAMEWORKS AND POWER PLAYS ————

A number of influential 'traditional' Romanists present their work as either
or both of two distinct aspects of archaeology:
1) discovery and recovery;
2) interpretation (or explanation).
Yet there is an intermediate stage of crucial importance, which should be
more explicitly debated, and which evokes Collingwood's epistemological

assumptions: the formulation and adoption of the conceptual or inter-pretive frameworks with which to interpret that which is discovered. I'm not the only working archaeologist who is dissatisfied with many of the standard implicit conceptual frameworks for the Roman Empire. Large-scale power, domination, control and submission are required subjects of study and interest, with an emphasis on the lives of the wielders of power, not on the means by which differential social power relations were created and maintained. As the means included the manipulation of meaningfully constituted material culture, including configurations of domestic and public architectural space, Roman archaeology is clearly failing to exploit its glittering wealth of material culture for theory building.

The description of powerful institutions, rather than analysis of the origins, manipulation and artificial maintenance of power, indicates all too well the nature of the concerns of the dominant group in Roman archae-ology in Britain. This is partly a hangover from the days of Victorian anti-quarians and some later archaeologists who saw the Roman Empire as some kind of natural precursor of the British Empire (see Hingley this volume), and were obsessed with the idea of military control and gracious living. It is clear from many writings that the Roman army was viewed un-questioningly as a positive force; and Roman villas were interpreted as the country houses of gentlemen farmers – indeed the word 'villa' entered the vocabulary of an aspiring middle class from the late nineteenth century on-wards. Chedworth villa, Gloucestershire, was redesigned by Victorian anti-quarians in a stylised and idealised manner, through the levelling and land-scaping of the site, the perching of little roofs on surviving walls, and the building of a country house – now the museum – in the middle of the site.

It is disturbing that many Roman archaeologists have not yet eschewed Victorian-Edwardian notions of human relations (Scott 1990a). It has also been mooted that a patriarchal hierarchy of Establishment figures is espe-cially evident in Roman archaeology, and that the Romanist hierarchy seems to 'reflect' the perceived hierarchies it studies.

I would argue with the 'traditionalists' that there are powerful and excit-ing reasons for change.

a) Roman archaeology can avoid the more painful adventures of the fundamentalist-theorists (e.g. processualists).
b) A concern with gender relations is currently revolutionising archaeology in a way that a concern with social structures did in the eighties.
c) It is increasingly being accepted that political and social theory

has an influence on archaeological practice and theory, and thus on archaeological interpretation.

d) Archaeology has matured enough as a discipline for us to allow ourselves alternative hypotheses to explain the same data, rather than searching for The Answer.

e) Roman archaeology is so 'rich' (see below) that it can, if it so desires, make a major contribution to theory within the archaeology of material culture.

All of the above are healthy academic developments, and theoretical debate in Roman archaeology should be encouraged as an intellectual exercise, at the very least.

Dominant Concerns: 'the Comfort Zone'

Because people have their own particular idea of what their present means, depending upon such factors as the social theories which they are prepared to accept, and because this is their primary knowledge, they tend to project this present back into their past; their present is their perspective for finding meaning in the relics of the past; and with some influential Romanists this present includes the Comfort Zones of dominant social groups.

The past is seen as a powerful place, where structures and events were somehow more 'natural' and 'right' than now; and people use this past to legitimise their present. They say, 'that's the way things happened; that's the right way to do things; that's the way things should happen; these are natural and good aspirations.' It is a circular story, that becomes more intense with the telling. It is a means of social control, and has been used to regulate the activities and aspirations of 'naturally' subordinate groups. There are many presents and many pasts to be narrated, but the losers in the game are often the same subordinated groups. One group's legitimised present is gained at the expense of another group's past and future; and it is for this reason that critique and remedial research in the archaeology of women, for example, are crucial, especially at a time of a general 'backlash' by the New Right against feminism (Faludi 1991).

The Marginalisation of Women in Roman Archaeology

The comments above are no mere abstractions. There is, I believe, a pressing need for an archaeology of gender relations. Romanists should not feel exempt from this call just because they have information about 'real' women in the form of texts, epigraphy, sculpture, paintings and small finds. On the contrary, the cultural meanings of this data need to be critically assessed. Further, the information presented for study tends to represent the existence of only a small proportion of women from particular social groups, leaving the vast majority of women historically disenfranchised. These women, the majority living and working in agricultural communities, are continually screened out of archaeological narratives. Yet importance in the world – power – lies in whose stories get to be told and heard and credited with significance. What a different Roman archaeology we would have if we let those who otherwise go unconsidered tell their stories and be important within their small-world but universal lives.

But instead we have volumes like *Who Was Who in the Roman World* (ed. Bowder 1980), a work of 'meticulous scholarship' where 'every effort has been made to include all historical and cultural figures of importance' (ibid., 9). Only a small number of these figures are women – a sample of the sections A-D reveals a 7% share – though interestingly a much higher percentage appear in the supplementary index of persons mentioned in the text but 'not important enough to be given their own entry' (ibid.); but there is no discussion of whether this number is a fair, proportionate and useful representation of the available material evidence, so one is left to wonder how 'importance' is assessed. The entries of those women who are included tend to have certain common themes: they were the wives, mothers or daughters of important cultural figures (Julia Paula, Tranquillina, Constantia); they were victims or perpetrators of violence (Julia Soaemias, Lucilla, Domitia Longina); they were reknowned for their beauty (Clodia, Lollia Paulina); they were reknowned for their chastity or their promiscuity (Antonia, Verginia, Clodia); their production or non-production of offspring (Agrippina the Elder, Sabina); or they were the 'real power behind the throne' (Julia Maesa, Julia Mammaea). There is a disparity between the length of the women's entries and the men's. Julia Domna receives only 17 lines, whereas relatively unknown male military and political figures receive 2 to 3 times as much text. Statilia Messalina receives only 5 lines, and Messallina only 9. The message which comes through is that women are of secondary importance. Within Julia Domna's entry, more space is given to the activities of her sons – Caracalla and Geta – than to her studies of philosophy and literature. It is also notable that in Caracalla's own personal entry, he 'arranged to have Geta stabbed to death', while in Julia Domna's entry 'Caracalla, having persuaded Julia to summon them for a reconciliation, stabbed Geta to death in her arms', associating her especially with a psychologically disturbing image of familial violence.

The Roman World (ed. Boardman et al. 1986, jacket), an Oxford History of the Classical World, is presented as the work of

> seventeen contributors [who] are acknowledged authorities in their field. They have taken great pains to present the latest position of modern scholarship in an accessible narrative, concentrating on those aspects of the Roman world that are both important for the understanding of the period and of lasting interest to today's reader.

But a depressing use of androcentric (sexist) and exclusionary language pervades the pages. Take Matthews's contribution, for example: 'in the cities of the Empire most men lived . . . in the plain tenement blocks' (p. 346). It is not good enough to counter this charge with the assertion that the word 'men' is used to denote 'people', and that the existence of women is implied. I do not want to be *implied*; I want historical existence. On the following page we learn that at Chedworth villa 'the owner's wealth was probably based upon stock-breeding and wool-production', but this statement begs many (undiscussed) questions of cultural structures. The assignation of ownership of wealth to a particular member of a rural working family should not be done automatically, almost by default. Matthew's paper assumes the primacy of patriarchal society throughout his discussion of the Empire, so one is left with the impression that the 'owner' of this British farmhouse raking in the 'wealth' is of course male. A promising paragraph (p. 348) about the 'great majority of the population', the rural peasantry, drifts quickly into a discussion of landed magnates and 'men of substantial private means'. Women are to be found, within the confines of one page (p. 357), which opens with: 'The women of the community [the Empire] would generally be seen in terms of the socio-economic categories assigned to the men'. (Is this *true*? If so, why, and how? And what about ideological categories?) However, 'their rights at law were . . . much more extensive than one might have expected.' (Again, why? Why should Matthew's breathtaking assumptions lead us to expect *anything*?) Later in the page women appear 'sharing in their husbands' work and its organisation' (is women's work not their own work? Or are their expendable ergs the property of their husbands?), 'particularly in the finer crafts . . . such as perfumery'. Following this we are then launched straight into a twee passage on women's 'service occupations', viz.: prostitution, which concludes with mention of women's only other discussed activities, 'the home' and childcare. There is no discussion of the evidence for, and social and ideological implications of, the placing of the women of the Roman Empire firmly 'in the home'. I question the validity of Matthews's conceptual framework which categorises women into helpmates, whores and madonnas.

Another recent academic survey of the Empire, also titled *The Roman World* (ed. Wacher 1987) and written by 'acknowledged authorities' (ibid., jacket), reveals androcentric concerns amongst the contributions. In the light of large-scale ethnographic and United Nations data on agricultural societies which indicate that women do over 80% of the actual work, though they control a minority of the resulting 'wealth', Blunt's very first sentence in his 'Labour' chapter seems surprisingly forgetful of women: 'The economy of the Roman Empire was predominantly agricultural; for the rich land was the safest, and therefore the most honourable investment and most men worked on the fields' (Blunt 1987, 701). Women are at home, watching spinning wheels (ibid.). He continues, 'Most men of course lived in the country, or in small towns, many of whose inhabitants went out daily to till the adjoining fields' (p. 702). All categories of labour, from 'freedmen' to debt bondage to slaves are discussed in terms of men and a male world (p. 704–14). His discussion of slave labour culminates in the observation that the presence of Black female slaves in the United States 'in healthy conditions' allowed the slave population to 'more than reproduce itself'. He then asserts that 'To judge from the Roman agronomists, women and children were not much used out of doors, and . . . it therefore seems probable that as a result of a deficiency in women slaves breeding could not have kept up numbers' (p. 715). Leaving aside Blunt's irritatingly ethnocentric and adaptive framework for the study of slavery, it may be noted that he does not cite any specific Roman agronomists in support of his down-playing of the role of female (and child) agricultural labour. It is not wise to use unnnamed Roman literary sources to make generalisations about Empire-wide labour forces. Blunt's argument begs careful handling and critical assessment in light of the ethnographic data alone; we might also consider: the general unreliability of Roman *agri cultura* sources when writing about reality rather than an idealised world; their unreliability when writing about the daily lives of members of other social classes; the un-representative nature of these sources for non-Italian and non-slave-estate agricultural societies; and, as noted above, the tendency of some male writers, including perhaps Roman agronomists, to write of 'men' when they should perhaps write of 'men and women'.

The history of women fares little better in the hands of some women scholars, whose works on the Roman period have included desperately effete studies of 'the traditional concerns' of 'girls', 'ladies' and 'women-folk' such as childcare, housework and gynaecological problems.

Breaking Out of the Comfort Zone

It would be infinitely more useful to study women in the Empire within critical frameworks of social classes, ideologies, changing configurations of social space, artistic and prosaic depictions of women, references to women in literature/rhetoric, and the supply and manipulation of 'female' material culture, and then to approach the 'male' world in relation to this.

In broad terms it may seem that women were and are socially and economically subordinated in very many societies. If this generalisation has any truth it is of supreme importance to the study of human societies, as are the reasons why. But *is* it a fact? Or is it just the way we write history which puts women down? Can writers who operate from a society which still maintains that it is a woman's biology which determines her poor economic status (Faludi 1991, passim) really hope to distinguish between natural and cultural 'reasons' for women's status in past societies?

Archaeologists may not be concerned with the future, and neither are they social engineers. Yet they have been, are, and will continue to be the pawns of social engineers, and must be explicit, possibly to the point of tedious repetition, about the origins of their interpretive frameworks. Archaeologists must particularly emphasise the cultural construction and historical specificity of social behaviour in the past, displaying a concern with how the dominant groups in past societies legitimised their decision-making processes through symbolic 'narratives' such as the manipulation of material culture, iconography, and mythology. Narratives have powerful social meanings, and they work because the 'reader' understands and is affected by them. Narratives drip with information and knowledge which range from the obvious and potent to the hidden, esoteric and subliminal; these can be structured as layers of interacting or even contradictory symbolism. Sometimes cross-cultural correlations may be recognised (such as the common human themes of fertility, and madonna-and-child iconography), but archaeologists should beware that what they recognise has emic meaning, and is not a carefully selected self-made narrative to support their personal or group perspective.

The dominant group in any society , when challenged with a new credo that is outside its Comfort Zone, does not easily change. Unfortunately there is much self-protection even in the bowery groves of academe, even though this self-protection is counter-productive to ongoing intellectual debate. The dominant group in academe, faced with the argument that their self-interests are actually devaluing historical analyses, will simply retreat into the Comfort Zone and protest their correctness.

THE QUESTION OF HUMAN STRUCTURES AND HUMAN AGENCY

Roman archaeologists might fruitfully tackle the question of what is power. Hodder (1991, 15) understands

> power to be the ability to act in relation to interest, including the interest in controlling others and resources . . . power may be based on the control of social or esoteric knowledge rather than on the control of economic resources.

Human agents occupy

> the material world, permanent and decaying, constructed and demolished, exchanged and accumulated . . . a potentially powerful system of signification (Barrett 1988, 9).

On the theme of power Hodder (1991, 15) continues:

> goods, labour, and land have to be evaluated within a symbolic system before they can be used as the basis for social domination.

Thus he argues that the power to act assumes some knowledge of an interest, but that interest is itself constructed within a system of signification. From this he contends that therefore all power relations depend on the structures of signification within which they take place, and that the central issue is the relative importance of prestige and economy in constituting power. In other words, are human actions determined more by cultural values and systems of prestige or by the distribution of economic resources?

> Archaeologists might hope to contribute to this debate by examining over the long term the durability of symbolic codes in the face of changing relations of production. As radical economic change takes place, associated with changes in structures of social domination, do the symbolic codes seem to determine or be determined by the changes in the economic structures? Is it possible, as Duby (1980) has argued in another study of long term processes, in Medieval Europe, that the superstructure can at times act as infrastructure, playing a dominant role? (Hodder 1991, 15–16).

The implications and potential for Roman archaeology are enormous, for here is a chance for Roman archaeology to contribute very clearly to theory building. Although Hodder is discussing social and economic transformations of the European Neolithic, he offers an underlying unifying theme: that it is sets of symbolic concepts that are central to social and economic change; we must interpret this symbolism however within its specific historical and cultural context, by teasing it out, identifying various associations, and, perhaps, oppositions (see below).

Perhaps also we might look forward to a change in the unequal social and economic power structures of Roman archaeology itself when conceptual transformations occur?

One of the failings of theoretical work in prehistorical archaeology – particularly processualism – has been the lack of understanding of the importance of *human agency*. Romanists, on the other hand, tend to obfuscate the complexities of human behaviour with the introduction of 'historical' human stories, often in the style of the ripping yarn. This brings us back not only to the Comfort Zone, but to the issue of human agency, and the question of individual choice in the acceptance of codes and practices.

The degree of determinism involved in human action is discussed by Hodder. He asks what role can be given to human agents and appears to offer parameters. At one extreme he believes it possible to argue that all human actors are entirely determined by structures in relation to events (ibid., 14–15).

> Thus, given an array of symbolic and social structures, and given a set of concrete conditions, certain solutions can be predicted. Within this view, human agents provide the medium for the playing out of structures, but they are entirely determined by those structures. According to this view history could not have been otherwise, except perhaps for random variation or 'error'.

At the other extreme (ibid., 15)

> social life is generated by knowledgeable human actors, monitoring the results of their actions, conflicting in their demands, pursuing varied social goals. Even if agents act within and through symbolic and social structures, they are able to transform the structures strategically. According to this view, history could have been otherwise. It is not fully predictable.

Barrett might appear to regard human or social agency as more complex,

and discusses the issue within an argument stressing that we must use archaeological evidence not as a *record of* past events and processes but as *evidence for* particular social processes (Barrett 1988, 6). Barrett (ibid., 7–8) is

> seeking not only to break with the functionalism which characterises
> much of current archaeological thinking, but also with the more
> recent demands for an 'archaeology of meaning' as propounded by
> Hodder. In his own attempt to escape functionalist explanations
> Hodder has shifted the attention of archaeology towards consider-
> ing the intentions and motivations of human agents . . . we are sim-
> ply moved from a position where social structures govern human
> behaviour to one which reasserts the primacy of the individual.

And elsewhere Barratt (1990, 46–7) asserts that

> To engage in writing an archaeology of human agency which is
> understandable primarily by reference to the meaningfully con-
> stituted world within which that agency operated, does not require
> us to find out the meanings an object might have had for individual
> participants in the ancient cultural system. More to the point is the
> historical problem of understanding the way dominant meanings
> were sustained over time and space through those participants'
> engagement in different regions of social discourse. Clearly this
> argument emerges from a general theoretical consideration of
> exactly what we need to understand when talking about other
> societies.

Again, it would appear that Roman archaeology might have a valuable
positive contribution to make to the debate on human agency. With its
wealth of material culture in the form of houses, farms, public architecture,
art and decoration, texts, an unbroken carpet of pottery over the landscape, etc., encompassing a period of many centuries, one might reasonably expect the data to provide evidence for the relationship of human
agents with social and economic structures and systems of signification,
and changes therein.

PROCEDURES, FRAMEWORKS AND THEORETICAL APPROACHES ———

Recent attempts by Romanists to 'get trendy' include the tactic of mention-
ing almost anecdotally the existence of 'the New Archaeology' (reviewed
Scott 1990b: I mention the term here to dispose of it), particularly in terms

of the Hypothetico-Deductive method or the testing of models in the scientific mode. But, as has been argued elsewhere, the kind of certainty hoped for by the H-D method's proponents can never be achieved. A blend of inductive and deductive reasoning is needed, with an active realisation that material culture is meaningfully constituted, that people continually create and re-negotiate narratives to maintain and subvert dominant meanings, and that the history we write about the past is itself such a narrative.

There is no one 'New Archaeology', but rather a pot brimming with ideologies and approaches, all rich with potential for making sense of the data, none of which is necessarily wrong, and none of which is necessarily right: structuralism, post-structuralism, post-processualism, critical theory, feminist archaeology, post-modernism, hermeneutics, Marxist and Marxist-structuralist theory, which all overlap to some extent, are commonly used frameworks. (Definitions of these terms are available now in many accessible publications, e.g. Hodder 1986; Renfrew and Bahn 1991.) For the orderly and ordered Romanist this may seem an intolerable state of affairs: is there no *procedure*? Well, no. But this is not new, as the Collingwood quotation at the start of the paper was intended to demonstrate. There are technical procedures for the recovery and processing of data, certainly, but even these are affected by interpretive priorities. Collingwood knew that the ways we deal with evidence are related to 'philosophical presuppositions' about that evidence, and our subsequent interpretations are always affected by 'epistemological assumption'. The archaeologist can taste from the pot, suck it and see. There is no hard science in archaeological interpretation; there is no hard science. Even physicists don't have 'proof' – good practitioners obtain increasingly better and better descriptions of the data.

Could it then be true that 'anything goes' with regard to interpretations of the past? Could there not be fascist archaeologies, for instance? This is a question that the post-modernists have yet to answer satisfactorily, but suffice to say a socially responsible moral content is usually anticipated for theoretical approaches. For example, many conferences and publications specifically discourage discriminatory language of a sexist or racist nature. This particular issue is frequently denigrated and trivialised by senior academics, but they are presumably fighting for the territory of their Comfort Zone. I don't believe that they are stupid enough to believe recent feminist critiques to be bad academic excursions, but rather that they feel threatened. Gilchrist's recent discussion of women in archaeology (present and past) (1991, 495–500) was a fine piece of work for both its intellectual content and its accessibility; it should interest the discipline of archaeology as a whole, as a subject *per se* and as a guiding strategy. The general framework for the 'engendering' of archaeology identified by other recent authors (Ovrevik 1991, 738; Gero and Conkey 1991, 5) could usefully be taken on board by Roman archaeology: critique; remedial research; theory-building.

Symbols, Context, Associations and Categories: some Examples

How might we then go about critique and conduct remedial research and build theory? I believe this can best be done by methods which have a place for the traditional skills of observation and intuition: the recognition of broad archaeological contexts, associations, and categories. However the new ideas for Roman archaeology expressed above and throughout this volume may help to throw new light on old problems.

Symbolic Structures

For example, I was recently asked to consider the relative absence of villas in Britain north of the Severn-Humber line; by my reckoning only about 6 per cent of the known total of certain, suspected and possible 'villas' lie here (Scott 1988, fig. 85). The 'obvious' solution to this question is first that one shouldn't really expect to find villas in a military zone with in-hospitable climate and terrain. But the *gsur* settlement in Tripolitania, for example, would appear to argue against this. Further, in Britain, one must consider that villas are absent from areas north of the Severn-Humber line where arable agriculture could have been and probably was practised; Collingwood (1923, 41) observed this long ago. Even if sheep and cattle farming were predominant in northern Britannia, it has always been accepted that these formed the basis of the wealth of the Cotswold villas (e.g. Matthews 1986, 347). The second reason usually given, after Rivet (1969), is that the pre-existing social and economic conditions were all wrong for villa settlement in the north of England and Wales. In fact he says (Rivet 1969, 204):

> Taking the distribution of villas as a whole, they present very much the picture we should expect . . . we find them to be fairly evenly distributed over that part of Britain which we defined as economic-ally viable at the time of the conquest.

The south-east of England is deemed by Rivet to have become 'eco-nomically viable' through its late Iron Age contacts with the Roman world. Apart from the etic language, no one would really have a problem accepting that contact with the Roman world in pre-Roman Iron Age

Britain was important. But unfortunately for Rivet's analysis, it ignores the fact that, after AD 43, the north of England had contact with the socio-economic structure of the Roman world for over 350 years, and the argument thus ignores its own belief in Romanisation as a civilising force and a mechanism for provincial change. There is also evidence that the earliest Roman villas in Britain were imposed, utilising a blueprint plan from Gaul and early Romano-British towns, and thus were not eagerly adopted by Britons seeking enhanced prestige (Scott 1990c, 158–9). This view is further supported by the simple fact that during the intense contact period of the late pre-Roman Iron Age, no villas were built in south-east England.

It may be that, where there is an apparent 'resistance' to the rural villa ideal in particular regions, it is not the pre-existing social and economic conditions which are all wrong, but rather the symbolic conditions which are wrong. How indeed should we expect people to take to life in a villa, a new building type involving different shapes, proportions and colours, with new ways of using social space, new ways of using fire, water and natural materials, new ways of processing and storing agricultural produce, new ways of stalling and butchering animals, new ways of dealing with the Roman economy and administration, and new types of art, decoration and furniture? Such ideological changes would have involved profound annotations to the existing cultural map. It is a lesson that many third world aid workers have been trying to teach the west for years.

Regarding northern Britannia, it has long been noted that there is a distinct paucity of Romanised material culture on the rural native sites (L. Allason-Jones, pers. comm.), lending some weight to the idea that there was a conflict of symbolic codes between native and Roman. The question still remains why the Roman administration sought to impose or 'encourage' a villa landscape in the south of the province in the early years of conquest. It was of course imperial policy to build public buildings and monuments and private houses, and the effect of this would be the creation of an environment in which the administrators would feel more comfortable and in control. The distribution of villas and towns appear complementary throughout the Empire, and in Britain the early towns – Verulamium, Chelmsford, Colchester, Canterbury, Chichester, Winchester, Silchester – are in the south-east (Wacher 1974, 25), which is why the earliest villas were imposed here, and why the villa system always concentrated here. Gradually the imposition of Romanised culture did have an effect on the symbolic structures of southern Britannia, which in turn allowed for greater social and economic changes, and it can be observed that these changes, evidenced by the material culture, were a uniquely 'British' response to the new external and internal influences (Scott 1988). But the lesson is that Romanisation was possibly not the unstoppable cultural force and sought-after commodity which some scholars have deemed it to be.

Contexts and Associations

It is perhaps ironic that whereas Romanists are adept at looking for 'parallels' and artefactual contexts for material culture, especially where small finds are concerned, they are less happy seeking associations and broad social contexts for material culture, other than trying to look one up in an historical text. This dependence on literary sources as 'objective text' is inherently problematic because the texts are themselves material culture, the authors being human agents acting within and through symbolic and social structures, whose work must therefore be interpreted through reference to these structures; but these structures in the Roman world have not yet been identified. The literary sources are also unrepresentative of the Empire's inhabitants and settlements. Varro does not travel well to northern England. And it is being demonstrated increasingly by field survey in the temperate and semi-arid lands of the Empire that cities and luxury villas were not isolated features in an otherwise empty landscape (e.g. Gaffney and Tingle 1985; Barker and Lloyd 1991); the Roman countryside was densley packed with farmsteads, small villas, villages and shrines (see van Dommelen this volume; Alcock this volume). We need archaeological theory to understand human behaviour in the Roman Empire.

It is suggested in this volume that Professor Branigan's analysis of the contents of the well at Brislington villa (1972) is undertaken in terms of a 'good story', rather than in terms of broad archaeological-social context (Poulton and Scott). That the deposits contained fragments of mosaics and a set of pewter vessels was taken as evidence of a clearing-up operation after 'the occupants were attacked in their dining room.' Parallels were sought, in the form of comparable well deposits from villas in south-western England, but only to confirm the interpretation, gleaned from the literary source Ammianus Marcellinus, that a war with the Picts occurred in Britain in AD 367. The broader archaeological context, of other pewter and debris deposits, in a variety of contexts, including those which might be termed ritual, was not explored; and the dating evidence used to assign all the well deposits to 367 is thus dubious.

Similarly, a great many conjectural stories have been put forward to explain the 97 infant burials at Hambleden villa: the burial of 'little corpses'

'secretly, after dark' (Cocks 1921, 150); the 'surreptitious evidence of un-
official births on the villa' (Johnston 1983, 11); 'evidence of infanticide'
(Watts 1989, 373); and the exposure of unwanted female offspring of a
slave-run establishment (Frere 1967, 266–7). If, however, the Hambleden
infant burials are viewed within the broad archaeological context, we find
that we are probably dealing with an infant cemetery (Scott 1988, 246ff.).
At Barton Court Farm villa (Miles 1986), as at Hambleden, the infants were
buried in an outer farmyard, and in an area of agricultural installations
such as ovens and 'corn driers'. This means that these were not 'simply'
cemeteries, for the associations between the burials and the agricultural
features are part of the 'otherness' of Roman societies which is all too frequently unacknowledged. From this overall realisation it is possible to
explore the meanings of these associations (Scott 1991).

Categories

This leads us to categories (see Rippengal this volume). Is the world organised by people into sets of categories (Miller 1982)? Information available
for examination, such as the components and contents of a villa, can be put
into categories of opposition (e.g. in, out; culture, nature; male, female;
public, private; clean, unclean; sacred, profane) to enhance analytical understanding or 'reading' of the narrative. The problem, as Ian Hodder
pointed out in the TRAC discussion, is how to recognise categories. But
the accessible and vast material world of the Roman Empire should allow
for much stimulating and rich debate on the primary contention that
material culture sets reflect the organisational principles of human categorisation processes, and that it is through the understanding of such
processes that we may best be able to interpret changes in material culture
sets over time (ibid., 17).

ENDPIECE——————

It may well be that Roman archaeology with its wealth of material culture
can substantially contribute to the debates about archaeological critique,
research and theory building. Roman archaeology should not and need not
merely download the 'agendas' of prehistoric theorists into the discipline:
it has its own contribution to make and its own future to build, whilst
simultaneously improving its communications with the rest of archaeology.

I also hope that Roman archaeology will be able to bury the academic
hierarchical elitism of the past, and become a more exciting and egalitarian

discipline. I think that TRAC has served this purpose, attracting a broad sweep of delegates (many of whom would not attend TAG), and conducting itself in an open and good-natured rather than a rarified atmosphere.

Ultimately a theory about a set of data (or, if you like, interpretation of a body of evidence) will be deemed to hold good because, by common or majority consensus, it will be the best available to make sense of the data. It is therefore my desire and my intention that in the future the majority consensus will incorporate re-examinations of attitudes, aspirations and conceptual frameworks – the social and symbolic structures of archaeology itself – because we all have a Roman Empire to write.

Bibliography

Baker, F. and J. Thomas (eds) 1990 *Writing the Past in the Present*. Lampeter; St David's University College Wales.

Barker, G. and J. Lloyd (eds) 1991 *Roman Landscapes. Archaeological survey in the Mediterranean region*. London.

Barrett, J. C. 1988 'Fields of discourse – reconstituting a social archaeology' *Critique of Anthropology* 7 (no. 3).

Barrett, J. C. 1990 'Sciencing archaeology: a reply to Lewis Binford' in Baker and Thomas (eds).

Boardman, J., J. Griffin, and O. Murray (eds) 1986 *The Roman World The Oxford History of the Classical World*. Oxford; Oxford University Press.

Bowder, D. (ed.) 1980 *Who Was Who in the Roman World*. Oxford; Phaidon.

Branigan, K. 1972 'The Romano-British villa at Brislington' *Proceedings of the Somereset and Avon Natural History Society* 116, 78–85.

Branigan, K. and D. Miles (eds) 1988 *The Economies of Romano-British Villas*. Sheffield; Sheffield University.

Brunt, P. A. 1987 'Labour' in J. Wacher (ed.), 701–16.

Cocks, A. H. 1921 'A Romano-British homestead in the Hambleden Valley, Bucks.' *Archaeologia* 71, 141–98.

Collingwood, R. G. 1916 *Religion and Philosophy*. London; Macmillan.

Collingwood, R. G. 1923 *Roman Britain*. London; Oxford University Press.

Duby, G. 1980 *The Three Orders*. Chicago.

Faludi, S. 1991 *Backlash: the Undeclared War Against Women*. London; Chatto and Windus.

Frere, S. S. 1967 *Britannia*. London; Routledge and Kegan Paul.

Frere, S. S. 1987 'Roman Britain since Haverfield and Richmond' address to All Souls College Oxford reproduced in *History and Archaeology Review*.

Gaffney, V. and M. Tingle 1985 'The Maddle Farm (Berks.) project and micro-regional analysis' in S. Macready and F. H. Thompson (eds).

Garwood, P. et al. (eds) 1991 *Sacred and Profane*. Oxford; Oxford University Committee for Archaeology.

Gero, J. M. and M. W. Conkey (eds) 1991 *Engendering Archaeology: Women and Prehistory*. Oxford; Blackwell.

Gilchrist, R. 1991 'Women's archaeology? Poltical feminism, gender theory and historical revision' *Antiquity*, 495–501.

Gregson, M. 1988 'The villa as private property' in K. Branigan and D. Miles (eds), 21–33.

Hodder, I. (ed.) 1982 *Symbolic and Structural Archaeology*. Cambridge; Cambridge University Press.

Hodder, I. 1986 *Reading the Past: current approaches to interpretation in archaeology*. Cambridge; Cambridge University Press.

Hodder, I. 1991 *The Domestication of Europe* 2nd edition. Oxford; Blackwell.

Johnston, D. E. 1983 *Roman Villas* 2nd edition. Shire.

Macready, S. and F. H. Thompson (eds) 1985 *Archaeology and Field Survey in Britain and Beyond*. Society of Antiquaries Occasional Papers 6. London.

Matthews, J. 1986 'Roman life and society' in J. Boardman et al. (eds), 338–60

Miles, D. 1986 *Archaeology at Barton Court Farm, Abingdon, Oxon*. Council for British Archaeology Research Report 50

Miller, D. 1982 'Artefacts as products of human categorisation processes' in I. Hodder, (ed.).

Ovrevik, S.E. 1991 'Engendering archaeology' review article in *Antiquity* 65 no. 248, 738–41.

Renfrew, C. and P. Bahn 1991 *Archaeology, Theories, Methods and Practice*. London; Thames and Hudson

Samson, R. (ed.) 1990 *The Social Archaeology of Houses*. Edinburgh; Edinburgh University Press.

Scott, E. 1988 Aspects of the Roman Villa as a Form of British Settlement. Newcastle upon Tyne; PhD thesis University of Newcastle upon Tyne.

Scott, E. 1990a 'A critical review of the interpretation of infant burials in Roman Britain, with particular reference to villas' *Journal of Theoretical Archaeology* 1. Oxford; Oxbow

Scott, E. 1990b 'In search of Roman Britain: talking about their generation' *Antiquity* 64, 953–56.

Scott, E. 1990c 'Romano-British villas and the social construction of space' in R. Samson (ed.), 149–72.

Scott, E. 1991 'Animal and infant burials in Romano-British villas: a revitalisation movement' in P. Garwood et al. (eds), 115–21.

Thomas, C. 1990 review in *Antiquity* 64, 183–84.

Wacher, J. 1974 *The Towns of Roman Britain*. London; Batsford.

Wacher, J. (ed.) 1987 *The Roman World* 2 vols. London; Routledge.

Watts, D. J. 1989 'Infant burials and Romano-British Christianity' *Archaeological Journal* 146, 372–83.

3

ATTITUDES TO ROMAN IMPERIALISM

Richard Hingley

It is argued that Romano-British studies have been influenced by the existence and organisation of Britain's own empire. A positive conception of Roman imperialism is still current and this indicates that many Romanists have yet to escape from moral precepts derived from our own imperial past. In recent years a number of authors have criticised the use of pro-imperialist models, but reviews of models outlined by members of the post- imperial generations should be equally critical. One influential model outlines the nature of the Roman Empire as a gigantic 'common market': it will be argued that the Common Market/European Community also forms an inappropriate model for the study of the Roman Empire.

During the Theoretical Roman Archaeology Conference at Newcastle I presented two papers: one concerned with the nature of past studies of Roman Britain in the context of British society, and the other with the organisation of household space in Iron Age and Roman Britain. Both papers have been published recently (Hingley 1990; 1991) and I do not intend to repeat any of that discussion in detail in this volume. Instead, this paper provides an extension of some ideas expressed in the *Scottish Archaeological Review* paper (ibid.) and forms part of an ongoing debate concerning the motivation behind Roman imperialism (see Hingley 1982; 1991; Millett 1990a; 1990b).

In *SAR* I argue that research directives in the study of Roman Britain have been biased by the parallel which has been drawn between the Roman Empire and the British Empire. This has led to a conception of the motivation behind the creation and maintenance of the Roman Empire as positive. In other words, it has often appeared that the motivation behind expansion and conquest was a moral obligation to bring civilisation to barbarian societies on the periphery of the Roman world; a motivation akin to the so-called 'white-man's burden' (Hingley 1991).

In my article the works of a number of authors who wrote about the Roman Empire during the first three decades of this century are reviewed (including Haverfield, Stobart and Nilsson) and it is argued that much work of this date derives from a positive conception of imperialism. This positive attitude survived the end of Britain's own empire and the establishment of the Commonwealth, forming the basis of most modern accounts of the archaeology and history of the Roman province of Britain (Jones and Miles 1979; Hingley 1991). That this concept of the motivation of the Romans remains dominant in the minds of some scholars is evident from Professor Thomas's suggestion that the approach I adopted in my book *Rural Settlement in Roman Britain* (Hingley 1989) invites us to 'share in a communal, retrospective guilt not just for the British Empire . . . but . . . for the *Roman* imperial presence; and for drawing entirely valid parallels between the advances towards civilisation that both such imperial ventures brought about' (Thomas 1990, 184).

This is obviously an emotive topic for some academics. Freeman's critique of my *SAR* paper (Freeman 1991) is more lengthy and complex, but also appears to contain a number of misconceptions which I will attempt to correct elsewhere. In recent years, however, a number of authors of 'the post-imperial generation' (Millett 1990a, xv) have attempted to acknowledge and take account of a perceived bias in research perspectives. Several Dutch scholars have been particularly involved in this process and some British authors have, in Millett's words, attempted to remove the debate from 'one based on a prevailing pro-imperialist attitude to another which takes a more neutral view of the available evidence' (1990b, 37).

To what extent are these supposedly post-imperial accounts actually neutral? It will be argued in this paper that the positive view of Roman imperialism is still dominant among British archaeologists and ancient historians in the 1990s.

Millett has quoted the work of Badian (1968) and has argued that, after the initial prizes of conquest had been taken, a deeply embedded set of social conventions acted to dissuade the Roman elite from excessive economic exploitation of provincial populations. This, it is argued, reflects a tradition whereby the conqueror became patron and protector of the conquered (Millett 1990a, 3). Wealth and prestige were gained by the Roman elite through the ownership and exploitation of land rather than by the amassing of wealth through trade.

It is necessary to be critical when utilising ancient written sources in order to assess the motivation of the Roman Empire's elite. Garnsey and Saller have argued that the degree to which this elite were involved in trade and industry has been underestimated. On the basis of diverse, mainly non-literary, sources it would appear that individual aristocrats were owners of large warehouses, brickyards and pottery works. It is also known that the elite was the source of loan-capital invested in shipping and other activities (Garnsey and Saller 1987, 8; see also the thorough recent survey of 'capitalism' in the Roman world by Love 1991). Indeed the elite of the British Empire generally avoided direct involvement in industry and trade. That the elite in both empires kept trade and exchange at arm's length does not however indicate its failure to exploit economic possibilities.

It is necessary therefore to be critical of all existing interpretive models that are used in the study of Roman imperialism and to acknowledge the economic and political motivation behind all acts of imperialism.

Other approaches to Roman imperialism have been developed in recent years, but if we do not adopt a critical perspective to these, we may stray into the operation of models that are just as inappropriate as the British Empire. For instance Mann, in his discussion of the stability of the Roman Empire, utilises an idea derived from A. M. H. Jones (1966, 311) that the empire was a gigantic 'common market', in which a balance of interests existed between the state, the producers, the middlemen traders and the contractors (Mann 1986, 278). This model appears to bear the particular stamp of later twentieth-century studies. It is important to remember that the Roman Empire was not established or maintained as a free-trade institution. Indeed many areas were only incorporated and controlled by force, and many barriers existed to trade and exchange; for instance the state's control of grain and minerals and the control of markets within the Empire by the state and the elite (MacMullen 1970, 333–4). In addition one wonders about the degree of influence of certain producers within the empire; is the concept of the balance of interests really useful in this context?

Any model which is based on the concept of a balance of interests will never produce a realistic picture for the political and economic context of Britain within the Roman Empire. I would argue the need for a critical perspective on the motivation behind imperialism, leading to an analysis of the relationship between different elite groups in certain areas of the Empire and also the relation between the elite and the producers within and between particular *civitates* in Britain. It is only through the use of this type of critical perspective that British scholars will escape from the mental constraints imposed by their recent past and present and be able to construct a coherent Roman archaeology.

Acknowledgements. I wish to express my thanks to Dr Eleanor Scott for inviting me to contribute to the conference and to this publication, and to Christina Unwin, Dr David Breeze and Dr Lesley Macinnes for comments and advice on this paper.

Bibliography

Badian, E. 1968 *Roman Imperialism in the Late Republic.* Oxford; Oxford University Press.

Blagg, T. and M. Millett (eds) 1990 *The Early Roman Empire in the West.* Oxford; Oxbow.

Burnham, B. C. and H. C. Johnston (eds) 1979 *Invasion and Response: the Case of Roman Britain.* Oxford; British Archaeological Reports.

de Ste Croix, G. E. M. 1981 *The Class Struggle in the Ancient Greek World.* London; Duckworth.

Freeman, P. W. M. 1991 'The Study of the Roman period in Britain: a comment on Hingley' *Scottish Archaeological Review* 8, 102–4.

Garnsey, P. D. A. and R. Saller 1987 *The Roman Empire: economy, society and culture.* London; Duckworth.

Hingley, R. 1984 'Roman Britain: the structure of Roman Imperialism and the consequences of imperialism on the development of a peripheral province' in D. Miles (ed.), 17–52.

Hingley, R. 1989 *Romano-British Rural Settlement.* London; Seaby.

Hingley, R. 1990 'Domestic organisation and gender relations in Iron Age and Romano-British households' in R. Samson (ed.), 125–48.

Hingley, R. 1991 'Past, present and future – the study of the Roman Period in Britain' *Scottish Archaeological Review* 8, 90–101.

Jones, A. M. H. 1966 *The Decline of the Ancient World.* London; Longman.

Jones, M. and D. Miles 1979 'Celts and Romans in the Thames Valley: approaches to culture change' in B. C. Burnham and H. C. Johnston (eds), 315–25.

Love, J. R. 1991 *Antiquity and Capitalism: Max Weber and the sociological foundations of Roman civilisation.* London; Routledge.

MacMullen, R. 1970 'Market days in the Roman Empire' *Phoenix* 24, 333–4.

Mann, M. 1986 *The Sources of Social Power. 1. A History of Power from the beginning to AD 1760.* Cambridge; Cambridge University Press.

Miles, D. (ed.) 1984 *The Romano-British Countryside.* Oxford; British Archaeological Reports.

Millett, M. 1990a *The Romanisation of Britain: an essay in archaeological interpretation.* Cambridge; Cambridge University Press.

Millett, M. 1990b 'Romanisation; historical issues and archaeological interpretations' in T. Blagg and M. Millett (eds), 35–41.

Roskams, S. 1986 'Later Roman towns'. Paper presented at conference at Rewley House, Oxford.

Samson, R. (ed.) 1990 *The Social Archaeology of Houses.* Edinburgh; Edinburgh University Press.

Thomas, C. 1990 'Review of R. Hingley's *Rural Settlement in Roman Britain*' *Antiquity* 64, 183–4.

4

THEORY AND ROMAN ARCHAEOLOGY

Richard Reece

The paper seeks to find the proper, or at least current, role of theory in Roman archaeology. It sets up a project to study the settlement pattern of Roman Britain from purely material sources and tries to investigate the presence or need for theory in each of the successive steps of the project. A division is found between the gathering of observations and their manipulation, which can be relatively explicit, and the interpretation of the observations which has to have an an element of theory and subjectivity. Three basic questions arise from this title. Which theories? To which areas of Roman archaeology should they be applied? What is the purpose of such application?

Two simple, and polarised, objections against any such activities are clear: (a) we know what happened, we don't need theory; and (b) we do not yet have a good enough data base to justify the application of theory.

Perhaps we ought first to sort out some objectives and so find a possible archaeological problem which could act as an example. If our aim is to describe a dinner-party-orgy as it might have taken place in South Italy around the middle of the first century AD – a worthy and interesting aim – we should apply to the *Satyricon* of Petronius rather than an archaeological data base. If our aim is to analyse the changes in settlement pattern in Britain between AD 1 and 500 then we might be on the right archaeological track. I would go so far as to say that the settlement question could only exist in the context of information on material, that it could not have occurred without a sample of basic material. In that sense it is a 'material' subject and can only be answered from material evidence. We are in the business of archaeology. How would an archaeological answer to the question be found?

Taking nothing for granted we might be able to define a type fossil for the period in question, a general Roman type fossil as a theme for those five hundred years. If any recourse to history is allowed then Pompei might be a good place to look for a specifically Roman type fossil, because there you have a site sealed at a historically known date. If historical sources are not allowed then tree-ring dating must be pressed into use. Rings must be counted back from AD 1990 to AD 1, and a site with a sealed deposit of that sort of date examined. Perhaps the London water-fronts will do if an error of a decade or so is allowable. I do not see for the moment any theoretical help for either tree-ring-dated deposits, or possible theoretical refinements in the date of the destruction of Pompei. Let us, for the sake of argument, take Samian pottery as our type fossil, our Roman Type Fossil, or RTF; I like to use the S sometimes, and only a sickly pedant would forbid it.

A map of finds of Samian would be a first step towards the settlement pattern of Roman Britain. Given extensive field-walking and field-survey the map could have quite a lot of dots on it. It would of course not be a map of settlements in Britain 1–500, but a map of find-spots of Samian pottery. Perhaps this is where theory comes in?

If so, our two polar objections come in as well.

(a) This map is clearly so far from the real state of Roman things that no injection of theory could improve on what we already *know* from other sources. Viz. Britain to the 18th century was agricultural, and the distribution of settlement mirrored the distribution of cultivable land. Work therefore on modern land-quality maps, and distribute on the maps random dots in proportion to the usability of the land, and you will have a far better, if generalised, map of settlement in Roman Britain than from any other source. Set your parameters so that the number of dots is greater than the number of Samian dots, and perhaps give four or five ascending numbers of sites. Then moderate your possibilities by reference to one or two examples of highly detailed field-work. The land will give the generalised distribution; the moderating field-work will give the level at which the sites are to be scattered.

(b) The Samian map is such obvious nonsense that to apply any theory to it would simply compound the folly. We are clearly not yet ready for theory.

Or am I already indulging fairly heavily in theory? If so I find the word and the concept a nonsense, for all I have tried to do so far is to think in stringently careful and analytical terms.

Can we agree to summarise so far? I doubt it, but I might as well try. The first purpose of archaeology is to define material accurately, to know which material is where, and when. This gives three main parts to the basic primary functions of archaeology: definition of material, description of spatial spread, and description of chronological context. The second purpose may be to interpret this evidence gathered.

Before we try to go on theoretically let us try to improve our map. We must improve our RTFs. A more common fabric than Samian pottery, but sometimes in the same contexts, is Black Burnished Ware category 1, or BB1, and its copies, BB2. We define it as a second RTF by its common association with Samian, but we may note that it often occurs without Samian. We can therefore plot new maps of Samian, with or without BB1. When we take a closer look at BB1 and take into account form as well as fabric it becomes clear that certain forms occur with Samian in primary contexts, and other forms never occur in those primary contexts but in others, higher up the stratigraphic record, where Samian, if it occurs at all, may be re-cycled. We therefore get Samian phase BB1 dots and post-Samian phase BB1 dots. From constant observation of super-position of deposits we conclude that this involves early BB1 and later BB1. We now have period maps. Some dots on the map can be associated with marks such as soil-marks, plough-marks, aerial photographs or even humps and bumps. Some of the sherds gathered from field spreads can be associated with assemblages more or less described from sites more or less excavated.

So spreads can be measured and dated. Maps can reflect the dimensions and dates of scatters. Is theory likely to elbow its way back in?

Objection (a) will now have changed to

(a2) We know the date and distribution of field scatters; we don't need theory.

This objection seems set to change and keep on cropping up as your information is improved. It will not go away when the first set of problems are overcome. It may well turn up in a different guise as follows.

(a3) If your sophisticated maps of distributions of RTF scatters is seriously, detectably, even 'significantly', different from what we *know* (i.e. from agricultural land) then it is clearly nonsense and no amount of theory will help it. I don't believe it.

(b2) The data base is as good as it will ever be; why subject it to theory?

We begin to approach a possible area of agreement. In order to have a good idea of how the past still exists in the present we need to know:

    i) how the material is defined;

    ii) where it is in space;

    iii) when it was in time.

Our objectors will go on from there, in unison: and this is the nearest we can ever come to what was, so why add theory?

Because, we answer, of the next stage. We asked questions not about scatters of RTFs but about settlement patterns. We have to turn scatters into settlements. In short we have to interpret. But before we go on to that stage we need to have a closer look at some of the things we have done to see whether theory has crept in unnoticed.

We move on now to the Definition of Material. Some ardent theorists will insist that the material is already theory laden, and that to define it further only adds to the theory. I see the force of argument for a flint 'arrowhead' or a bronze 'razor', where an attribution of use has been foisted on a piece of material in order to define it, when that object is part of an indivisible continuum. The dividing line between 'spear-shaped arrowheads' and 'arrowhead-shaped spears' may either be totally arbitrary or non-existent. In the Roman period I doubt whether this is a major problem if we stick to material objects. And it is part of my thesis that most material of the Roman period in Britain can be described, and even defined, in modern terms, without necessarily introducing interpretation.

For about thirty years excavators have sent me their Roman coins. They want as many scraps of bronze to be coins as possible because far more information can be obtained from coins than from scraps of bronze. After the first batch have come from a large excavation a second batch, much smaller, usually follows of further hopeful scraps which have emerged from cleaning. I therefore tend to see too many scraps and have to reject a few. But the number of bronze scraps which I have to label 'not a coin' are few, less than 1 in 1000, and the number of scraps about which I am not sure is even less than that. For the objects I accept as coins there are places in voluminous *corpora*. Note that I do not say that every 'coin' is described in a *corpus* somewhere; this is because if you understand the material you can find the place in a well constructed system in which your previously undescribed coin belongs. Since the indeterminate scraps to which I can attach no classification are so few, less than 1 in 10,000, I cannot take seriously any claim that there is a serious and important doubt about what is a Roman coin. I therefore take the simple descriptive definition 'Roman coin' to be relatively theory free. If anyone were to object that to define something as a coin involved countless theories of economics, market forces, and politics, they would have completely missed one of my main theme-songs, that we do not know what 'Roman coins' were to the Romans, nor have we any idea, *a priori*, what they were used for. All that is theory, and none of it follows from the descriptive definition 'coin'.

Or Samian, which is the result of a highly centralised, organised and standardised production. The number of borderline sherds – is it, or is it not Samian – is small in anything other than a viciously acid soil. Snap decisions probably affect the total archaeological record very little, and if they do matter they could be decided chemically.

Or BB1, the result of highly standardised but loosely organised production. There is little or no doubt about fabric, and that could be resolved petrologically. There is strong agreement on the general forms. That is a BB1 pie-dish, this is a BB1 cooking pot.

The word Samian obviously carries no hints of the island of Samos, big or small s, pie-dishes suggest nothing about pies, nor cooking pots cooking. But BB1 is black and burnished.

Once the material has been well defined then it either has been found at National Grid co-ordinates WXYZ or it has not. And if there is doubt, it has not. It was found at that point in the stratigraphic sequence or this, and if there is doubt choose the later. It was in context a or b and if uncertain it was unstratified. It commonly occurs in upper stratigraphic groups, or lower ones, or both.

All this, our data base, has been arrived at without any obvious application of explicit theory, and quite probably without direct involvement of specific theory. Applications have involved certain principles which are thought to be important in almost any endeavour. Any definition ought to be clearly comprehensible, ought to avoid uncertainty, and ought to be universally applicable. If possible it should be susceptible to testing by physical or chemical means. If either definition or test involves theory the theories are likely to be diverse rather than convergent, so any support of definition by test will probably be in spite of the theories rather than due to the theories. Add to definitions precise observations of what was found where, and in what combination with other objects, and I think you have the basis of the information.

If people wish to niggle they may. But if they wish their niggles to be taken seriously they must show how the application of the niggle would change the data base created by more than one per cent or keep quiet.

It is possible that potential critics will have followed me this far, just out of bored curiosity, in the sure and certain knowledge that I shall collapse in an untheoretical heap in the next stage – if I attempt it. For, to a number of Roman archaeologists, the next stage must be interpretation. If I want to pursue my original goal of changes in settlement pattern then I probably do have to interpret. My tendency would be to stop at the data base and say 'The settlement pattern is represented by the spreads of material mapped. Changes over time can be seen on the phase maps provided.' In fact I shall briefly stop there, but I will go on after to see where interpretation leads.

I could say that scatters of BB1 and Samian have been measured (5 yards across and 20 yards long) and have been assigned to either an early group, a late group, or a general group. All scatters of more than 50 yards across are early or indeterminate; no late scatters are 50 yards across. Of course no one would quote this, or perhaps even take it in. They would interpret it, and Reece would have shown that large villas were exclusively an early phenomenon. I would rather say that above ground rubbish heaps which plough out to large scatters were the early form of rubbish disposal, and rubbish pits, which plough out, if at all, to small scatters, were the late form. But the villa interpretation is much more interesting.

So how do we interpret? By what theories can interpretations be constructed, compared, proved or disproved? What is the interpretative theory which transforms what may be relatively objective categories or Roman material into stories? What is done with the material and what ought to be done with it?

To embroider material into interpretation we must have some concepts in our minds, some ideas of parallels ready to apply, and we must have some reasons for sticking the concepts to the material. You have to have the idea of a threshing floor ready to hand in order to apply it to a layer of worn stones set in a particular way. When it is pointed out to you that the stones are set in, and covered with, water-borne silt you may have to give up your interpretation in favour of a paved river ford. You must search your mind, or the minds of colleagues, or the library, for analogies, but give them up if they conflict with the material evidence.

We interpret by analogy. Some people are horrified at this, and want to believe that archaeology can be more exact a science than this. They would do well to heed Prof. Mary Hesse's warning (given in seminars, but not yet, so far as I know, published) that by doing this archaeology is working alongside the 'hard' sciences. Analogy is not a poor relation, but, according to a respectable professor of the History and Philosophy of Science at Cambridge, what scientists have often done and do now.

The next question concerns the way in which analogies are chosen, and then, how they are judged. The cynical and destructive, if truthful, answer is that they are neither explicitly or even knowingly chosen and that only the unpopular ones are judged.

Many Roman villas were dug up on estates. Many estates produced only one villa, and, almost by definition, estates have one comfortable if not stately home. There were clearly too few villas known to accommodate more than a small part of the Roman population of Romano-Britons, and they were too well appointed compared with other houses of the Roman period to be for the poor. It was therefore obvious that the villa was the home of the Roman estate owner just as the comfortable or stately home was the house of the modern estate owner. Other facts followed, such as occupation of the house – *the* house, singular – by a single family, with dependants if necessary to fill up the rooms, and a fence round a nice discrete property to give a comfortable few hundred acres at least. And the majority of Romanists are too blind to distinguish this plausible and possible fiction from fact. That it has never been explained in a *locus classicus* shows, not that it is a heap of rubbish, but that it is fact, for fact does not need to be explained, only to be quoted and used.

Hence we arrive at a definition of theory in archaeology. Theories are unsuccessful ways of arguing against facts. Facts are what are set out in the text-books of Roman Britain. Therefore anything which goes against the text-books is merely theory. This is neat, but it does hold a problem now that Frere's *Britannia* has imitators and dubious offspring. So as not to be misunderstood I had better say that I regard all sub-*Britannia* offspring, that is all books modelled on *Britannia*, as dubious, if I am polite. *Britannia* by itself was internally consistent, and I admire it for that, while not agreeing with it. Imitators have jiggered with bits of it and the results contain argumentative holes through which objectionable carts and horses can be driven. With *Britannia* you either accept it whole and its world to go with it, or you do it yourself. With various Roman Britains about, judgements need to be made, and that can only be done with the help of theories. So, in a sense, sub-traditional Roman Britains have fostered the need for a theory of interpretative judgement. Nutty Roman Britains just make things worse, or better, depending whether you want to bring interpretation out of the closet or not.

So far have our standards of common decency declined that there are now books on Roman Britain which show explicit interpretation. Richard Hingley (*Rural Settlement in Roman Britain*, 1989) had the nerve to take a Roman villa plan, and populate it as if it were a collection of savages' huts. North American savages, I think, at that. Which clearly makes it wrong, since Rome was the colonial power, so villas ought to be interpreted by analogy with weather-boarded, white-washed, colonial mansions. Which of course helps us to understand the role of slaves.

So, to leave polemic for a little, we interpret by analogy. This has all the known problems, in particular the impossibility of interpreting a pottery kiln as a knuft-herping site since no one knows what knuft-herpers needed for their job. Remains need to be consistent with the firing of pottery, as known at present, or observed in primitive contexts, or read from early manuscripts, or dictated by technological considerations, reaching at least 500 degrees C and staying there for some hours, in order to be interpreted as pottery kilns. It may be that they also need to be consistent with human beings. It is no good suggesting an interpretation which simply will not work for human beings as we judge for ourselves. Here we may be seeing the entrance not of the interpretative theory, but the theoretical framework. It is too loose a method to leave each person with his or her individual perceptions and peculiarities to judge the humanity of each interpretation, we need a human scheme, a human theoretical framework, a common frame of reference, within which to interpret. Several of these frameworks exist, and we can both ease our own task, and that of our readers, by explicitly siting our interpretations in a chosen model of the world. It may be the Marxist model, or the market economy model, or the religious (flavour to taste) model. It is not so much importing a load of theory into our interpretation as doing our interpretation within a framework of theory.

This proliferation of theory worries me. We have theory level 1: interpreting by analogy, and all the needs of method, testing and evaluating. We have theory level 2: the theoretical framework in which we see human beings operating. We have theory level 3: the theory to which we apply the two lower levels, the theoretical construct which is the Roman Empire.

How do these levels relate in practice? To what extent are they explicit? And to what extent are they controllable?

The Roman Empire is based partly in historical references and partly in the pious hopes that material has been well gathered and used as a commentary. As it stands it is quite immune from valid theoretical niggling unless the nigglers were to start afresh and build their own Empire. Even that would be of questionable value since it would be unique to them. We have to live with the construct as it is, recognise that it has no more reality than the physicists' constantly changing pictures of the atom, and try to knock some sense into it whenever we get the chance.

If we come down to the level of a province, of Roman Britain, then there may be more hope. But we only have control over the theoretical construct that is Roman Britain if we go back every time that we do anything to the actual material. If we take secondary sources then we are incorporating other people's theories into our theory as if they were material facts. Thus we may use a secondary summary, like John Wacher's *The Towns of Roman Britain*, 1974, provided we do no more than use it as a guide to the original sources. We must draw a very hard line between talking about material and talking about what people thought about that material. This almost restricts us to bibliographies, for any connected text in the chapters of such books is interpretation, and so is laced with personal theory. Such text is only usable for a study of 'twentieth century views of Roman Britain', it says nothing at all about Roman Britain.

This suggests that we can get at some aspects of Roman Britain if we go back to our sources, but we have to push further. Wacher on towns may guide us back to an original excavation report. Here we must be extra vigilant. We may trust a drawn section, though work at Stanwick shows how Wheeler could bend his sections to fit in with his historical preconceptions. We can probably trust explicitly described material since few reports describe material that was *not* found on the site, but found somewhere else. Yet context is vital. It would be true for a report to say that Ptolemaic coins had been found at Winchester; but it would be a *suggestio falsi* unless it added that they were found on a spoil-heap and not in excavation. If the context is given then it is clear that they have rather less validity than the coins in grand-father's box which he always said came from his allotment. Where material is well described, this is good. Where it is not described it is not necessarily proof of absence, for every printed and even archive report is a selection of what was actually found.

At this point I need a parable, and the only one that springs to mind involves the world of the word-processor. I hope it will not put off those who are not yet properly programmed. A conference organiser decides to publish the proceedings of the conference. Contributors are asked to supply their text on a word-processing disc. The discs come in and the editors, not realising there are any difficulties, but thinking that all word-processing is the same, send the discs off to a little publishing company which has otherwise intelligent customers, and they manage to plug all the discs into their system and print the results. The firm are surprised, but the organiser did say it was a very abstruse conference. The editors are horrified, for most of the papers are blocks of signs and letters and spaces which make no sense at all. The company comes to their help and explains that it all depends on the framework within which each contributor worked, an Amstrad here, an IBM there and a Mac somewhere else. And even when you have found out what general theoretical framework each contributor was working in, you still have to find out the individual programme, Word, Word Perfect, Wordstar, Macwrite, that each was using to fit the basic information of words and phrases together, to interpret the material.

Our Roman Britain is just such a jumbled conference proceedings; the trouble is that we think we can read it, and we never notice that each person is working in an individual theoretical framework. We may sort out the Mac user, the Marxist, from the IBM user, the liberal – I steer clear of equating any computer with Thatcherism; it would be an actionable slur. But we are not even aware that there are different programmes, different ways of interpreting, and we read the results as if they all fitted together.

To try to sort things out we might have conversations more often in the following vein. The scene is set by a non-Marxist arguing with a Marxist:

NonM: I could never work in a Marxist framework, I need freedom.

M: So you say that outside Marxism, and other like isms, there is total freedom?

NonM: I do.

M: Which framework do you work in then?

NonM: I don't.

M: I know you to be a Capitalist Imperialist Swine; I therefore assume that you work in a CIS framework

NonM: That is rubbish; I work in post-Thatcherite, success oriented, Britain which is free from all theoretical constraints.

M: Thank you.

In other words, if they are needed, you cannot avoid a framework within which to pursue archaeology. You, just by being you, have taken in so many things that anything you do to material is heavily theory laden the moment you begin to interpret it, and perhaps long before. Your framework may not be an identifiable, taggable framework, it might be all your own. As a person living a full life, which is different from all other lives, this may well be a very good thing; as an archaeologist helping to build a picture of what went on in the Roman Empire it is disastrous. Disastrous because no-one else knows exactly why you gathered this material in this way and said that about it. And of course the trouble is that many archaeologists are people at the same time.

Is there a recipe for a better future? It sounds suspiciously as if everyone must write Their Roman Britain, and all will be revealed.

5

THE STUDY OF ROMAN TECHNOLOGY: SOME THEORETICAL CONSTRAINTS

Kevin Greene

This paper criticises attitudes to the history of technology exemplified by the Routledge Encyclopaedia of the History of Technology *(1990), which displays ignorance of the nature and achievements of archaeology, compounded by failure to distinguish between the materials and methods of archaeology and history. The* Encyclopaedia's *emphasis on individual inventions leads to linearity and diffusionism, while questions of gender are hardly addressed.*

This paper draws attention to technological change resulting from the reorganisation of existing skills and resources, and suggests that innovation must have been more important than invention in a Roman context, and rejects the judgement of Roman technology in terms of an unquestioned desire for economic growth. Fortunately, there *is* now genuine debate about the theory of the history of technology, and much potential for research exists in the Roman empire. This paper was delivered in outline at the TRAC conference in March 1991 as an unashamed tirade against prevailing attitudes to the history of technology. I do not attempt to provide a detailed account of any existing theoretical framework, let alone propose a new one. For those speakers at the conference who voiced routine criticisms of 'Romanists' and their supposedly deficient outlook and deafness to theoretical considerations, my paper has a simple message – you have not heard anything yet . . .

HISTORIANS OF TECHNOLOGY ───────

A View from 1990

What I have to say in this section was provoked by reading *An Encyclopaedia of the History of Technology*, edited by Ian McNeil, published by Routledge in

1990 (hereafter *EHT*). *EHT* begins with an examination of the place of technology in history, which emphasises the role of individuals, and broadly equates technology with invention (p. 2) An interesting distinction is drawn between science and technology, based upon function; thus, because people who can be described as scientists *used* telescopes, they are left for another encyclopaedia; musical instruments are excluded on similar grounds, 'although the craftsmen who originally made them were undoubtedly technologists' (p. 4). Editorial convenience is the stated reason, rather than a theoretical functional classification based on different economic or social contexts.

By definition, any history of technology that perceives inventive individuals as prime movers will automatically skate over the entire undocumented prehistoric and protohistoric past; early historic periods lacking texts that 'name names' will also be relegated to an inferior position. The position is worsened by McNeil's ignorance of the nature and achievements of archaeology in the post-war period, compounded by his failure to distinguish between the raw materials and methods of archaeology and history, culminating in the following astonishing assertion (*EHT* p. 4):

> The neglect of technology, the near-contempt in which archaeologists and historians seem to hold it, is all the more surprising when one considers that it was one of the former who originated what is now the standard classification of the archaeological ages, and which is based on technological progress.

The archaeologist in question and the 'standard classification' turn out to be C. J. Thomsen and the three-age system. The only advance in archaeology in the twentieth century is credited to Childe, 'who was convinced that we should look upon pre-history primarily as a history of technology.' TRAC participants may or may not be reassured to learn that 'Of recent years more and more archaeologists have been adopting Professor Childe's approach' (p. 5).

McNeil then proposes 'the seven technological ages of man', which reveal even more about the attitudes that underlie the whole of *EHT*. The ages are defined very briefly (p. 5), and then used to structure thirty-eight pages of fuller discussion. I will summarise the seven ages from these definitions, and illuminate some with words from subsequent section headings, placed in parentheses:

1 the era of nomadic hunter-gatherers ('man, the hunter, masters fire');
2 the Metal Ages of the archaeologist ('the farmer, the smith, and the

wheel');

3 the first Machine Age;

4 the beginnings of quantity production ('intimations of automation');

5 the full flowering of the Steam Age;

6 the rapid spread of the internal combustion engine ('the freedom of internal combustion');

7 the present Electrical and Electronic Age ('electrons controlled').

Although these ages are described as 'to some extent overlapping', it is clear from McNeil's fuller definitions that they are viewed entirely from a First World perspective, and that they are based on very inconsistent criteria which blur the distinction between causes and effects, events and processes. Nothing is made of potential comparisons between the social organisation and energy expenditure of hunter-gatherers and settled farmers, yet extraordinary claims are made for the social influences of copper and iron (p. 12); copper was divisive and created hierarchies, supposedly for the first time, whereas iron 'has rightly been called the democratic metal, the metal of the people'. These potentially fascinating ideas are not justified or explored in any way, however, and no archaeological sources (other than Oakley's *Man the Toolmaker*) are provided in the further reading section (p. 43).

Inventions: a First World Viewpoint

A further problem with most histories of technology is that only those items that led to modern western 'high' technology are considered really interesting. Anything military or mechanical is always valued above the ingenuity of ordinary ceramics, textiles or basketwork, despite the greater benefit of the latter to a larger number of people. Likewise, almost everything is judged in terms of saving time and labour, which are unlikely to have been conceptualised, let alone commoditised, in anything like the same manner in pre-industrial societies.

The history of technology and inventions also tends to be perceived as a score-chart of temporal 'firsts' divorced from their spatial and cultural contexts. Once again, the basis of information is primarily European, and governed by texts, although China always receives honourable mention on account of its early literary sources, explored by the indefatigable Joseph Needham. When the history of technology is text-centred and geographically restricted, and envisaged in terms of individual inventions, it tends towards linearity and diffusionism. If texts are absent, and inventions cannot be located in a precise place or time, the linear model degenerates into an extremely naive sequence of causes and effects; thus, *EHT* manages to condense the origins of farming and the introduction of individual hand-tools into four sentences (p. 11–12):

> It started some time about 10,000 BC, when a great event took place – the end of the last Ice Age when the melting ice flooded the land and brought to life a host of plants that had lain dormant in seeds. Among these was wild wheat as well as wild goat grass. It was the accidental cross-fertilisation of these that led to the much more fruitful bread wheat, probably the first plant to be sown as a crop, which was harvested with a horn-handled sickle with sharpened flints set into the blade with bitumen.

Just like that. Exactly the same linear model is proposed for the 'invention' of containers (p. 15):

> The development of both tools and weapons increased the demand for containers in which to remove the spoil of excavation or to preserve or to cook the winnings of the hunt. Basketwork is characteristic of the Neolithic Age and is a development of the weaving of rushes to make floor coverings for mud huts. Such forerunners of the carpet date from some time before 5000 BC. The same weavers learned to work in three dimensions so as to produce baskets in which grain could be stored. By 3000 BC the skill was widespread.

I do not wish to labour this point any further, but it must be pointed out that this kind of simplistic reductionism is less obvious to the uninitiated when it is cloaked in the apparent respectability of literary texts from the Graeco-Roman world or early medieval Europe.

PROBLEMS OF PERCEPTION ————

The theoretical and interpretative ground has been shifting rapidly all around the general issue of technology, and many new factors affect traditional interpretations of Roman technology.

Ethnic Stereotypes: Greeks and Romans

At this point, I will turn to another problem affecting the study of Roman technology, which is well illustrated by a quotation from a book on ancient pottery that encapsulates the traditional view of classical scholars. This interpretation of the relative merits of Greek and Roman culture permeated most branches of classical archaeology, and then progressed into the canons of the history of technology (Walters 1905 vol 2, 430):

> Roman vases are far inferior in nearly all respects to Greek; the shapes are less artistic, and the decoration, though not without merits of its own, bears the same relation to that of Greek vases that all Roman art does to Greek art.

What do we find eighty-five years later in *EHT* (p. 18)?:

> The Greeks were great builders but, apart from a few exceptions such as Archimedes, were theoretical scientists rather than practical technologists. . . . The Romans, although a far more practical people, invented little of their own but did much to adapt the principles, used by the Greeks only for their temple 'toys', to large-scale practical applications such as could be used 'for the common good'.

Later, in the context of a section on weapons and armour, the same sentiment is echoed by Charles Messenger (*EHT* p. 970):

> Unlike the Greeks, the Romans were not innovators but very practical engineers, who applied the ideas of their predecessors.

I have explored elsewhere the question of 'Greek science', which was in fact largely Roman in date, developed in Alexandria, and extensively applied, for example in irrigation agriculture (Greene 1990). I also stressed the need to modify our concepts, as the classical world developed from city-states to a vast empire with very disparate needs, differing greatly in areas of dissimilar geography and economic development.

Gender

Questions of gender are (at last) of growing importance in archaeology, but have hardly been addressed in relation to the industry or technology of the Roman period. The function of women in this context is hardly touched upon by Dickinson, Hallett, or other contributors to Grant and Kitzinger's *Civilisation of the Ancient Mediterranean: Greece and Rome* (1988), in contrast to aspects such as social status, prostitution, and the enjoyment (or otherwise) of sex. The reason is that these accounts rely upon the same documentary and literary sources which neglect many other aspects of economic life (Lefkowitz and Fant 1988). Work by Berg (1984; 1985) on recent industrial societies has underlined the fact that women remained a very important part of the labour equation, but it hardly needs to be said that they make little or no appearance in the 'roll of honour' of inventors. We can safely assume that many of the technical developments of the pre-industrial period were the result of women's endeavours, particularly in the context of food-processing and storage, and household industries such as ceramics and textiles (Westwood and Bhachu 1988).

In almost provocative opposition to late twentieth-century avoidance of conspicuously gender-specific language, it is depressing to find that *EHT* designates the period before farming as 'The first age: man, the hunter, masters fire' (p. 5), and to learn that 'Metal workers were a class of specialists . . . who depended for their sustenance on the labours of their fellow men.' (p. 13). Presumably the neglect of 'low' technology such as basketry, in contrast to the attention paid to machinery, also reflects feminine/masculine associations.

The Industrial Revolution

The lack of a Roman 'Industrial Revolution' in response to technical and infrastructural change need not worry us (Greene forthcoming), for Roman economic growth consisted primarily of proliferation and intensification, in the favourable circumstances of an expanding empire. The Industrial Revolution only happened once, initially in Britain and then in parts of Europe, and can therefore hardly be considered to be a 'normal' path of economic development. Technological change is now seen as more of a consequence than a cause of the Industrial Revolution of the eighteenth century, and the leading lights no longer appear to have been self-made craftsmen/entrepreneurs, but the very same rich industrialists and landowners of the pre-industrial period.

Technology Transfer

Experience of failures of high-technology investment in Third World economies has forced donor nations and banks in the First World to recognise the importance of the social context into which new technology is introduced, and to acknowledge the necessity for a suitable infrastructure. I have explored aspects of this phenomenon in a recent paper (ibid.) and drawn attention both to the diversity of forms of technology transfer, and the fact that change can take place purely in terms of the reorganisation of existing technical skills and resources, rather than new equipment or inventions. This concept is likely to be particularly useful in a Roman context, where innovation must have been more important than invention (Greene 1986; Hopkins 1988).

Appropriate Technology

The concept of appropriate technology is inextricably bound up with the careful use of global resources, ideally from renewable sources, without ecological or social damage. Obviously, we cannot look for values such as these amongst Roman engineers or manufacturers, but they remind us to avoid the pitfall of judging Roman technology purely in terms of progress, led by an unquestioned notion of the desirability of economic growth. *EHT* is dedicated 'To the memory of THOMAS NEWCOMEN who built the first engine to work without wind, water or muscle power'. The final irony is that the 'liberation' of humans and animals by Newcomen's steam engine of 1712 simply helped to increase the number of other ways in which they could be exploited, and sealed the fate of the world's atmosphere and forest cover by accelerating the use of fossil fuels.

CONCLUSIONS ————

Fortunately, there *is* genuine debate about the theory of the history of technology. Whether implicitly or explicitly, all modern prehistorians are involved in exploring the implications of technology (in its broadest sense), and Childe has not been alone in according technology a central determining role in human society.

In 1979, Bugliarello and Doner published a collection of papers on the history and philosophy of technology originally presented at a symposium held at Chicago in 1973. The symposium was prompted by unease amongst the participants about the impact of contemporary technology, and its retrospective implications ('Are we so bemused by our own age of anxiety that we have become insensitive to the impact caused by technological innovations in earlier times? How has man absorbed the technology of his own time in all the ages past?' (p. xi)).

The World Archaeological Congress held at Southampton in 1986 included a theme session entitled 'The social and economic contexts of technological change', subsequently published under the rather more dynamic title *What's New? A closer look at the process of innovation* (Leeuw and Torrence 1989). In the editors' preface, they describe the session as 'the only main theme . . . that was conceived of as being in the non-fashionable, functional and technological sphere' (p. xix). The reason for the change of title is interesting in the light of my comments on the First World orientation of *EHT*: 'Many scholars emphasised the continuous production of innovations in all social settings and protested against the prevailing attitude that non-western peoples are backward and unchanging, and depend entirely on the developed world for their ideas and technology' (p. ix).

The many contributions to *What's New?* raise the subject of the *context* of technology and innovation to a sophisticated level, which succeeds in combining theory and observation in case-studies from all over the world. Set alongside recent work on the Industrial Revolution and Third World economics, I hope that it is apparent that the attitudes displayed in *EHT* in 1989 are in fact the bones of a very large, but almost extinct, dinosaur. More than ten years previously, Kranzberg had already stated that 'innovation most nearly resembles an ecological process and requires a dynamic systems model.' (Bugliarello and Doner 1979, xx). This biological metaphor has been extended by Basalla's recent book *The Evolution of Technology* (1988), which argues against the role of individuals.

I hope that these concluding remarks give some indication of the vitality of this 'non-fashionable, functional and technological sphere', and the potential for research that exists in the Roman empire – a relatively sophisticated society with a significant element of information-flow through literacy.

Bibliography

Basalla, G. 1988 *The Evolution of Technology*. Cambridge; Cambridge University Press.

Berg, M. 1984 *The Coming of Industry: Innovation and Work 1700–1820*. London; Fontana.

Berg, M. 1985 *The Age of Manufactures: Industry, Innovation and Work in Britain 1700–1820*. Oxford; Blackwell.

Bugliarello, G. and D. B. Doner, (ed.) 1979 *The History and Philosophy of Technology*. Urbana; University of Illinois Press.

Dickinson, S. K. 1988 'Women in Rome' in M. Grant and R. Kitzinger, (eds) 3, 1319–1332.

Grant, M. and R. Kitzinger, (eds) 1988 *Civilisation of the Ancient Mediterranean: Greece & Rome* 3 vols. London; Collier Macmillan.

Greene, K. 1986 *The Archaeology of the Roman Economy*. London; Batsford.

Greene, K. 1990 'Perspectives on Roman technology' *Oxford Journal of Archaeology* 9.2, 209–219.

Greene, K. forthcoming 'How was technology transferred in the Roman Empire?' in M. Wood et al. (eds).

Hallett, J. P. 1988 'Roman attitudes toward sex' in M. Grant and R. Kitzinger (eds) 2, 1265–1278.

Hopkins, K. 1988 'Roman trade, industry, and labour' in M. Grant and R. Kitzinger (eds) 2, 753–777.

Leeuw, S. van der and R. Torrence (ed.) 1989 *What's New? A Closer Look at the Process of Innovation.* London; Unwin Hyman.

Lefkowitz, M. R. and M. B. Fant B. 1988 *Women's Life in Greece and Rome: a source book in translation.* Duckworth.

Walters, H. B. 1905 *History of Ancient Pottery: Greek, Etruscan and Roman* 2 vols. London.

Westwood, S. and P. Bhachu 1988 *Enterprising Women: Ethnicity, Economy and Gender Relations.* Cambridge; Polity Press.

Wood, M. et al. (eds) forthcoming *Opposition or Opportunity?: Romanisation in the West.*

6

THE PRE-INDUSTRIAL CITY IN ROMAN BRITIAN

Simon Clarke

By detailed examination of the location of different types of building within a range of urban sites, the functions of Roman towns are considered. This paper rejects the suggestion that the form of the Roman town can be explained solely as the imposition of an alien culture. Indigenous social forces must be considered primarily responsible for the maintenance and adaptation of an institution which survived for over three hundred years within the province. Various theoretical models of the pre-industrial city are considered. With these in mind possible explanations are sought for the variations in the form of Romano-British urban topography. The differences in size and amenities offered between early civitas capitals and small towns are considered the product of radically different social conditions in each. This is quite contrary to the still frequently expressed opinion that small towns simply represent a later version of urbanism which had discarded as unnecessary the trappings of classical civilisation. The possibility that general principles exist which may extend throughout all periods is suggested by parallels in the medieval period.

INTRODUCTION ─────────

Rarely have there been systematic attempts to consider in detail the functional implications of the urban topography of Roman sites. There is a belief that we already know all about the major Roman towns. Though rarely explicit there is an assumption that towns are a facade, an alien imposition, part of an ideology accepted by the local population during a vague process known as Romanisation (Reece 1985, 37). Such faith in diffusionism has largely disappeared from other periods in archaeology. Though there is no doubt that a significant flow of people from the continent did occur, the possibility that early towns served functional purposes for the indigenous population must be considered.

THE ORIGIN OF ROMANO-BRITISH URBANISM ─────

In discussing the function of early public towns it is worth quickly reviewing the evidence for their origin. Two factors have traditionally been considered highly significant in the development of the early urban centres in
Roman Britain. Both are essentially diffusionist explanations for the spread
of towns: official encouragement, and the economic stimulation provided
by the presence of the army.

The reference by Tacitus to 'private encouragement and official assistance' (*Agricola* 21) regarding the foundation of public buildings has been
seen as tantamount to a deliberate official policy of urbanisation (Frere
1987, 98–9; Wacher 1974). However no other references to an official
urban policy are known to exist (Mann and Penman 1978, 61). Others have
seen this passage as indicating the informal use of tax remissions and the
use of the local nobility's client system to raise funds and gather necessary
resources (Blagg 1980; Millett 1990, 72). Millett has suggested that 'private
encouragement and official assistance' are much more likely to have origin-
ated at the *civitas* rather than provincial level of government, with Agricola
receiving undue credit for the actions of his political subordinates (ibid.,
74).

Similarly the theory that skilled military personnel were used to carry out
official policy has lost favour in recent years. Blagg notes that the military
have a quite distinct style of stone masonry (Blagg 1980; 1984). Furthermore masons were far from always present in army units stationed in
southern Britain. Cirencester's fort apparently had none, its timber buildings (probably of two phases) being of post-in-trench and sill beam construction (Wacher and McWhirr 1982).

The theory that major early towns were stimulated by economic activity
originally focused on a fort (Webster 1966) has also been questioned. On a
general level for southern Britain it is now considered highly unlikely that
camp followers were able to determine the location of political centres in a
society in which local government continued to be in the hands of the
traditional land owning elite (Jones 1987, 48–9). Certainly the traders and
craftsmen known to have existed at fort *vici* are very unlikely to have
possessed the resources to carry out a major public building programme.
Although Corinium directly overlies at least one fort, it perhaps provides
one of the best examples of the weakness of the military origin theory. On
the creation of the public town neither buildings nor existing road system
appear to have been incorporated into the town's fabric. In fact the levelling of the fort and surrounding civilian settlement seems to have been so

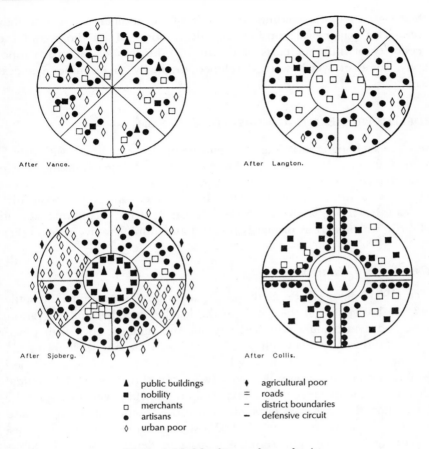

▲ public buildings	✦ agricultural poor
■ nobility	= roads
▢ merchants	‒ district boundaries
● artisans	‒ defensive circuit
◊ urban poor	

Figure 1. Models of pre-modern urbanism.

complete that the construction of the basilica, one of the first tasks undertaken, failed to make provision for possible subsidence over the fort's defensive ditches (Wacher 1974, 298).

A more plausible suggestion is that a fort was located at Cirencester largely for political reasons, being just a short distance from the existing elite centre at Bagendon. It was this settlement which provided the origin of the Roman town. The creation of the public town at Cirencester signifies nothing more than a minor shift in the location of the region's political centre, in order to take advantage of the new communications network focused on the fort (Jones 1987, 48-9; Millett 1990, 74).

In the light of this the development of major towns should be studied

with a view to understanding the needs of the indigenous society they
served. This paper will consider the distribution of buildings and the
accessibility of different parts of the town, using models of urban topography, some of which were developed originally to examine medieval
towns.

PROBLEMS WITH EXISTING MODELS OF URBANISM ─────────

There are such great variations between the models concerned with urbanism that it must be wondered whether any useful generalisations can
be transferred to the Roman period. A great many classifications of ancient
and medieval urban settlement have been made. However a basic division can be made between those originating from economic stimuli
and those which start as primarily political and administrative centres (Fig.
1).

Commercial Urbanism

Vance (1971) pictured the medieval city as primarily a commercial settlement. Authority was in the hands of the leading members of the various
guilds, and as a result towns had not one but multiple foci, with practitioners of different crafts tending to live and work close to their own guild-
hall. The aristocracy, while it may have possessed town houses, was peripheral to urban life. Nevertheless society continued to be essentially feudal,
guilds providing an alternative overlordship (ibid., 106), with strong ties being maintained across class divisions, hence the absence of zoning according to class. Because the society lacked a strong central authority no sense
of planning is visible. The result is a mass of densely packed buildings
served by a network of narrow irregular streets which were frequently en-
croached upon and built out over (ibid., 102).

A slightly different picture is proposed by Langton (1975), who described
the pre-capitalist city based on observations of seventeenth century
Newcastle. He recognised that a single mercantile quarter provided the
focus to a town zoned by both class and occupation. The aristocracy was
also present in the city, but as with Vance's model was not of central
importance occupying its own high class residential district away from the
city's centre. These observations are less acceptable as a model for urbanism in Roman Britain, however, for Newcastle was on the eve of the Industrial Revolution and is perhaps more aptly thought of as a hybrid pre-
modern/modern city.

Public Urbanism

Sjoberg's (1960) pre-industrial city, like Finley's (1975) ancient city, was dominated physically and symbolically by the edifices of administrative and religious institutions. Important commercial buildings were to be found in the central area, but were dwarfed by administrative and religious structures. These formed a single focus around which the residences of the aristocratic elite clustered. Sjoberg noted that most cities were multi-functional, usually fulfilling administrative, religious, cultural and economic roles. However the city was essentially geared to serving the needs of the landed elite, economic activity being of secondary importance. Finley stated that in defining the city, 'the economy did not enter into consideration at all, apart from the requirement that the material goods indispensable for civilised amenities had to be available somehow' (ibid., 124). Unlike many other writers Sjoberg saw the aristocracy as an urban class, in spite of their ownership of rural estates. To them the city was an essential tool of social control. It allowed the maintenance of communication within the elite class, provided physical safety, perpetuated their value system, confirming their 'divine rights' and provided consumer items which were the symbols of elite status. Outside the core area, isolated from it and each other by poor communications, and sometimes internal city walls, were further distinct districts. Each had a fairly homogeneous character, zoning being according to ethnic origin, family ties (including patronage) and occupation. A significant low status population (slaves and outcasts) was to be expected throughout the city and just outside the city walls, where rural poor were also to be found.

Gradual Development

Each of these theories has some basis in fact, but they are clearly incompatible. Collis (1984, 123) simply saw them as flawed by their 'lack of historical depth', leading him to construct his own 'model of gradual development' (Fig. 2) to describe the evolution of a defended oppidum (ibid., fig. 8.15). This model has much to commend it, the settlement created closely resembling Silchester, which Collis takes as the Roman ideal (ibid., 124). However I do not believe that failure to consider the temporal dimension can completely account for the differences between the models of Vance and Sjoberg. A more reasonable suggestion is that they represent two distinct brands of urbanism.

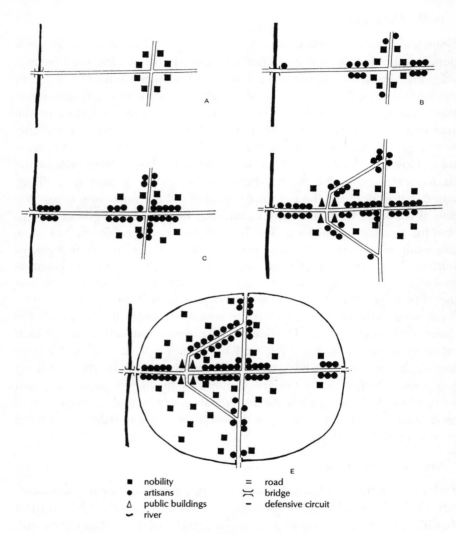

Figure 2. Model of gradual urban development (after Collis).

CORINIUM: A PUBLIC TOWN HISTORIANS OF TECHNOLOGY ──────

Cirencester (Fig. 3) like most major Roman towns had a relatively low density of buildings set within a highly regular grid of streets. These were generally between six and nine metres in width but could be as much as twelve

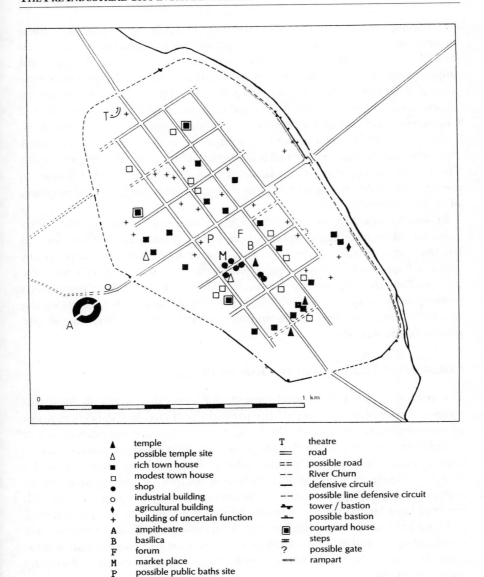

▲	temple	T	theatre
△	possible temple site	═	road
■	rich town house	══	possible road
□	modest town house	‒‒	River Churn
●	shop	▬	defensive circuit
○	industrial building	‒‒	possible line defensive circuit
◆	agricultural building	⚓	tower / bastion
+	building of uncertain function	⚊	possible bastion
A	ampitheatre	▣	courtyard house
B	basilica	☰	steps
F	forum	?	possible gate
M	market place	᠁	rampart
P	possible public baths site		

Figure 3. Roman Cirencester: functions of buildings.

metres across in central areas of the town (McWhirr 1981, 30). Far from
lacking a single strong focus, the town was dominated by a large basilica

and forum, with a large temple precinct probably occupying the insula immediately to the south-east and public baths possibly to the west (Wacher 1974, 300). The theatre next to the city's north gate, the amphitheatre just outside the west gate and a number of possible temple sites, at locations scattered throughout the city, detract somewhat from the impression of centralisation of public buildings. Only very limited commercial and industrial activity is suggested from existing excavations. These are confined to a limited area adjacent to the central public buildings with a single light industrial building located just outside the west gate. The rest of the city displays no sense of zoning by building type, houses of the highest quality being scattered fairly evenly amongst domestic premises of more modest character.

In further contrast to Vance's model of medieval urbanism the aristocracy seems to have been central to the life of Roman cities. Corinium, as has been argued above, served as a replacement for the elite native settlement at Bagendon. It may perhaps even have been named after Corio, the last pre-Roman ruler of the Dobunni (Wacher 1974, 293). Cirencester's service community was probably consistent with serving the needs of the resident population without providing a central place facility to the surrounding countryside.

COMMERCIAL URBANISM IN THE ROMAN PERIOD

The nature of the urban development at Cirencester outlined above fits quite well with Sjoberg's view of the pre-industrial city, but Vance's concept of commercial urbanism, in which the landed elite are peripheral, is not completely alien to Roman Britain. Roman Britain appears to have had no equivalent to the medieval guilds and very little evidence exists as to the Roman attitude to land holding in urban centres. However small towns appear to have a great deal in common with Vance's medieval model. Some at least lacked much cohesion, being strung out along a great length of highway. The Roman settlement at Bourton-on-the-Water seems to have consisted of a number of occupation areas both on and some distance away from the Fosse Way. Small towns nearly always lacked either the will or the means to establish a regular street network. Where the building land provided by the frontage of a highway was not adequate small tracks often seem to have been laid to serve individual buildings as the need arose. A reasonably full street pattern of this type is known at Wycomb. Only two branch roads are known from the patchy investigation of Bourton Bridge

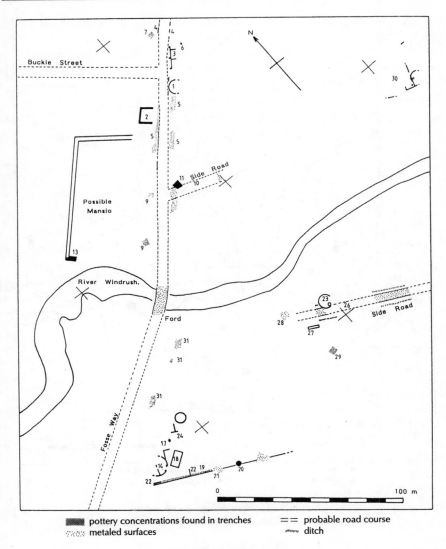

Figure 4. Bourton Bridge settlement.

settlement (Fig. 4). Even from the very short lengths of these side roads so far recognised it is clear that encroachment by buildings was a regular occurrence.

So far relatively minor commercial settlements have been discussed. A

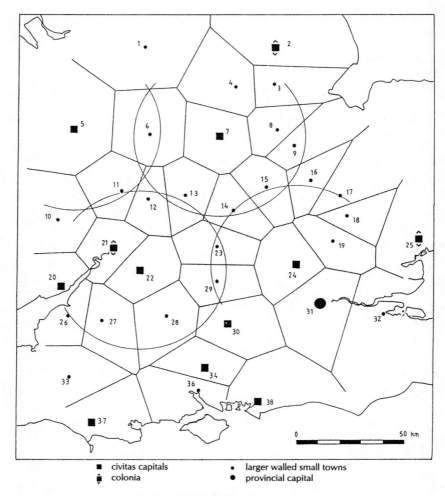

*Figure 5. Thiessen polygons applied to
larger Romano-British walled towns (after Hodder 1972).*

site like Kenchester however, with the resources and the will to build a defensive circuit, is more interesting. This suggests that the wealth generated
from commercial activity was enough to support a large population, with
fairly high material standards, but did not lead to the urban planning and
strong central architectural focus which characterised the public towns.
Even in the ancient period it is clear that such sites were confused with pub-

lic towns. However Strabo (3.4.13) emphasises that they represent something quite different when he protested against the term city being applied to the large villages (*komai*) of the Spanish peninsula (Finley 1975, 124).

The Temporal Development of Classical Urbanism?

It might be argued that the differences between the public towns, which were mostly early foundations, and the small towns, which often did not reach their maximum extent until the later Roman period, were due to changes in the nature of urbanism. It has been said (e.g. Reece 1980) that classical urbanism was in decline by the late period, the population of *civitas* capitals having failed to grow, their public buildings falling into decay or at least not being added to by new foundations. The larger walled small towns which grew spontaneously on the fringes of the early *civitas* territories (Hodder 1972) may have performed essentially the same role as an early *civitas* capital (Fig. 5). Their 'natural' growth, without the public trimmings, was sustained by the rising power of the money economy. The term 'false start' has been applied to the public towns (Jones 1987), their *genus* being seen as an artificial creation of a foreign ideology which was ultimately unsustainable by the native population.

However the image of public towns as failed social institutions by the fourth century is denied by the distribution of villas. These late Roman expressions of landed wealth generally occur in distinct clusters centred on the public towns, but are noticeably absent around most larger walled small towns. Some of the so-called small towns enclose areas not much less than that of the smaller public towns, and with their extensive extramural settlements may have had populations somewhat larger. But similarities in the size of the settlements were not matched by similarities in form. The larger small towns were very often heavily involved in industrial activity. The largest, Water Newton, was a major centre of the pottery industry. Worcester, another large walled site, was heavily involved with iron production. In contrast, even in the late Empire public towns were not important production or redistribution centres. Even their own needs had to be met by importation from areas some distance away; north Wiltshire and Oxfordshire supply Cirencester's pottery, for example. The absence of a regular street grid already commented upon should also not simply be dismissed as a degeneration of urban style in the later Empire. Drinkwater has noted that the *insula* system was most inflexible. Once laid down the network was not easily added to or altered, even to accommodate the largest and most important subsequent building programmes (Drinkwater

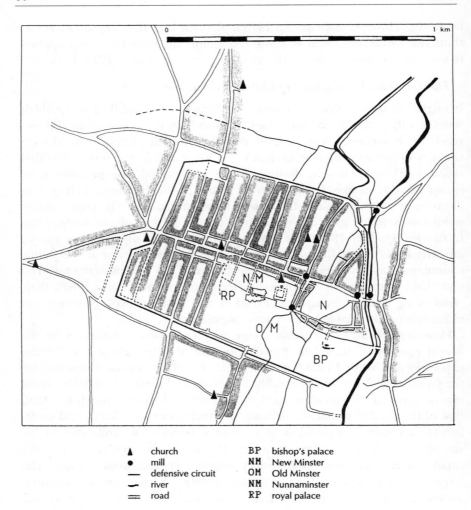

▲	church	BP	bishop's palace
●	mill	NM	New Minster
—	defensive circuit	OM	Old Minster
⌒	river	NM	Nunnaminster
=	road	RP	royal palace

Figure 6. Late Saxon Winchester.

1985, 53). This inflexibility was apparently acceptable in public towns throughout their history in spite of the inefficient use it made of space, but was not considered appropriate in small towns.

These differences argue very strongly for public towns continuing to have very different functions, in relation to the surrounding countryside, to even the very largest small towns.

MEDIEVAL PUBLIC TOWNS ————

In spite of frequent references to the dissimilarity between classical and medieval urbanism (e.g. Reece 1985), commercial urbanism was not absent from Roman Britain. Nor does public urbanism appear to have been confined to the Roman period. Saxon Winchester (Fig. 6) would appear to fit the public town model much more closely than Vance's model of a medieval city supported by commercial activity. Between the seventh and ninth century the city's population seems to have comprised four main elements. These were a royal residence, a cathedral church and its attendant community, an unknown but probably small number private estates belonging to nobles and a small service population (Biddle 1976, 119). The latter was numerically small and dependent on the other three elements in the town and certainly did not perform a central place function as a market for the surrounding countryside (Hodges 1982, 42). What is particularly startling however was the towns provision around AD 900 with a highly regular street grid planned and executed as a single feature (Biddle 1976, 119). While the town had probably started to take on certain trade and production roles from the late ninth century, the impetus for this administrative and cultural capital in Wessex clearly came from society's traditional elite: king, nobles and church. Hodges sees this as the result of the kings of Wessex looking to southern Europe where the classical street grids still persisted as a fossil from the Roman Empire (Hodges 1988, 5), but this is surely a weak argument for so strong a similarity. For such a massive expenditure of labour as the creation of a planned town, there must have been sound practical rather than purely sentimental reasons.

THE SEPARATION OF PUBLIC AND COMMERCIAL URBANISM ————

Sjoberg has characterised public towns as populated by a significant merchant class, as well as an aristocratic elite, and lists a number of reasons why the two elements of urban society should be located together (Sjoberg 1960). Prime amongst these was the elite's need to maintain a firm grip over all potential sources of social power. Elite control of the means of production is a central theme in Marxist social theory and is seen by Hodges as the driving force behind early medieval urbanism (Hodges 1982; 1988). However there are sound reasons why these two important elements of urban life should repel as well as attract each other. Sjoberg himself noted that the religious-philosophical value systems promoted by most landed elites in pre-industrial societies depreciates non-intellectual activity as degrading, while glorifying leisure, literary pursuits and conspicuous consumption. These values had the effect of maintaining the status of the elite over the common classes. A secondary consequence of this mentality however is that initiative and enterprise is stifled, as there is little incentive to increase productivity (Sjoberg 1960, 186). This may help to explain why so little industrial activity is situated in the public towns. The presence of the elite while providing a natural market, also provided a powerful disincentive to the initiation of commercial activity. The lack of evidence for industrial activity at Cirencester is almost complete. This is largely explained by the site's complete unsuitability as a redistribution centre. Although the city is at the hub of a road network, bulky items like pottery become prohibitively expensive unless water transport is possible. Cirencester's lack of a navigable river therefore effectively prevented its development as a commercial centre. However, that such a site should be chosen as a capital is telling in itself. There may be a similar division between planned towns and organic development at small towns in Gaul. Drinkwater noted that sites like Arlon St Ambroix, while not possessing a classical planned layout, displayed a higher level of commercial and industrial activity than many *civitas* capitals (Drinkwater 1985, 54).

Over Britain as a whole most Roman period industrial activity can be seen to have been situated either in the countryside or in small towns, the largest of which seem to have developed at the political periphery. The development of these small towns away from the political centre might represent displacement of merchant and artisan classes to locations with more favourable social conditions.

GLEVUM: COMMERCIAL URBANISM WITH PUBLIC TOWN TRAPPINGS? ——

Of all the major towns which developed in the early Roman period, the *colonia* at Gloucester provides evidence for the best objections to the theory for public towns as set out above. Figure 7 is based on the extensive excavations published by Hurst (1972; 1974; 1975; 1988). Glevum developed on the site of a legionary fortress and its attendant civilian settlement. Both would appear to have made significant contributions to the material development of the *colonia*. The fortress street grid was inherited almost intact, as in all probability were at least some of the barrack blocks (ibid., 56). This is in stark contrast to Cirencester where, as already noted, levelling seems to have been total. The tilery and much of the civilian settlement outside Glevum's north gate also experienced a high level of continuity. Therefore the suggestion that the city developed from the commercial activity stimulated by the fortress seems not unreasonable in this case. Furthermore the city was established in an area marginal to the pre-existing Dobunni tribal grouping and for this reason it must to some extent have been a conscious decision to create a new centre of urbanism. By this I mean not simply the material trappings of a monumental town but also its social fabric, as no naturally urban, landed elite previously existed in the area of the *territorium*.

Certainly there is little evidence for a landed elite in the area immediately surrounding the town, villas being relatively sparse and small in scale by comparison with the nearby Cotswolds. However, that some sort of elite was extracting surplus in the form of rent or some other unearned income seems almost certain to be due to the *colonia*'s lack of a visible means of support. In spite of Glevum's promising location as a commercial centre, at the lowest bridging point of a major river system, manufacturing on the site actually declined after the military's withdrawal.

In many ways the commercial elements of the city remained separate from the monumental town in the same way that the military and civilian settlements had been. Although a few manufacturing premises were present within the walled area the main concentration of shops seems to have been outside the north gate, where a building interpreted as a market hall has also been noted. Wealthy houses are very definitely concentrated within the walled town along with a cluster of monumental buildings. In many ways Glevum was two communities, a walled settlement of the landed elite dominated by public buildings, and a commercial settlement, without a street grid and consisting mainly of strip buildings fronting the main road. This situation has some similarities with Langton's model in which elite residential and commercial districts were quite separate.

CONCLUSION ⸺

In conclusion, public cities as exemplified by Corinium cannot be explained purely as a facade of classical culture which was dropped in favour of 'natural' town development. Rather the form of the classical city should be considered highly functional. An emphasis on public buildings and a strong sense of planning would appear to be diagnostic features for towns of all periods which had their origins as political, administrative, cultural, educational and religious central places. In their earliest stages it is doubtful that such centres can truthfully be described as urban. Winchester

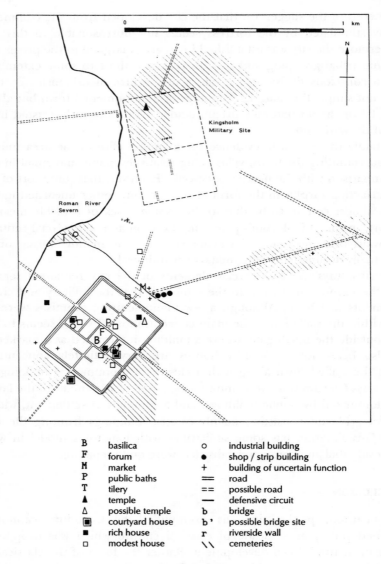

B	basilica	o	industrial building
F	forum	●	shop / strip building
M	market	+	building of uncertain function
P	public baths	═	road
T	tilery	══	possible road
▲	temple	—	defensive circuit
△	possible temple	b	bridge
◙	courtyard house	b'	possible bridge site
■	rich house	r	riverside wall
□	modest house	\\	cemeteries

Figure 7. Roman Gloucester.

was not urban until the late ninth century at least (Biddle 1976, 120), while few would consider the oppida of southern England to have been. Nevertheless they performed the role of *urbs* as understood by Roman writers and should be thought of as one of two quite distinct origins of urbanism. The other was commercial urbanism in which the town, lacking the central authority of the aristocracy, developed organically without any sense of planning and often without a single strong central focus to the settlement. While several writers, Sjoberg in particular, have noted that there are many reasons why these two elements of urbanism should come together to form a single settlement, forces also seem to exist which repel merchant and aristocratic classes from one another. In the Roman period the two types of urbanism seem to have remained particularly rigidly separate. This has given rise both to towns with segregation of the commercial from administrative elements, such as Glevum, and to towns in which the landed elite and their administrative infrastucture are largely or wholly absent, such as Kenchester.

Bibliography

Biddle, M. 1976 'Towns' in D. Wilson (ed.), 99–150.

Blagg, T. F. C. 1980 'Civilian and military architecture in the province of Britain' *World Archaeology* 12 (1), 27–42.

Blagg, T. F. C. 1984 'An examination of the connections between military and civilian architecture in Roman Britain' in T. F. C. Blagg and A. C. King (eds), 249–64.

Blagg, T. F. C. and A. C. King (eds) 1984 *Military and Civilian in Roman Britain*. Oxford; British Archaeological Reports (British Series 136).

Clarke, D. L. 1972 (ed.) *Models in Archaeology*. London.

Collis, J. 1984 *Oppida*. Sheffield; Sheffield University, Department of Prehistory.

Drinkwater, J. R. 1985 'Urbanisation in the three Gauls: some observations' in F. Grew and B. Hobley (eds), 49–55.

Finley, M. 1975 *The Ancient Economy*. London.

Frere, S. S. 1987 *Britannia* 3rd edition. London.

Grew, F. and B. Hobley (eds) 1985 *Roman Urban Topography in Britain and Western Empire*. Council for British Arachaeology Research Report 59. London.

Hodder, I. 1972 'Locational models and the study of Romano-British settlement' in D. L. Clarke (ed.), 887–909.

Hodges, R. 1982 *Dark Age Economics*. London; Duckworth.

Hodges, R. 1988 'The rebirth of towns in the Middle Ages' in R. Hodges and B. Hobley (eds).

Hodges, R. and B. Hobley (eds) 1988 *The Rebirth of Towns in the West AD 700–1050*. Council for British Archaeology Research Report 68. London.

Hurst, H. 1972 'Excavations at Gloucester, 1968–1971, first interim report' *Antiquities Journal* 52, 24–69.

Hurst, H .1974 'Excavations at Gloucester, 1971–1973, second interim report' *Antiquities Journal* 54, 8–52.

Hurst, H. 1975 'Excavations at Gloucester, third interim report: Kingsholm 1966–1975' *Antiquities Journal* 55, 267–294.

Hurst, H. 1988 'Gloucester' in G. Webster (ed.), 48–73.

Jones, R. F. J. 1987 'A false start? The Roman urbanism of western Europe' *World Archaeology* 19 (1), 47–57.

Langton, J. 1975 'Residential patterns in pre-industrial cities. Some case studies in seventeenth century Britain' *Transactions of the Institute of British Geographers* 65, 1–27.

Mann, J. C. and R. C. Penman 1978 (eds) *Literary Sources for Roman Britain*. London.

McWhirr, A. 1981 *Roman Gloucestershire*. Gloucester.

McWhirr, A. 1988 'Cirencester' in G. Webster (ed.), 74–90.

Millett, M. 1990 *The Romanisation of Roman Britain. An essay in archaeological interpretation*. London.

Reece, R. 1980 'Town and country: The end of Roman Britain' *World Archaeology* 12 (1), 77–92.

Reece, R. 1985 'Roman towns and their plans' in F. Grew and B. Hobley (eds), 37–40.

Sjoberg, G. 1960 *The Pre-Industrial City*. New York.

Vance, J. E. 1971 'Land assignment in the pre-capitalist, capitalist and post-capitalist city' *Economic Geography* 47, 101–120.

Wacher, J. 1966 (ed.) *The Civitas of Roman Britain*. Leicester.

Wacher, J. 1974 *The Towns of Roman Britain*. London.

Wacher, J. and A. McWhirr 1982 *Early Roman Occupation at Cirencester*. Cirencester.

Webster, G. 1966 'Fort and town in early Roman Britain' in Wacher (ed.) .

Webster, G. (ed.) 1988 *Fortress into City. The Consolidation of Roman Britain, First Century AD*. Batsford; London.

Wilson, D. 1976 (ed.) *The Archaeology of Anglo-Saxon England*. London.

7

WHEN (AND WHAT) WAS THE END OF ROMAN BRITAIN?

Kurt Hunter-Mann

A failure to distinguish archaeology from historiography has led many archaeologists to become over-reliant on the sub-division of British history into periods such as Roman and Anglo-Saxon. Furthermore, the unquestioning use of such normative racial/cultural terms as 'Roman' obscures the view of socio-economic change during the Roman period. This paper discusses the end of the Roman period as part of a continuum of social, political and economic change that refers back at least to the Iron Age and greatly influenced the Anglo-Saxon period. Marxist theory is used to suggest why British society changed so much during the fifth century. The model employed involves three basic revisions to the Marxist explanation of diversity and change: the pre-eminence of the societal superstructure; greater interaction within and between social classes; and the potential of any individual to promote change.

INTRODUCTION

The study of Roman Britain is dominated by dates. Historical events provide convenient chronological markers – not just AD 43 and 410, but also 55 BC, AD 61 and 367, for example. Some of the more fiercely debated topics also revolve around dates: just when exactly did Agricola subjugate Scotland, and when was the Antonine Wall manned? I do not wish to suggest that historical events are not important to archaeologists, but neither should they dictate the archaeological agenda. Whereas Roman Britain is seen as ending in 410 (if not 402), studies of the Anglo-Saxon period prefer to use a date of 'circa 450' for its commencement. Consequently, relatively little attention has been paid to the interface between the two periods, to the detriment of both. For example, Simon Esmonde Cleary recently suggested that 'there is a discernible post-Roman but non-Saxon interlude over most of the country of half a century at least' (1989, xi). Such historicism is self-perpetuating in that it confines evidence of *romanitas* to the period before circa 400, implying that society after 400 was no longer Roman; this view is normative in the extreme.

An Alternative Perspective

This paper is based on the Marxist assumption that the primary causes of social change are the contradictions between the forces of production and the relations of production; such contradictions result in conflict between those classes controlling production and the classes exploited in this process. Marxist-inspired Western archaeologists have developed a spectrum of views on the relative importance of economic and non-economic phenomena, such as ideology, in dictating the nature of the socio-political superstructure; there is also disagreement among neo-Marxists as to the dominance or reciprocity of the economic base and the socio-political superstructure (Trigger 1989, 340–1). In order to avoid over-emphasis on the economy, I prefer to see social change as the result of contradictions between the forces and relations of *society*, rather than of production; this means that non-economic factors, such as ideology, can have a direct influence on society.

One problem with Marxist theory is its division of society into classes (traditionally, the exploiters and the exploited), as this tends to reduce the possibilty of conflict within classes or consensus between classes. The potential for reciprocity between the socio-political superstructure and the relations of society has to be considered. This would allow sub-classes to contribute to the relations of society, whether or not they belonged to classes controlling the means of society; such a process, operating across classes rather than upwards between classes, can be regarded as lateral relations of society.

The elaboration of the class system acknowledges the potential of the individual to contribute to the relations of society, something not easily accommodated in traditional Marxist theory. Formal economic models, for instance, include an error term because it is recognised that any individual can make an impact on the group norm (Anderson 1991, 13–14).

IMPERIAL EXPLOITATION AND ROMANISATION ⸻

Unlike modern capitalist imperialism (conscious, systematic economic exploitation of the periphery by the core), Roman imperialism was largely the product of social struggle within the Roman elite (Millett 1990, 6–8).

Such socially motivated action, operating within classes (often for personal prestige), incorporates the three refinements to Marxist theory outlined above.

There was a degree of economic exploitation of the Roman imperial periphery, but in the case of Britain this took the form of an opportunity for the developing provinces (such as those in Gaul) to enter a new market; the process involved was casual, lateral interaction between provinces – not planned, hierarchical exploitation by a centralised imperial economy.

The provincial administrative system suggests a desire on behalf of the imperial authorities to avoid an excessively centralised system of government. If there was an imperial strategy, it was the use of Romanisation to encourage its subjects' participation in each provincial socio-economic system. Romanisation is generally seen as a gravitational form of cultural assimilation, with the aristocracy being the first native class to adopt aspects of Roman culture in order to be identified with imperial authority, thus maintaining their status within native society (ibid., 68); the lower levels of native society followed suit later for both social and economic reasons.

The question relevant to this paper is how 'Roman' the Romano-Britons had become by circa 400. The two main infrastructural elements of Romanisation, the towns and the army, have long been the focus of archaeological investigation in this country, yet they encompass probably less than ten per cent of the population of Roman Britain. The more common agricultural establishments and the small towns, displaying less evidence of *romanitas*, are severely under-represented in the archaeological record investigated thus far. A consequence of this is an over-estimation of the degree of *romanitas* in Romano-British society. The pragmatic nature of Roman imperialism meant that suitable elements of the LPRIA (late pre-Roman Iron Age) socio-economic system were accommodated in that of the Roman province. The maintenance of the native aristocracy within the provincial system probably involved the continuation of the LPRIA socially-embedded economy. As far as the bulk of the land-based native population were concerned, isolated as they were from much that was 'Roman' about Romano-British society, there was little inherent need for widespread adoption of Roman cultural attributes.

Towns are considered to have played an important role in the process of Romanisation, acting as foci of the imperial socio-economic system. Yet there is evidence of a decline of the urban functions within towns, beginning as early as the second century (Reece 1980). As the need or desire of the imperial government to maintain towns as infrastructural elements of Romanisation diminished, so the level of the government's investment in towns decreased. Consequently, the towns had to rely on their functional roles as social, economic and administrative central places within the local socio-economic system. In addition, increased investment in both rural society and economy – which is evident in the increasing numbers of villas and rural temples, and the location of later Roman pottery industries away from the larger towns (Millett 1990, 167–8 and fig. 52) – suggests that towns were possibly centres of trade, but not of industry. The documented troubles of the third century, with inflation, and disruption of trade with Gaul, probably saw a decline of trade via the towns. Although towns retained some social and trading importance, they acted primarily as centres of administration and, where walled, defence.

Although the army may have contributed to the Romanisation of Britain, its role in this process has been exaggerated. The military never totalled more than 50,000, whereas the civilian population numbered several millions, the vast majority of whom had no regularised direct contact with the army. Furthermore, a large proportion of the army consisted of auxiliaries, who would themselves have been Romanised only to a degree at first. As time passed, the army became less a beacon of *romanitas* and more a military wing of Romano-British society, hardly distinguishable from the civilian population. Consequently, the socio-economic influence of the army is considered to have been limited and largely indirect.

The concept of Romanisation filtering down from the native aristocracy to the rest of the population has merit, but requires qualification. Romanisation was a protracted process which occurred at varying, inconsistent rates in different places; the adoption of the villa house at the expense of the round-house may be a case in point. LPRIA society differed greatly across Britain, and the reaction to Romanisation would have varied accordingly (ibid., 11ff.). Clearly, Romanisation was not a normative process; the rate of assimilation (and the meaning it had to its subjects) would have varied from tribe to tribe, and within these groups between communities, families and even individuals.

In short, there was no classical Roman society in fourth century Britain; indeed, there probably never had been as far as the majority of the population were concerned. The socio-economic system displayed signs of reversion to the socially-embedded, land-based LPRIA system that had been maintained in the Roman period to form the foundation to the 'Roman' superstructure of Romano-British society. Accordingly, the role and nature of the infrastructural elements (notably the towns) differed greatly from the early Roman period. Finally, it is unwise to envisage a single Romano-British society; there was a multitude of perpectives of social identity, held by individuals and groups.

FIFTH-CENTURY ROMAN BRITAIN

Keeping this view of later Romano-British society within a continuum of socio-economic change, we may now be able to look for evidence of change in the fifth century and try to determine what it represents.

A rapid decline in coin circulation has been cited as an indication of the rapid collapse of the economy circa 400. However, it may be that the presence of Roman coinage in Britain largely represents central government expenditure, at first to pay the army, and later as remuneration for civil work and offices (Reece 1987, 125 and fig. 7.4). Copies of coins were often made during the fourth century, but arguably because the diocesan government had to produce coinage for its own administrative purposes. Copying tended to occur when silvered bronze coins were in circulation, perhaps because it was the intrinsic value of the metal that mattered, rather than the nominal cash value. This suggests that the bronze coins were largely the product of the administration's use of coins, with site finds representing the discarding of intrinsically relatively worthless, unsilvered coins, rather than loss as a result of circulation within a cash economy (ibid., 43–44). The increasing vigour of the Romano-British pottery industries during the later Roman period suggests that pottery was supplied on a more regional basis. Relatively little fourth-century Romano-British pottery was exported out of the diocese, and the level of pottery imports from the continent was much lower than that of the earlier Roman period (Millett 1990, 161 and fig. 65); a decrease in such long-distance trade probably reduced the need for large-scale cash transactions.

The use of coinage may not have ended so abruptly anyway. Coins issued after 402 do occur, albeit uncommonly, on British sites; moreover, the lack of post – 402 bronze issues from the continent may have been partly the product of an abundance of issues from the preceding period (388–402), a pattern of coin usage evident throughout the fourth century. Assuming a use half-life of twenty years, approximately a quarter of the coins issued during 388–402 could still have been in circulation by circa 430. Such a diminishing coin supply could have facilitated a gradual change to a cashless economy. Turning this argument on its head, there is no reason why the Romano-British could not have minted their own coins for use in a cash economy after 402. The abrupt cessation of the importation of imperial coinage after 402 is more in keeping with the end of imperial administrative and military involvement in Britain circa 410. The evidence of the coinage is therefore inconclusive, and must be considered in its socio-economic context.

Another widely accepted sign of the collapse of the Roman economy circa 400 is the apparent decline of pottery production. Yet the fourth century saw the emergence of manufacturers of both coarse and fine wares, and hand-made wares (ibid., 224 and fig. 95). It is possible that the hand-made wares represent a phase of pottery production operating at a lower technological level after either the demand or the ability to supply wheel-thrown fine wares had ceased. Such regionalised industries, not widely distributed far from the centres of production and so less likely to be influenced by imported forms, may have developed a degree of typological conservatism. It is possible that such pottery production could have continued well into the fifth century, involving forms not readily distinguished from those of the early fifth century.

Whereas the archaeological evidence is inconclusive, there is documentary evidence pointing to a degree of continuity of Romano-British society beyond 400. A council appears to have been governing the diocese in the middle of the fifth century (Gildas, 23.1), and at least one dynasty of the Romano-British aristocracy maintained their political eminence throughout the fifth century and into the sixth in central southern Britain, for example (ibid., 25.3). Documentary sources in fifth and sixth century Britain do not perceive any abrupt end to Roman Britain. They do identify the conflict between British and Germanic elites during the third quarter of the fifth century as a most serious disruption, if not a catastrophe, and it is perhaps at this point that the society and economy was forced to change markedly from that of the fourth century. The use of central places with a primary defensive function, particularly evident in the re-use of Iron Age hillforts (Burrow 1981), indicates a fragmentation of society into chiefdoms, albeit perhaps grouped together into petty kingdoms. Some of these kingdoms in the east were controlled by immigrant elites, but native kingdoms survived in the West for centuries after AD 400.

The Social Fabric of Later Roman Britain

The differences between fourth and sixth century British society and economy do suggest great change in the intervening years. In addition, the ultimate dominance of Germanic authority and language also requires explanation. It may be useful to look at the various social, economic and political factors that influenced the nature of the diocesan society in the early fifth century; it is these factors that dictated the development of a subsistence economy, through an exchange economy, and ultimately (perhaps) to a market economy. Economic stability was directly related to political stability: the Roman imperial system provided that by preventing internal conflict as well as rivalry with neighbouring political groups. The fifth century Romano-British diocesan authorities, on the other hand, had to maintain this control after circa 410.

Adopting the revised Marxist theory propounded earlier, the forces of society were the result of interaction between the means and the organisation of society. The 'means' in this case refer not only to subsistence, but also to any factor required in the maintenance of the existing standard of living. In later Roman Britain, technological development evident in the rural economy – such as corn-driers/malting kilns – imply a relatively vigorous land-based economy. The construction of walls around some towns in the later Roman period is thought to be the result of government investment in these administrative nodes.

Of course, such investment assumes the success of subsistence farming, to provide the basic means of life. The demographic stability required to maintain a subsistence economy was subject to the determinist factors of climate and disease. Gildas (22.2) refers to two famines and a plague in the earlier fifth century: 'a deadly plague . . . in a short period laid low so many people . . . that the living could not bury all the dead.' There had been a climatic deterioration in the later Roman period, and regular pandemic diseases appear to have been encouraged by empire-wide trade and travel. It is likely that there was a significant fall in population, which could have been one reason for the settlement of *foederati* on under-populated land. Consequently, determinist factors may have weakened Romano-British society. On the other hand, such problems were not unique to fifth-century Britain; there had been epidemics and pandemics during the Roman period. Climate and disease should be seen only as indirect causes of political instability.

In order to maintain the socio-economic system the workforce had to be organised. One element of this organisation was the military, needed to prevent the loss of resources to neighbouring powers through either raiding or annexation. A sign of increasing regimentation of rural society was the growth of the colonate system, a result of the desire to ensure not only subsistence production, but also the generation of wealth for the land-owners. The *coloni* were tied to estates on social and legal grounds.

The government had to pay for such elements of the infrastructure as the army, the bureaucracy and town defences. This was simply obtained from the inhabitants of the empire by either taxation or service. The curial classes, for instance, were expected to support their local municipalities.

But while the forces of society were attempting to maintain the status quo, and extract an economic surplus to benefit the exploiting groups, there was an inevitable desire on the part of the exploited to overcome such inequality. We have already seen that there was a tension between the process of Romanisation and the need or desire of the British to accept cultural assimilation. Even in the fourth century, it is not clear to what degree Romano-Britons saw themselves as Roman, rather than British with Roman influences, or even as tribal, with only superficial diocesan and imperial loyalties.

Romano-British society, compared to that of the LPRIA, was cosmo-politan. Initially, foreigners dominated the administration and economy. Imperial exploitation of Britain, such as to pay for defence – a large fraction of the economic surplus – was likely to be merely tolerated, and only then when some benefit to the contributors was evident (the Western Empire's military forces were relatively more costly than those of the wealthier Eastern Empire). The failure of the imperial system to both provide services and maintain its political control would have encouraged the manifestation of hitherto suppressed socio-political discordances within the province during the fifth century.

Even during the fourth century, it appears that both the *coloni* and the curial classes were attempting to evade either the provision of services or the payment of taxes, or both; hence the government's attempts to enforce services and taxation by law. Another source of tension was the exploita-tion of the poor by the wealthy. The land-owners tried to avoid supporting their local towns, investing resources into their rural estates instead. Land-holding was increasingly concentrated in fewer and fewer hands. Con-sequently, the *coloni* found themselves not only having to shoulder a pro-portionally greater share of the tax burden, but also working as mere tenants, unable to take their labour elsewhere.

The Germanic immigrations, notably during the fifth century, gave scope for further racial conflict. Martin Millett (1990, 219ff.) has suggested that political authority became personal rather than constitutional during the fifth century. Consequently, whereas in Gaul the political framework could accommodate immigrant groups by, for example, the legalised transfer of lands, the personalised politics in Britain encouraged a more personal and inconsistent response to such immigrations into the local socio-economic systems, which were increasingly socially-embedded; in particular, there may have been some reluctance to accommodate the immigrant elites within the political superstructure. This may have resulted in tension developing against such constraints.

Religion is another factor that should be considered, perhaps as a lateral tension. The success of the Romanisation of Britain has already been questioned above, and the degree of acceptance of the Roman pantheon by the British is a part of that debate. In view of this, it is likely that the adoption of Christianity as the official imperial religion in the fourth century had little immediate effect, as is indicated by an increase in the number of pagan temples in use (ibid., fig. 83). If Christianity spread as a form of assimilation, it may have been accepted more readily by those officials and aristocracies most dependent on the imperial government, but this means that Christianity had yet to reach the lower orders. Faced with struggles for political control during the fifth century, one wonders how a pagan Briton, perhaps ambivalent to *romanitas*, would have viewed the relative merits of being subject to a Romanised Christian native, or a pagan German. Germanic people had long resided in Britain, and the settlement of *foederati* was an established policy. By the middle of the fifth century, there may have been a considerable Germano-British population, probably considerably larger than the number of first and even second generation immigrants, integrated into the lower orders at least. It may be significant that Cerdic, claimed in the *Anglo-Saxon Chronicle* as the founder of Wessex, is a British name.

Overall these social factors indicate a fragile Romano-British society, divided both hierarchically and laterally. This echoes Michael Grant's (1990) view of internal weakness within the Roman Empire as a whole. It is simplistic and normative to regard the upheavals of the later fifth century as a struggle between two distinct groups (Arnold 1984, 122ff.) – (perhaps) ten thousand Angles, Saxons and Jutes, against three million Britons; it was much more complicated than that.

Even if society was stable internally, overall political stability was also dependent on external political conditions. Hostile neighbours attempting to increase territories, wealth and influence could raid or annexe weaker rivals. In the case of late Roman Britain, the diocese was subjected to raids rather than annexations, and indeed these had occurred in the earlier

Roman period. In the fifth century Germanic settlements in the east of the
diocese could be regarded as an external threat, but it has already been
suggested that this may have been more of an internal, socio-political problem. However, many parts of the country, particularly the coastal regions,
seem to have suffered from an intensification of raiding (and limited invasion). An inability to counter such threats on a diocesan scale would surely
have led to a fragmentation of authority. Although the barbarian invasions
were an important factor in the fall of the Western Roman Empire (Ferrill
1986, 164), Britain was lost by the empire for political rather than military
reasons.

POLITICS AND THE ECONOMY, A LONG-TERM VIEW

The Roman Empire satisfied the requirement for economic stability by
imposing political stability on Britain. The Empire also facilitated the
development of long-distance trade links, which would promote an
exchange economy.

The exchange economy, with close interaction and greater competition
throughout the system, may be evident in more rapid technological
development and typological innovation. In later Roman Britain technological development occurred within the rural economy, presumably as a
result of the increased investment in the countryside at the expense of the
towns. However, the decline of urban functions, and typological conservatism evident in the pottery, for example, betrays a decline in aspects
of the economy, particularly long-distance trade.

It can be argued that there is a correlation between the magnitude of
political authority and the scale of the economy in southern Britain during
the first millennium AD. The imposition of the Roman imperial system
clearly had an impact, but arguably only in terms of (initially) accelerating,
and in particular providing a stable political framework for, the development of the LPRIA socio-economic system. The political fragmentation of
the later fifth century presumably caused a major economic recession that
continued through to the seventh century. However, an exchange economy
continued in the Romano-British kingdoms of western Britain, involving
some long-distance trade with Gaul and the Mediterranean which included
imports of pottery (Thomas 1981), perhaps associated with items such as
wine and olive oil (Thomas 1990), and exports of raw materials, including
salt (Hurst 1990). Such trade is comparable with that of the LPRIA, and it
also has similarities with British long-distance trade links of the fourth and

earlier fifth centuries; this may represent the continuation of socially-embedded long-distance trade from the LPRIA through the Later Roman period. From the seventh century onwards, the increasingly stable socio-political situation in eastern England facilitated an expansion of the economy. This coincided with similar developments on the continent, so that the reciprocated trade encouraged an exchange, and finally a market, economy. One wonders if this political and economic consolidation would not have occurred sooner without the imposition of the Roman imperial socio-economic system.

CONCLUSION

Due to a bias in the settlement hierarchy sample taken thus far, the influence of *romanitas* has been over-estimated; there is reason to doubt that Romanisation permeated through to all levels of LPRIA society. The Romano-British socio-economic system was essentially the LPRIA system with 'Roman' embellishments. Once the initial phase of imperial government investment had ended, the influence of the embellishments (such as towns) declined in favour of a more socially-embedded, rural economy that is best explained as a development of the LPRIA society and economy. Consequently, the vision of a fully-Romanised, town-based socio-economic system suddenly collapsing at the end of the fourth century is illusory. Instead, with a society in flux, and a steadily changing economy, it is very difficult to identify from the archaeological record any major changes before the later fifth century. It is then that diocese-wide authority ends, and the Romano-British economy ends with it. Yet even then, there was no clean break with Roman Britain. Within the fragmented society and economy, the forces and relations of society would have changed, but persisted; and they would have had a great influence on the nature of the succeeding socio-economic system.

Romanists have tended to examine Romano-British society in isolation, only paying lip-service to the need to see it as part of a continuum of social and economic change (Anderson 1991). Anglo-Saxon scholars are just as guilty of this tunnel vision, preferring to concentrate on the origins of the Germanic immigrants rather than their interaction with the native population (Arnold 1984, 5). Archaeologists should be as concerned with material culture as with historiography; the compartmentalisation of time into historical periods should be seen as a convenience, intended to facilitate the archaeological debate, not to dictate it.

Bibliography

Anderson, J. L. 1991 *Explaining Long-Term Economic Change*. Basingstoke; Macmillan.

Arnold, C. 1984 *Roman Britain to Saxon England*. Beckenham; Croom Helm.

Burrow, I. 1981 'Hill-forts after the Iron Age: the relevance of surface fieldwork', in Guilbert (ed.), 122–49.

Esmonde Cleary, A. S. 1989 *The Ending of Roman Britain*. London; Batsford.

Ferrill, A. 1986 *The Fall of the Roman Empire: the military explanation*. London; Thames and Hudson.

Gildas see Winterbottom 1978.

Grant, M. 1990 *The Fall of the Roman Empire* 2nd edition. London; Weidenfeld and Nicolson.

Guilbert, G. (ed.) 1981 *Hill-Fort Studies*. Leicester; Leicester University Press.

Hurst, D. 1991 'Major Saxon discoveries at Droitwich – excavations at the Upwich brine pit' *Current Archaeology* 126, 252–55.

Millett, M. 1990 *The Romanisation of Britain. An essay in archaeological interpretation*. Cambridge; Cambridge University Press.

Reece, R. 1980 'Town and country: the end of Roman Britain' *World Archaeology* 12, 77–92.

Reece, R. 1987 *Coinage in Roman Britain*. London; Seaby.

Thomas, C. 1981 *A Provisional List of Imported Pottery in Post-Roman Western Britain and Ireland*. Redruth; Institute of Cornish Studies.

Thomas, C. 1990 '"Gallici nautae de Galliarum provinciis" – a sixth/seventh century trade with Gaul, reconsidered' *Medieval Archaeology* 34, 1–26.

Trigger, B. G. 1989 *A History of Archaeological Thought*. Cambrdige; Cambridge University Press.

Winterbottom, M. (ed. and trans.) 1978 *Gildas' The Ruin of Britain and Other Works*. Chichester; Phillimore.

8

'Villas as a Key to Social Structure'? Some Comments on Recent Approaches to the Romano-British Villa and Some Suggestions Toward an Alternative

Robert Rippengal

The paper makes a critical examination of one of the more influential pieces of 'social archaeology' to have come out of Romano-British studies – J. T. Smith's 'Villas as a key to social structure'. Smith's suggestions that many villas were occupied by 'extended families' is found wanting under a more detailed examination of the evidence. Instead, while there may sometimes be more than one domestic structure on a site, or even indications that individual buildings were occupied by more than a single nuclear family, it is suggested that it is the nature of the relationships involved that should be under scrutiny. To this end, a brief outline is given of an alternative approach to the material. This takes up Bordieu's notion of habitus with its emphasis on the role of material culture, and some examples are given to illustrate how it might expand our perceptions of the material from Romano-British sites.

INTRODUCTION ———

In his recent and important volume *The Rural Settlement of Roman Britain* Richard Hingley has felt able to state that 'considerable evidence exists to indicate that extended families were typical of the rural areas of the province' (Hingley 1989, 149). That he did so is perhaps a testament to the influence of J. T. Smith, for although Hingley's discussion is itself an elaborate one, it is in essence an extension of the paper by Smith published ten years earlier and entitled 'Villas as a key to social structure' (Smith 1978). It is the propositions set forth in that formative paper that are of primary interest here.

J. T. Smith's Unit Theory

Written explicitly as an antidote to the perceived stagnation of villa studies, Smith's paper sought to argue that 'a great deal can be learnt by comparative study of . . . known house plans', and in so doing to provide a new framework for the examination and understanding of a large part of the body of known villas. Followed up by a series of papers dealing mainly with the interpretation of individual sites (e.g. Smith 1985; 1987), this paper has come to form one of the most important of villa studies in the last 30 years. Indeed, in some quarters his position represents almost a standard interpretation, adopted or at least acknowledged in a series of recent works (Hingley 1989; Reece 1987; Miles 1986; Millet 1990).

It is by no means denied that his ideas represent a novel departure, one that appears to enliven what had become a rather sterile area of research, and this is surely where their appeal lies. However, it will be suggested that for all their impact, acceptance of these ideas has tended to be somewhat uncritical. There exists a *perception* that certain points have been demonstrated in this paper when in fact they clearly have not; it has become one of those many archaeological myths, widely cited without detailed reference as one might cite a fact.

The essentials of his argument are relatively straightforward. He suggests that an examination of the plans of a great many villas reveals evidence of joint occupancy. Sometimes this involves the presence of more than one domestic structure on a site, but as often as not it is discerned in the divisions of what is termed the 'unit system' within a single building (after Hemp and Gresham 1943, 98). This, it is claimed, represents an expression of 'existing social relations' based on the 'kindred or extended family' and indicating the survival of a pre-conquest, so-called 'Celtic' society (Smith 1978, 170–2). It is then briefly contrasted to what are termed 'hall villas'. These do not show indications of multiple occupation but instead stand in a position of superiority to various other buildings, 'the houses of social inferiors, of people who were dependants rather than equals' (ibid., 170).

CRITIQUE

In the course of elaborating such a position, a considerable number of illustrations are offered and these will be considered more fully below. However, before doing so a number of more general points are perhaps worth making.

At the outset, then, Smith outlines several basic principles that underpin the subsequent argument. Thus, he starts with the proposition that: 'every villa should be regarded as an expression, however humble, of classical architecture' and that 'any deviation from the accepted tenets of that architecture is significant' (ibid., 149). This represents a bland statement, as of fact, yet it is surely an assertion that demands some further elaboration, not to say justification.

Implicated is the whole process of Romanisation. This is something that has indeed been identified as central to the future development of Roman studies (Burnham and Johnson 1979; Slofstra 1983), yet nowhere is the nature of that process discussed here. Elsewhere it is claimed we are dealing with an essentially Celtic people, one that was actually very resistant to change, yet here we are told that classical architecture was taken on board lock-stock-and-barrel and that the slightest deviation is of profound significance. In contrast, it might be suggested that if native culture was so persistent it should be those classical elements that *were* adopted that require explanation, not deviation from classical forms. In fact, Smith is not even consistent in his application of this precept. Thus, for the purposes of the paper he lists 'symmetry of elevation and plan' (Smith 1978, 150) as one of the basic tenets of classical architecture to be assumed, yet elsewhere a considerable number of the sites he lists are denoted as examples of the unit system simply by virtue of their symmetry!

Elsewhere, it is suggested that a 'winged corridor villa' is more Romanised than an 'aisled house' (ibid., 153), or that it is fallacious 'to regard small villas of the type of Lockleys or Park Street as vernacular architecture', that they are really 'modest manifestations of classical architecture' (ibid., 170). Once again, however, we might ask *why*, what are the distinctions implied here and what is the nature of 'Romanisation' they embody? It is these issues that should surely be addressed in a paper of this kind whereas they are left unsaid, in the air.

It might be suggested that we know classical forms were adopted simply by virtue of the fact that we find houses with features such as the collonaded, winged facade. Therefore, there is something to explain if they do not also have an axial approach with central entrance into the main room of the house. In contrast, however, I would suggest that it is hardly surprising that in the middle of the British countryside, hundreds of miles and at least one sea crossing from Italy, on the fringes of the north-western part of the Empire, we do not find an exact transplantation of the Pompeiian villa, and therefore to assign any differences to profound social considerations needs considerably more justification. Indeed, Percival (1976, 58–9) notes that even in Italy when we are dealing with working villas as opposed to the limited class of luxury retreats archetypal forms are less important, layout being 'determined much more by the requirements of farming practice than by the dictates of architectural fashion' .

To this it might be added that the pedigree of Romano-British houses has been a subject of continuous and vigorous debate since the nineteenth century, within which tradition the nature of classical influence is generally seen as rather more equivocal than Smith allows for. Indeed, as long ago as 1911 Ward noted of Romano-British and Pompeian houses that 'the one set . . . is about as unlike the other set, in that most important point, the planning or arrangement, as both are unlike the houses of the moderns' (Ward 1911; see also Haverfield 1912; Collingwood 1923; Collingwood and Myers 1937; Richmond 1969; Hingley 1989).

Of interest in this respect is the second of Smith's presuppositions, the notion that 'a clear distinction must be drawn between a house plan which corresponds with the reality of contemporary social organisation, and the facade or other classical trimmings' (Smith 1978, 149). It is notable that Smith's own use of the term 'trimmings' would seem to assign a rather less over-bearing role to classical influence. Indeed, it would tend to bring him more into line with the bulk of thought on the matter, for there is, after Swoboda, a widely accepted contrast between the typical facade and the houses behind it (Swoboda 1919). However, the question becomes, how do we elucidate the 'reality of contemporary social organisation' these houses are supposed to represent. While Smith's attempt to elucidate such questions is certainly unusual in the context of Romano-British archaeology it is perhaps undermined by a lack of theoretical elaboration and the consequent failure to bridge the gap between theory and data.

Towards illustrating this, we may move on to the third and final of the initial conditions, the notion that (Smith 1978, 149–50):

> [those villas] in the provinces north of the Alps are particularly relevant to one another because the native peoples there are likely to have had more in common with one another than any of them had with Roman life, and consequently comparison of their villas should reveal those elements common to the social structures found by the conquerers. And from all this it follows that changes in type of plan or elevation correspond not only to variation in wealth but, more importantly, to changes in social structure.

Although one might be sympathetic to the basic notion expressed here, as stated it represents a series of *non-sequiturs*, leaps that are never addressed more fully. Perhaps two points may be made. Firstly, the notion of 'the kind of social relations characteristic of Celtic society', viz. the 'extended family', is simply stated, presented almost as a *fait accompli*. In fact, although the basis of the paper is clearly the notion that social questions may be addressed within the archaeology, what becomes apparent is that such issues are not really addressed at all. Instead, a largely meaningless term is thrust onto the material without further comment or elaboration.

In contrast, it may be suggested that the notion of a Celtic social form, particularly the 'pan-European' form hinted at, is one that demands rather more discussion. Kinship is of course notoriously complex, yet this merely makes the lack of such discussion all the more telling. Smith himself concedes how 'surprising' the idea of joint occupancy is, yet never takes up the challenge this represents. Indeed, this aside, if the social form at issue is essentially a pre-conquest one, it seems particularly surprising that no reference is made to any of the prehistoric material or to any of the work by prehistorians on this subject for whom the notion of extended families would certainly be controversial.

For all this, the very attempt to look at such questions as archaeological problems is an important one, for the all too limited horizons of Romano-British archaeology have for long tended to reduce its impact. However, even the basic proposition that villas indeed represent 'a key to social structure' is undermined by a failure to examine the relationship between 'society' and 'architecture', to provide a rationale for why we might be able to talk of kinship when we are simply looking at the floor plans of long derelict buildings.

Early in the paper it is implied that there are 'fundamental elements' of villa plans that 'express social structure', yet nowhere is it clearly stated what these elements might be (ibid., 150). Instead, Smith's conception of the link between society and architecture would seem to be rather limited. In effect, he seems to suggest that house plans in some way equate with society such that we may simply look at the plans and 'read off' the social form.

Lacking is any account of how this relationship operated in *practice* and, thereby, of why house plans should equate to social form. Equally, there is no concession that there may be other formative and potent influences on architectural form. Thus, in discussing the placement of certain water shrines, he notes, without elucidating *why*, that it was dictated 'by some profound social consideration', and that, somehow, 'architecture tells us what it was' (ibid., 157). In contrast, it is stressed here that architecture does not tell us anything *per se*. We might attempt to elucidate meanings within architectural forms, but Smith's simple equations are fundamentally misleading.

Central in this respect is the supposition that two or more domestic units equates with an extended family. In essence this rests on the notion that where such discreet units are encountered they are of equal status: 'it appears not only that some villas comprised two houses where the orthodox view would lead us to expect only one, but that far from there being any suggestion that one house was subordinated to the other . . . both houses, though they may be of different sizes, are of equal status' (ibid., 153). This assumption is fundamental, yet nowhere is it adequately examined, let alone justified with reference to the material. At this point we must turn to the examples for it is here that this issue must be pursued.

Initially, then, Smith suggests that there are a number of sites on which we may identify two such houses: Newton St Loe (Fig. 8); Gayton Thorpe (Fig. 9); Beadlam; Arquennes; and Paulton. As an initial observation, it is perhaps to be conceded that most of the examples given do appear at least plausible as two houses. However, what is so striking is that even if there are two domestic units on these sites, they are buildings of different character whose equality of status must be open to some question.

In criticising Smith's notion of equivalent status, it is conceded that while he is somewhat ambivalent on the point he does not mean that each house or 'unit' is literally exactly the same as the other(s). Instead, differences are taken to be of degree rather than of kind. This, one assumes, is where we may see the contrast with hall villas where differences were somewhat more profound. However, what is stressed here is that if we are claiming to work from the archaeology, the material differences seen in the archaeological remains are often such that to *start* with an assumption of equality seems inadequate. Instead this is something that Smith needs to demonstrate as being the case in spite of the obvious material differences. Indeed, so far from assuming equality and working from this basis, it is surely the nature of the relationships between the various elements on these sites that should be the very subject of investigation. Are they such that we should talk in terms of kinship or differences of degree, or do they suggest differences of kind, perhaps better discussed in terms of dominance and dependence and/or mode and relations of production?

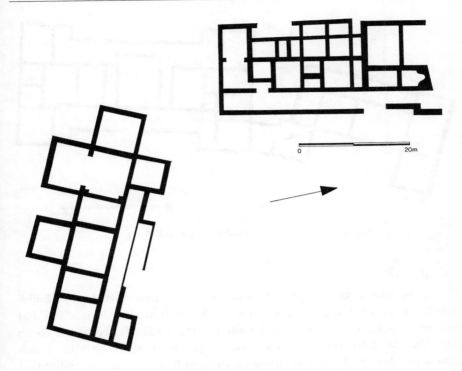

Figure 8. Newton St Loe (redrawn by Rob Rippengal).

Newton St Loe

To return to the examples, at Newton St Loe while both buildings are of
similar size they nevertheless appear quite different : one is made up of a
series of large apartments, the other of a great many small rooms. Clearly
this means very little as an observation on its own. However, it does suggest
that there may be more to them than is encompassed in Smith's description. Unfortunately, this site is only poorly reported (*JRS* 26 (1936), 43–6;
VCH Somerset i, 302), yet even these limited descriptions tell us that the
westerly building was considered the more interesting of the two and was
the only one with baths, hypocausts or tessellated floors, including several
mosaic pavements. What this means might be open to some question, and
again it is stressed that the standard of reporting is poor. However, what is
clear is that to talk simply of two equivalent houses begins to look rather
inadequate, particularly if this is to be cited as a primary example.

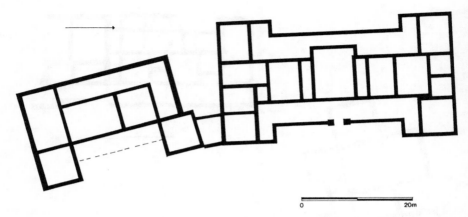

Figure 9. Gayton Thorpe (redrawn by Rob Rippengal).

Gayton Thorpe

We might look next to Gayton Thorpe, for to say here that the two build-ings are equivalent seems a nonsense on the basis of size alone – one has five rooms, the other thirteen. Smith, however, specifically notes: 'Both have the standard type of facade with the portico and wing rooms which proclaim a house of some standing', using this to reject the possibility that the smaller one could have housed farm labourers (Smith 1978, 153).

This is an interesting statement, and might be contrasted with his earlier suggestion that all may not be what it seems hidden behind such a facade. Once again, the standard of reporting is rather limited. However, it is suffi-cient to tell us that the facade on the southern building might be a case in point – it does not seem to denote a 'house of some standing' as Smith suggests, but stands in front of and *masks* a building that is in stark contrast to the one next to it.

The latter, as well as having a far more elaborate ground plan also has baths, other heated rooms and a large central room that produced a mosaic pavement, painted plaster and fragments of Italian marble. The southern building, in contrast, is rather different. The facade is, we are told, well constructed and the wing rooms contain a geometric mosaic pavement and a tessellated floor respectively. However, even here it is to be noted that the facade does not quite match that of the building next door. While the latter includes evidence of a columned entrance and dwarf wall for a colonnaded varandah, here, while there is some evidence for a verandah in the form of a concrete floor, the lack of any more substantial remains indicates an altogether less imposing edifice. This aside, behind the facade the excavator notes that the standard of construction and setting out were clearly inferior. What is more, most of these rooms were furnished with simple rammed chalk floors, and nowhere in this building were there the baths, heated rooms or other signs of comfort and ostentation found next door.

The one surprising exception to this is that both buildings have a mosaic, something on which Smith places some little emphasis. However, without purporting to offer a 'solution' to this apparent enigma, it might be noted that in the southern building the mosaic is placed in a wing room. In contrast, the mosaic in the main building is laid in the large central room, perhaps a significant difference. The latter, then, marks the heart of a building built to a high degree of sophistication throughout. The former, in contrast, is perhaps the one room that affords such a degree of comfort in the whole of this otherwise inferior building. Once again, the meaning of this observation is open to some question. However, if we were actually considering the nature of the relationship between the occupants of the two buildings, might not this kind of thing be a starting point?

The aim of all this is not to try to demonstrate that there were not two domestic units on these sites. Instead, several points are intended: that to indicate that some sites have what appear to be two 'houses' and elaborate this no further is insufficient; that to assume a simple equality between the two elements is particularly inadequate to the point of being misleading; and that the evidence recovered on most of these sites provides far more useful and relevant information than Smith makes use of, a lack that can only do his argument harm. In sum, it is to be stressed that although Smith raises an interesting possibility he does not elaborate it in a way that would make it convincing.

Montacute-Ham Hill

Moving on from here, it is assumed in Smith's paper that he has thus far demonstrated that certain sites have two houses, a notion that is then expanded by drawing in a number of other sites where the evidence seems more equivocal. The first of these is Montacute-Ham Hill (Fig. 10), where one relatively typical domestic block is linked by a wall to two further elements: a single separate room with a tessellated floor and independent entrance; and what is described as a work-hall, on the *Wirtschaftshalle* model (i.e. including living accommodation). On this basis Smith compares it to

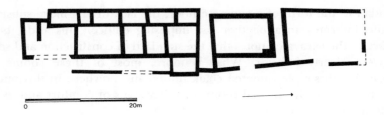

Figure 10. Montacute-Ham Hill (redrawn by Rob Rippengal).

those sites just described, where he assigns the separate houses equal status, and suggests 'something similar must underlie [this] curious villa' (ibid., 153). Without going into elaborate detail, the plan alone must surely make this a rather remarkable claim.

It might be countered here that, as noted above, Smith is not really suggesting literally equal status for these buildings. However, in this vein it might be noted that the differences between the various structures on this site appear to be differences not simply of degree but of kind and that if we are to believe the contrary somewhat more forceful arguments need to be brought forward. He attaches some importance to the fact that they are aligned together, but is this really an adequate ground for assigning them equal status?

It is of course possible for there to be considerable inequalities within a kinship system. Thus, a group linked through a common ancestor and living together might display such inequalities. However, if Smith intends such a scenario, several points might be made. Firstly, why all the talk of equal status? Secondly, the failure to explore these relationships leaves the notion of extended families, even if we take it on board, rather ephemeral: a bare starting point for more meaningful discussion. Finally, it is hard to see why sites like Montacute do not fall into the category so briefly described at the end of the paper where other buildings on a site are regarded as being subsidiary to the main house. Indeed, there is a widely held notion that such buildings housed farm labourers, a suggestion that seems on the face of it rather more convincing than Smith's ideas.

Maillen-Al Sauveniere

Among other sites with 'work halls' that are drawn into this *schema* is Maillen-Al Sauveniere (Fig. 11). Here a single extended *porticus* forms a unified facade behind which are two separate structures. Smith notes that the eastern one, a bipartite hall, is likely to have functioned as a work-hall.

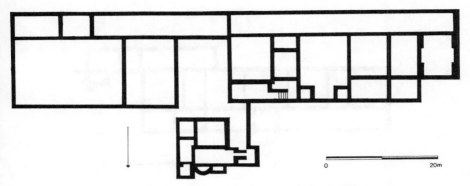

Figure 11. Maillen-Al Sauveniere (redrawn by Rob Rippengal).

However, he suggests that 'because the two are joined by a corridor the dwelling aspect of the work-hall is likely to have been important' (ibid., 153). As an initial reaction, it might be countered that the separation of the two buildings behind their facade is perhaps as significant as the link it forms between them. However, even if we accept Smith's rather tenuous piece of logic, once again it is to be stressed that these are quite clearly buildings of very different character, of nothing approaching equivalent status and certainly unlikely as the separate dwellings of two parts of an extended family.

From here, in a key extension of the argument, Smith goes on to suggest that: 'the social situation thus implied appears to have been embodied from the first in a few villas of unified architectural form' (ibid., 154). Towards illustrating this, he picks out as most obvious those sites where there are two entrances and where the obvious central approach is blocked. In particular, a number of sites have water shrines located where we might otherwise expect a central entrance. Given that there are sites, such as Rapsley, where water shrines were not so placed, it follows, as noted above, 'that the placing of a shrine just where it blocked the most obvious point of access was prompted by some profound social considera-tion' (ibid., 157), that, in other words, these buildings housed more than one domestic unit.

Downton

Of the sites used to illustrate this point, Downton (Fig. 12) is particularly interesting. Here the central room has no frontal access, 'so we are left with a hall common to two flanking houses' (ibid.). If we could show this to

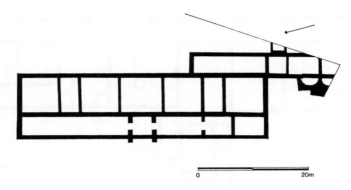

Figure 12. Downton (redrawn by Rob Rippengal).

be the case it would indeed be remarkable, for it comprises one relatively small and apparently coherent block. However, once again a more considered examination of the evidence would seem to leave Smith's interpretation rather lacking – it is all very well to *suggest* that there might be two houses here but he fails to develop this idea and demonstrate such a situation.

In contrast to his claims there clearly is, for example, a central entrance into the *porticus* itself. Thus, although there may not have been a central access to the main 'hall', there clearly was a single main entrance that split to run into the two halves of the corridor. Equally, the notion of two houses leaves the central room, the only one with a mosaic and the largest in the house, in a kind of limbo, as a no-man's land between the two blocks, surely a rather unlikely proposition. Indeed, if we take this to be the main room, is it really so surprising that there should not be immediate access from the outside world? Such direct access may be one of the canons of classical architecture and it may be the norm in the more temperate climes of the classical world, but is it really to be expected in the rather colder climate of Britain?

Indeed, it might be pointed out that the *atrium*, with which Smith is drawing a parallel, is not by any means an obvious equivalent to the central room of villas like Downton either in terms of form or function. Of the latter, the *atrium* is above all a public room and is therefore quite naturally linked to the outside, though not in fact directly but via the *fauces*. In contrast, the private apartments, including the *tablinium*, are set rather deeper in the house.

Regarding Downton, Smith's division would leave only the southern

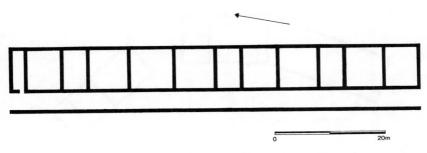

Figure 13. Eccles (redrawn by Rob Rippengal).

'house' with either a hypocaust or baths. The baths, in particular, are not sited where they would be accessible from both halves of the building, but are offset at one end and the corridor that gives access to them provides access only for the southern half of the building, surely an unlikely arrangement if we are really to believe that there are two such carefully laid out 'houses' here.

This is important, for it indicates that while there is a degree of symmetry in a strictly geometrical sense, there are not simply two equivalent units here. Given that mere symmetry is regarded as good reason to identify a unit system site, it cannot be too highly stressed that the failure to take account of the more detailed information is positively misleading. Nowhere is this more apparent than in the way in which Smith attempts to see the kind of units distinguished at Downton in a host of other sites, many of far larger and more elaborate design. As presented, these 'unit system' villas appear as empty shells. In contrast, if he used accompanying detail to demonstrate that they can be regarded as equivalent and discrete units in terms more meaningful than their geometry, his argument might be more convincing.

Eccles

What is needed is at least one more elaborate example that could stand as a model from which to view the others. Of the examples given, Eccles (fig. 13) stands out, recently and comprehensively excavated. Thus, it might be possible to go further than simply indicating possible suites of rooms and actually demonstrate them to be complementary sets.

In this vein, one thing that seems particularly striking about these sites is the question of scale. Eccles is an extremely large and complex site, quite clearly the product of considerable recources. However, if we compare it to

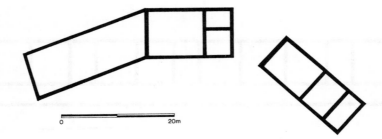

Figure 14. Bradley Hill (redrawn by Rob Rippengal).

Gayton Thorpe, where the different families at least live in sizeable 'houses', it seems odd that here its occupants effectively live in small apartments in the manner of a grandiose 'housing association', which somewhat belies the imposing nature of the site as a whole.

Bradley Hill

This is of course a rather superficial reaction. However, we might take it further, for if we compare the Eccles units to a site such as Bradley Hill (Fig. 14) the comparison becomes more telling. If we look at the accommodation here, we seem to have units that would pass muster within a site like Eccles, yet these are sites of radically different character, wealth and status.

It might be countered that this is simply an indication of the potency of the kinship relations involved. In answer, however, we might return to the fact that elsewhere the combination of wealth and status with kinship ties produces separate houses and certainly did not produce units that by their size and configuration suggest they could as well be occupied by the humblest of farmers.

TOWARDS AN ALTERNATIVE ——————

Much has been said thus far that is rather negative. Although the examples could undoubtedly be taken further, a more immediate question becomes, what is the alternative? How may we look, not just as villas but at any houses in order to answer the kind of questions raised here?

As a starting point, we might look to Heidegger, for he has suggested that dwelling is a fundamental human characteristic, that 'we do not dwell because we have built, but we build because we dwell, because we are dwellers.' Indeed, in pre-industrial societies most people will be conceived, born and die in houses; the house provides the focus of their daily lives both as a centre of domestic routine and as an important site for a range of productive tasks. Furthermore, most will build the house in which they dwell and as such their houses represent close indicators of how they feel this milieu of activities should be set and how they ought to proceed. In other words they are bound to what Bourdieu has termed a *habitus* (Bourdieu 1977).

This is a key notion. On one level it refers to what we might term a world view, a distinct orientation 'in the world'. However, it is rather more dynamic than this, including a key concept of *doing*. Thus, it refers not so much to a world view as to the very way in which we live in the world – a competance or, as Bourdieu himself puts it, a *modus operandi* (ibid., 79).

In attempting to understand this concept, material objects are seen, as Douglas and Isherwood point out, to have a very positive role; they are used 'to constitute an intelligible universe' (Douglas and Isherwood 1979). Thus, material culture represents far more than merely an embodiment of ideas and meanings but becomes an active force, an enabling element, a medium not merely for expression but for construction, working to produce reality, to order an otherwise chaotic world.

This reification lends material culture a particular potency. We are all of us framed in meaning, set within a vivid and tangible matrix of signification. Indeed, we do not simply construct this matrix, but, by virtue of its essential durability, are in turn constructed through it. Thus it is that Bourdieu talks of 'the mind born of the world of objects', and here we might return to the house, for he notes of 'inhabited space' that 'through the . . . divisions and hierarchies it sets up between things, persons and practices, this tangible classifying system continuously inculcates and reinforces the taxonomic principles underlying all the arbitrary provisions of . . . culture' (Bourdieu 1977, 89).

In other words, the house literally represents an embodiment of the *habitus*. What is more, once built it acquires an enduring role in the direction of future practices and, thereby, in the very process of social reproduction. Thus, to return to Smith for a moment, houses or villas must of course relate to social structure. However this is but one element, for the meanings embodied in the house are infinitely richer than he allows for. Rather than the formulation 'house = social structure', the house is bound to a whole way of living, of 'being in the world'. Thus, although things like the placement of entrances or the division of space may relate to kinship, before we begin to make claims of this kind, we need to develop a rather more profound understanding of the particular houses involved, of the 'way of living' they embody.

Towards developing such an understanding, we can perhaps begin by viewing the house first and foremost in its universal context, as a landmark, a manifest symbol of all that is cultural standing against the vastness of the world outside. Immediately, we have a link to the fundamental Levi-Straussian opposition of nature and culture and following it we might draw out a number of implications.

The Latin *domus* is the stem for a whole series of words – words such as domicile and domestic, but also domain, dominion or dominate. In this reading, then, the house speaks to us as a symbol of ownership, mastery and power. To dwell, in this sense, is to have conquered, to have made the world one's own. Thus, the house as domus is a product of our will-to-power wherein we impose ourselves on the world, locating ourselves within it, claiming possession and transforming the heretofore untamed into the means of habitation.

In contrast to this image of human potency, we might draw out a rather different series of associations. Thus, the word *house* carries us back to the verge of history, to the Dark Ages and beyond. In Old English *hus* means simply shelter, after the Germanic *huden*, to hide, conceal or cover, and it comes down to us not simply as house but also as hut, huddle, hoard and husband. It speaks, in other words, of our essential vulnerability, of the fragile, exposed side of our nature as dwellers.

We have, then, two contrasting and equally powerful images held and joined in a tension that is resolved in that most mundane of structures, the house. As described in etymological terms this relates specifically to our own culture. However, some negotiation of these two elements, of nature *versus* culture, of humans in nature *versus* humans set up over nature, is common to all houses, and if we return here to Roman Britain, an immediate potential for comparison is apparent.

We might begin by contrasting, albeit somewhat crudely, the 'native' round house and the most common of villa forms, the 'winged corridor villa'. The aim is not to provide a definitive analysis but a starting point, for these two forms perhaps exemplify the distinction drawn out above.

The classic round houses of Iron Age and post-conquest Britain seen, for example, at Whitton (Fig. 15), represent in many ways an essential acceptance of nature. It is often suggested that the circular form is of itself somehow natural or organic. However, without being committed to quite such a bold supposition here, it is suggested that their form, though

Figure 15. Whitton (redrawn by Rob Rippengal).

undoubtedly the realisation of an ideal, was largely unconstrained by either rigid notions of geometry or of 'accuracy' and precision. The straight line, the regular angle and so on, those ideals of systematised construction, are entirely alien to this tradition of building.

Similarly, these structures were built almost entirely of natural materials: posts for the basic framework were generally full trunks or limbs left 'as they came' rather than square sawn or hewn; over this, wattle and daub walls, thatched roofs and trampled earthen floors all represent nature essentially untransformed. What is more, there is no attempt to hide these elements or the details of construction – they exemplify what, more recently, modernist architects have dubbed 'honesty'. Finally, by virtue of their use of materials these structures are rather impermanent marks on the landscape, rapidly and inevitably subject to all the natural processes of decay and degeneration.

If we look next to the winged corridor villa, as exemplified by a site such as Newport (Fig. 16), we see a somewhat different picture. Smith places particular emphasis on the importance of classical influence without elaborating what it is that this expressed. Thus, it is here that we shall start, for in combining the Greek idealism of the classical orders with a typically heavy practicality, Roman building produced an architecture that expressed perfectly the unshakeable self-confidence that sprung from a steady assurance of their place in the world. It is an architecture informed by a very definite concept of the relationship between man and nature: a belief that the world has a basic immutable order; that men by powers of

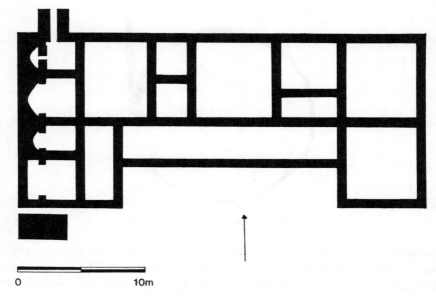

Figure 16. Newport (redrawn by Rob Rippengal).

reason can discover what that order is; and that, discovering it, they can control their environment as they will.

Outside official and public buildings, this is an architecture seen only in rather attenuated form in Roman Britain. Nevertheless, there was clearly exposure to it and it was certainly aped to some degree in the vernacular architecture of the period. Thus, while few villas produce clear expression of the classical orders *per se*, might they nevertheless indicate a similar shift in perceptions?

On one level, such basic qualities as the straight line, the level or 'true' surface, the right angle and the use of regular units of measurement, together with their expression in a language of geometric forms, symmetry and so on speak immediately of rationality and order, and if we look further this is mirrored in the changing nature of construction and materials.

Gone is the acceptance of nature taking its course, along with the 'organic' form, unworked materials and exposed construction that express-ed it. Thus, what is immediately striking about these buildings is their solid-ity, their permanence – these are structures that might stand for centuries, strong, upright, impervious to all that the elements might throw at them.

This solidity is exemplified in the use of stone. However, what is so notable about stone in this particular tradition is the transformation wrought upon it to produce, in the 'best' examples, carefully squared faces laid in regular courses. Similarly, the firing of clay to make brick and tile marks an even more striking transformation of the natural substance and contrasts directly with the earlier use of daub. Similarly, we see a host of new flooring materials. Whether concrete or mosaic, what is important is that the bare earth is hidden, shut away, the floor regular and true. So too the coating of walls; everything is hidden under an even, uniform covering of plaster. Even in the use of hypocausts to provide heat 'as if from nowhere', we see once again an isolation of the 'raw', 'natural' process of burning wood.

In all, this new architecture, with its substantial, permanent structures, neat, square rooms, decorated floors, carefully painted walls and impressive, well-proportioned facades exemplifies not man in nature, but man's conquest of nature. It is, I would suggest, not simply a change in degrees of comfort or even of 'manners', but something altogether more profound, a semantic shift, a key transformation of the way in which these people saw themselves and, indeed, lived in the world.

This is, of course, merely a starting point from which to develop a broader analysis. The aim of such an analysis would be to demonstrate how, by articulating a host of different forms of evidence, relating even to the most mundane of activities, we might hope to gain a fuller understanding of this way of living, of the *habitus*.

Categories of Information

To this end, I have drawn up two lists. The first gives, perhaps rather obviously, the kind of evidence available. The second is intended to illustrate how, by means of a comprehensive series of comparisons, the kind of articulation I referred to may be achieved:

A. Categories of information available for examination:

Site layout including position, orientation and plan of:
> 'main house', including features such as hearths, baths, hypocausts, mosaics, facade(s) and shrines; and the disposition of reception rooms, private quarters, bedrooms, kitchens and work rooms
> 'secondary' or other domestic units, including same features as 'main house'
> subsidiary buildings
> enclosures and/or yards
> other features – threshing floors, corn-dryers, hearths, pits, 'activity areas', boundaries and burials
> fields, roads and other outlying features

Constructional details of:
> walls
> floors
> roofs
> facade(s)
> doorways
> boundaries and enclosures

Building materials:
> stone (including e.g. origins and whether dressed)
> marble
> brick
> tiles
> timber
> wattle and daub
> thatch
> plaster
> render
> floors in particular: flags, other paving, gravel, cobbles, beaten earth, rammed chalk, concrete, *opus signinum*, tesserae, tegulae, mosaic

Decoration:
> painted plaster (inside or out)
> mosaics
> statuary

Faunal remains:
> species representation
> body part representation
> food residues
> 'economy'
> distribution

Pottery:
> fine/table-coarse ratio
> forms/uses
> fragmentation/trampling
> origins; distribution
> quantity

Small finds:
> tools
> utensils
> toiletries
> weapons
> votive objects
> other exceptional small finds
> coins
> distribution/find-spots

B. To shed light on (more formally):

    in:out
    front:back
    centre:periphery
    (up:down)
    (these including consideration of: boundaries, doors/thresholds,
       liminal areas, orientation, separation, inclusion, exclusion etc.)
    culture:nature
    male:female
    human:animal
    animal:plant
    clean:unclean
    sacred:profane
    fertile:infertile
    living:dead
    public:private
    (more difficult, though not necessarily impossible, e.g. day:night;
       light:dark)
    and relating to and cross-cutting these:
    dirt and hygeine including: personal cleanliness, especially related to
       the practice of bathing
    different categories of rubbish and other waste, such as domestic
       waste:farm waste; excrement:other rubbish/waste; human excre-
       ment:animal excrement; animal waste:plant waste
    processing of: animal products (e.g. butchery); grain (e.g. threshing,
       drying, milling); other (e.g. pottery production, metal working,
       woodworking)
    storage of: food; water; oil/wine; animals; grain; tools/utensils
    use of water: for drinking; for washing; sacred water/in shrines
    use of fire: for warmth; for cooking; for drying grain; for
       craft/industrial purposes
    burial of: animals; infants; adults
    decoration: of walls (in or out); of floors; of ceilings; furnishings
    activities such as: cooking, eating, sleeping, receiving guests, work
       (domestic:farm)

The whole is to be related to such conventional indicators of wealth and status as: fittings, features, decorative and architectural details; pottery; small finds; diet; economy; and contacts with the outside world.

CONCLUSION ————

Finally, and by way of a conclusion, it is important not to give an impression of uniformity here. The contrast between round houses and the winged corridor villa makes a point but is not the most meaningful comparison that could be made. The variety of domestic arrangements is quite striking and it is important to maintain this variety in our analyses for this is where Smith falls down. Thus, comparisons within and between round houses, simple one, two or three roomed houses, 'cottage' villas, winged corridor villas, courtyard villas, aisled buildings and even non-domestic sites such as shrines are central to the approach. Do they encompass the elements outlined above in the same ways; do they, in other words, express the same *habitus*?

Thus, in relation to Smith's argument, I suggested earlier that we ought to be addressing the relationships between the various domestic units on many of the sites he discusses. In particular, I suggested that there is good reason to doubt his notion of equality, that there may be differences not simply of degree but of kind. Here, then, we have a means of assessing differences of 'kind', for in comparing different expressions of *habitus* there are inevitably implications for the social conditions that lie behind them for, as Bourdieu notes, 'all the products of a given agent, by an essential overdetermination, speak inseparably and simultaneously of his class – or, more precisely, his position in the social structure' (Bourdieu 1977, 87).

Bibliography

Bourdieu, P. 1977 *Outline of a Theory of Practice*. Cambridge; Cambridge University Press.

Brandt, R. and J. Slofstra (eds) *Roman and Native in the Low Countries*. Oxford.

Branigan, K. and D. Miles (eds) 1986 *The Economies of Romano-British Villas*. Sheffield; Sheffield University, Department of Prehistory.

Burnham, B. and H. Johnson 1979 'Introduction' in Burnham, B. and H. Johnson (eds) .

Burnham, B. and H. Johnson 1979 *Invasion and Response: The Case of Roman Britain*. British Archaeological Reports, British Series; Oxford.

Collingwood, R. G. 1923 *The Archaeology of Roman Britain*. Oxford.

Collingwood, R. G. and J. N. L. Myers 1937 *Roman Britain and the English Settlements*. Oxford.

Douglas, M. and B. Isherwood 1979 *The World of Goods: towards an anthropology of consumption*. London.

Haverfield, F. 1912 *The Romanisation of Roman Britain*. Oxford.

Hemp, W. J. and C. Gresham 1943 'Park, Llanfrothen and the unit system' *Archaeologia Cambriensis* 97, 98–112.

Hingley, R. 1989 *The Rural Settlement of Roman Britain*. London.

Miles, D. 1986 'Villas and variety: aspects of economy and society in the Upper Thames landscape' in K. Branigan and Miles (eds).

Millet, M. 1990 *The Romanisation of Britain*. Oxford.

Percival, J. 1976 *The Roman Villa*. London.

Reece, R. 1987 *My Roman Britain*.

Richmond, I. 1969 'The plans of Roman villas in Britain' in A. L. F. Rivet (ed.).

Rivet, A. L. F. 1969 *The Roman Villa in Britain*.

Slofstra, J. 1983 'An anthropological approach to the study of Romanisation processes' in R. Brandt and J. Slofstra (eds).

Smith, J. T. 1978 'Villas as a key to social structure' in M. Todd (ed.).

Smith, J. T. 1985 'Barnsley Park villa; its interpretation and implications' *Oxford Journal of Archaeology* 4 (3), 341–51.

Smith, J. T. 1987 'The social structure of a Roman villa: Marshfield-Iron-mongers piece' *Oxford Journal of Archaeology* 6 (2), 243–55.

Swoboda, K. M. 1919 *Römische und romanische Palasta*. Vienna.

Todd, M. 1978 *Studies in the Roman-British Villa*. Leicester; Leicester University Press.

Ward, J. 1911 *Romano-British Buildings and Earthworks*.

Abbreviations in text:

JRS Journal of Roman Studies.

VCH Victoria County Histories.

9

A THEORETICAL FRAMEWORK FOR THE STUDY OF ROMANO-BRITISH VILLA MOSAICS

Sarah Scott

Studies of Romano-British villa mosaics have tended to be restricted to description, classification and typological survey. Little attempt has been made to go beyond the ordering of data, to consider the relationship between the mosaics, the villa, and the nature of the society itself. The aim of this paper will be to outline a new theoretical framework for the interpretation of villa mosaics. This framework involves a considera-tion of: the nature and 'meaning' of the designs; the relationship between the mosaics and their architectural context; the effect of the social position of the interpreter on meaning; and finally, the significance of the mosaics in the broader historical context. It will be suggested that such a framework could provide new and deeper insight into the nature of social relations and material practices within Roman Britain.

INTRODUCTION ─────────

The purpose of this paper is to outline an analytical framework for the study of Romano-British villa mosaics. It will hopefully be demonstrated that a new theoretical approach could allow deeper insight into the nature of social relations throughout the Roman period in Britain, and enable an interpretation to be made regarding the significance of the mosaics, both as products of, and 'participants' in, these relations.

The discussion will be based on the premise that material culture is a communicative symbolic field, and that it is structured in relation to social strategies and power relations (Hodder 1982). Although this symbolic field is already in place for an individual to use, it is through the manipulation of both material and other practices that the individual is able to establish him/herself within the social order, and is able to make changes to his or her position within this order.

The implication of this premise for the study of Romano-British mosaics is that they can be seen as having the potential to provide us with an insight into the nature of social relations within Roman Britain. These material practices are not simply a source of information about other aspects of society, however; they are a source of information in their own right. The mosaics should not be seen as a passive reflection of Romano-British society; they must instead be seen as integral to, and active within, social relations. Any attempt to interpret the mosaics therefore has to go beyond description and classification, and must endeavour to consider subjects such as: dating; style; the meaning of the art within a given cultural context; and the nature of the society producing them.

Bearing this in mind, the theoretical framework to be outlined involves four basic stages of analysis:

1) the collection and presentation of the data in a manner conducive to further study;

2) a closer look at the nature of representation within the mosaics, and an assessment of the way in which 'meaning' is encoded within the system;

3) an examination of the relationship between the mosaics and their architectural context;

4) the interpretation of the mosaics in terms of the historical context of their production and use.

Before discussing these analytical stages in more detail, however, it will be useful to consider briefly the nature of some previous work on Romano-British mosaics, and to identify some of the problems which have placed restrictions on interpretation.

The Nature of Previous Work

Work on Romano-British mosaics, such as that carried out by J. M. C. Toynbee (1962; 1964), and D. J. Smith (1969) falls very much within archaeology's 'traditional' culture-historical paradigm. Although extremely valuable in terms of descriptive detail and ordering of data, it has contributed very little to an understanding of the mosaics within the wider social context.

In the case of much of the work carried out on villas and mosaics, the manner in which the data has been classified and organised hinders rather than facilitates interpretation. For the most part, studies of the Romano-British villa are characterised by a tendency to divide the villa up into sev-

eral different components, these components then being analysed sep-
arately. A striking example of this type of work is Rivet's *The Roman Villa* in
Britain (ed. 1969), where various aspects of the villa are compartmentalised
and considered in turn by different authors. I suggest, however, that if any
one aspect – such as the mosaics – is to be interpreted more fully, it is essential that the villa be considered as an entity. The division of the villa into
these various components is artificial in the extreme, presenting a distorted
and incomplete view of 'villa life'. Additionally, if we are to make any attempt to go beyond the descriptive stage, it is necessary not only to consider the villa as an entity, but also to consider the changing historical context of the production of both the villas and the mosaics.

If we are to attempt to interpret the social significance of the mosaics,
the 'traditional' type of approach must be rejected in favour of an interpretive framework which integrates theory and data more fully. This integration of theory and data is necessary even at the initial stage of the collection and presentation of the archaeological material.

THE PRESENTATION OF THE DATA ———————

It is important not only to locate, identify and describe the mosaics, but
also to relate them to the plan of the villa. It is essential that the mosaics
can be seen in relation to one another, and in relation to the architectural
setting. Some of the eighteenth and nineteenth century plans of villas are
useful in this respect as they have the mosaics illustrated *in situ* (see e.g.
Figs 17 and 18 of Newton St Loe and Withington respectively). The draw-
ings of Samuel Lysons (e.g. 1797) are a particularly notable example of this
holistic craft.

Before any attempt can be made to relate the mosaics to their historical
context of production, it is also necessary to have some idea of their
chronological framework. It is suggested that a formal analysis of the
mosaics could prove extremely useful for building up a more detailed picture of the chronological and formal aspects of Romano-British mosaics. As
Miller (1985) has noted, formal analysis can also provide a description that
may be more useful than the mere listing of motifs, and may provide
alternative levels at which to examine the articulation between form and
society.

Having discovered the nature of the art forms, where they occur, and
how and when they were constructed, it is possible to move to the next
stage of the analysis. This will involve a closer look at the nature of

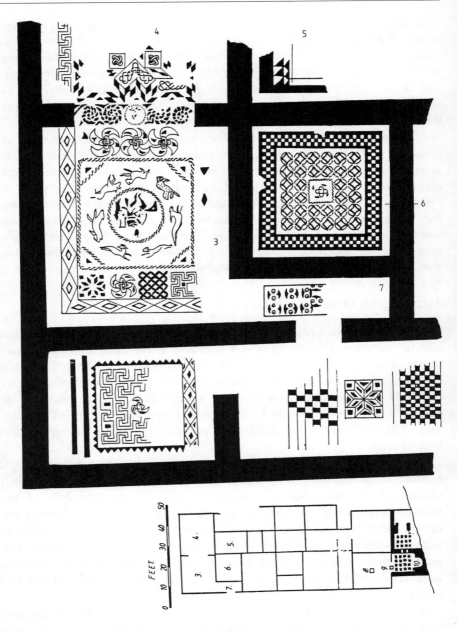

Figure 17. Newton St Loe: villa and mosaics.

representation within the mosaics, and an assessment of the way in which meaning is encoded within the system.

How Do the Mosaics Encode Meaning?

Regarding Romano-British mosaics, it is useful to make an analytical distinction between representational, or iconic forms, and non-representational, or arbitrary systems of representation.

Iconicity has been defined by Taylor as (1987, 198): 'the formal resemblance between the signifier, the painted form, and signified, the object or species represented.' Within an arbitrary, or non-representational system, there is no necessary relationship between the signifier and the signified.

It must be emphasised, however, that although there may be no necessary relationship between signifier and signified in arbitrary systems of representation, such a system may be far from arbitrary in that, in order to interpret meaning, it may be necessary to possess an in-depth knowledge of the code employed. Likewise, although the representational forms may be easier to interpret initially, they too may have meanings which require some kind of specialised knowledge.

It is useful to distinguish between the two systems of representation within Romano-British mosaics because, within Roman art, it is necessary to look at many of the representational forms in terms of contemporary mythology and religion. The non-representational forms, on the other hand, need to be understood as part of an historical, aesthetic tradition extending back to classical Greece.

It must be stressed, however, that if the full potential of the mosaics for encoding meaning is to be understood, it will be necessary to look at the relationships within and between the two systems of representation. In order to interpret an element within a mosaic, it is essential to look at its relationship with other elements within the mosaic, and also to look at the relationships between mosaics within a villa. For example, in terms of classical mythology, many figures may be interpreted very differently according to their context: who else, and what else they are represented with. By considering the relationships between various elements, it may be possible to screen out 'surplus' meaning. Additionally, various forms may be placed together in such a way as to imply a new meaning, which can only be grasped through an analysis of the relationships between forms. Eriksen's 're-reading' of the Hinton St. Mary 'Christian' pavement illustrates clearly the importance of this type of approach. He convincingly argues that the design represents a syncretistic allegory: 'where the Graeco-

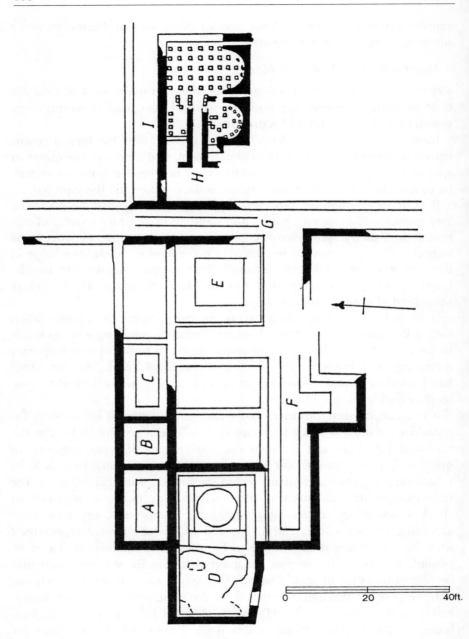

Figure 18. Withington: villa and mosaics.

Roman elements indicate the presence of the old religion, and where scriptural images are so interwoven as to create a striking thematic and symbolic unity' (1980, 48).

It is also important here to consider how the form of a mosaic, i.e. the way in which subjects or elements are presented, can affect meaning. I have suggested elsewhere (1991) for example, that the concentric circles of the Romano-British Orpheus design (e.g. Figs 18 and 19 of Withington) lend impact to the idea of Orpheus subduing nature in its strongest and wildest forms. It is argued that this particular feature suggests continuity, and emphasises the fact that the animals are unable to escape the power of Orpheus.

All of these factors have to be considered in terms of who would have seen the mosaics. The mosaics would obviously have been open to different levels of interpretation according to the social position of the interpreter. If we are to consider this question further, however, it will be necessary to place the mosaics within the architectural context.

THE ARCHITECTURAL CONTEXT ————————

It is important to remember that the mosaics themselves are an integral part of the villa architecture, being of a much more permanent nature than furniture, for example. The following quote from Vitruvius emphasises clearly the significance of the architectural context (Vitruvius in Preston-Blier 1987, 1):

> In all matters, but particularly in architecture, there are these two points: the thing signified, and that which gives it significance. . . . It appears then, that one who professes himself an architect should be well-versed in both directions. Let him be educated, skilful with the pencil, instructed in geometry, know much history, have followed the philosophers with attention, understand music, have some knowledge of the jurists, and be aquainted with astronomy and the theory of the heavens .

What this highlights is that the significance of architecture is grounded in the experiences and intellectual background of its makers and users. As Preston-Blier (ibid.) has pointed out, architecture is invariably anthropocentric, being bound up with human activity, experience, and expression. Architecture provides an objectification of pre-existent patterns and perspectives, ordering space, and therefore human action. Preston-Blier

Figure 19. Withington: Orpheus and other mosaics.

(ibid., 2) notes that when architecture borrows its imagery from human experience, it encourages those who move within it to reaffirm essential features of human identity and activity. However, at the same time, architectural meaning can also have a basis in metaphor; a structure may provide the means for seeing one thing in terms of something else. As such, it may bring a number of diverse ideas and activities together into a coherent whole.

In order to analyse the complex symbolism of architecture, however, it is obviously necessary to consider the occupants and their use of the architectural space and symbols. In particular, it is essential to account for the social position of the interpreter when attributing 'meaning' to the architecture. Interpretation is always bound up with social inequality and with power relations. It is particularly important to bear this in mind in the interpretation of mosaics. The question of physical access to the mosaics has to be considered in relation to the nature of representation. Access to the meaning of the mosaics may have been constrained both physically and through varying degrees of education and understanding. It is important to consider, for example, how the mosaics and architecture might have been viewed by the people who worked in the villa, or how they might have been viewed by women. This may be critical to understanding the ways in which they functioned within the social and political context.

In terms of Romano-British mosaics, therefore, it is necessary to look very closely at the various trends in design construction, and at the changing popularity of the subjects depicted. These patterns must then be related to developments in domestic architecture more generally. At this stage it will also be necessary to look at the ways in which Roman beliefs and ideals imposed on domestic architecture and interior decoration, and at the various functions of rooms within the villa. On the basis of this, the question of who may have had access to those rooms which possessed mosaics can be considered, and the relationship between these people and the owner of the villa assessed. It may then be possible to suggest reasons why a certain design may have been chosen, and to address the question of what the villa owner may have been trying to say about himself and his relations with the rest of society.

Integral to this stage of the analysis must be a consideration of the relationship between the architectural forms and their immediate environment. For example, how did the siting of a villa contribute to its overall aesthetic effect, and how did the villas relate to other buldings in the landscape?

THE SOCIAL, POLITICAL AND ECONOMIC CONTEXT ————

In order to explain the relationship between the mosaics, the villa, and society, it will be necessary to place them within the broader social, political and economic context.

If we are to understand why certain practices were employed in certain places at certain times, it is important to consider the social, political and economic context of their production and use. Material culture is always integral to power strategies and ideological practices. As Shanks and Tilley (1987, 72) point out, any analysis of power should be concerned with the social roots of power, attempts to achieve and maintain power, and counter attempts to subvert power strategies.

Regarding Romano-British mosaics, the data must be considered in all of its specificity, and must be related to the changing historical context. It will be necessary to consider who the elite were at any one time, and on what their power and wealth was based. The relationship between the elite and the other elements of Romano-British society also has to be taken into account. All of these factors then have to be considered in the light of Britain's changing relationship with the core provinces, and with other areas of the Empire. Having placed the mosaics and architecture within this wider context, it should then be possible to address the question of why certain material practices were employed at certain times, and to suggest how these practices may have played a role in maintaining or changing the very structure of society.

CONCLUSION ————

To summarise, it has been suggested that much of the pessimism inherent within studies of Romano-British villas and mosaics is due not to a lack of evidence, but to the nature of the approach employed. In order to move beyond the stage of description and classification, a new approach has been proposed, in which the mosaics are considered within their architectural context, and as integral to social strategies and power relations.

It must be emphasised that the analytical stages outlined above are not mutually exclusive. In practice, there will have to be a constant movement back and forth between the various levels. However, perhaps the most important feature of such an approach is that it provides a single framework within which to analyse the different levels of discourse inscribed in the material text. Within such a framework, it is no longer possible to consider various components of the villa in isolation, or to discuss the villa without placing it within its specific cultural context. An attempt must be made to develop theories regarding the possible function and significance of these material practices.

Although the integration of theory and data has only begun relatively recently in Romano-British archaeology, it has hopefully been demonstrated in this paper that the potential of such an integration is considerable. It is possible for an interpretation to be made regarding the significance of the villa mosaics and architecture, allowing new and deeper insight into the nature of social relations and material practices throughout the Roman period in Britain.

Bibliography

Coward, R. and J. Ellis 1977 *Language and Materialism.* R. K. P.

Eriksen, R. 1980 'Syncretistic symbolism and the Christian Roman Mosaic at Hinton St Mary: a closer reading' *Proceedings of the Dorset Natural History and Archaeological Society* 102, 43–48.

Hodder, I. 1982 *The Present Past.* Batsford.

Hodder, I. 1986 *Reading the Past.* Cambridge University Press.

Lysons, S. 1797 *An Account of the Roman Antiquities discovered at Woodchester.* London.

Lysons, S. 1817 *Reliquiae Britannico-Romanae* volume 2.

Miller, D. 1985 *Artefacts as Categories.* Cambridge University Press.

Moore, H. 1990 'Paul Ricoeur: action, meaning and text', in Tilley (ed.), 85–120.

Nichols, W. L. 1838 *Description of the Villa at Newton St Loe, Bath.*

Preston-Blier, S. 1987 *The Anatomy of Architecture.* Cambridge; Cambridge University Press.

Rivet, A. L. F. (ed.) 1969 *The Roman Villa in Britain.* London.

Scott, S. 1989 Symbols of Power and Nature: A Contextual Approach to the Orpheus Mosaics of Fourth Century Roman Britain. Leicester; unpublished BSc Dissertation University of Leicester.

Scott, S. 1991 'An outline of a new approach for the interpretation of Romano-British mosaics, and some comments on the possible significance of the Orpheus Mosaics of fourth-century Roman Britain' *Journal of Theoretical Archaeology* 2.

Shanks, M. and C. Tilley 1987 *Social Theory and Archaeology.* Cambridge; Polity Press.

Smith, D. J. 1969 'The Mosaic Pavements' in A. L. F. Rivet (ed.), 71–125.

Taylor, L. 1987 The Same but Different: Social reproduction and innovation in the art of the Kunwinjku of Western Arnhem Land. PhD thesis Australian National University.

Tilley, C. (ed.) 1990 *Reading Material Culture*. Oxford; Blackwell.

Todd, M. (ed.) 1978 *Studies in the Romano-British Villa*. Leicester; Leicester University Press.

Toynbee, J. M. C. 1962 *Art in Roman Britain.*

Toynbee, J. M. C. 1964 *Art in Britain under the Romans.*

Webster, G. 1969 'The future of villa studies' in A. L. F. Rivet (ed.), 217–249.

10

THE HOARDING, DEPOSITION AND USE OF PEWTER IN ROMAN BRITAIN

Rob Poulton and Eleanor Scott

The circumstances surrounding the deposition and hoarding of pewter in Roman Britain are examined – in particular material associations and broad archaeological contexts are analysed – and the conclusion is advanced that almost all such pewter material became buried as a result of ritual activity. It is further suggested that the deposition of pewter is but one element in a frequent and widespread use of seemingly everyday objects for non-rational purposes in Roman Britain, and that this reflects a development or re-invention of Celtic religious practices. Finally, the question of whether the character and distribution of the surviving pewter can be used to postulate a common domestic use for such vessels in late Roman Britain is considered. The arguments are advanced that much of the surviving pewter may have been specifically manufactured for religious purposes, and that the extent of domestic use cannot be directly inferred from the archaeological evidence.

INTRODUCTION

Pewter artefacts made in the Roman period have been described and discussed on a number of occasions (e.g. Wedlake 1958; Peal 1967; Beagrie 1989). Certain points have become generally agreed: while the circumstances and date of deposition of many of the known pieces of Roman pewter are obscure, the evidence from the remaining pieces suggests that the great majority were not manufactured until after circa AD 250 and that they were deliberately buried. In consequence, a common interpretation has arisen that the pewter represents the tableware of wealthy families, hoarded for temporary safekeeping in some time of crisis (e.g. Brown 1973, 201–4). Manning (1972, 248–9) suggested that religious activity lay behind the deposition of pewter hoards and Beagrie (1989, 179) agreed that the 'theory of religious deposition would . . . seem to offer the best explanation for the context of the majority of Roman pewter vessels.' It is the purpose of this paper to examine the interpretation of Roman pewter hoards in greater detail and consider how this affects our understanding of how pewter was used in Roman Britain.

CIRCUMSTANCES OF DEPOSITION ———

Hoarded material, by its very nature, is rarely recovered under controlled archaeological conditions. There is, therefore, very little that can be said with certainty about the circumstances of deposition of most Roman pewter, and even for the better known examples listed below the information is often inadequate.

Shepperton, Surrey (Poulton, in prep. a)

On 11 August 1987 a hoard of five pewter plates was brought up in the bucket of a mechanical excavator, which was removing the alluvial overburden in Shepperton Ranges gravel pit. The find was immediately reported and for this reason and also because the site was already under regular archaeological observation in view of the discovery of prehistoric finds of major importance (see, for example, Bird & Bird 1987, fig. 1) in the previous year, it was possible to determine the findspot with some accuracy and to assess the nature of its immediate context.

A bore-hole survey of the pit by the gravel company had indicated that there was considerable variation in the depth of alluvial deposits over the gravel, and site watching confirmed that this was due to the presence of a number of silted up river channels representing former courses of the Thames and tributary streams. These were evidently of various dates and it was from one such that the important prehistoric finds came. The pewter plates, however, were from an area between the channels, in what must certainly have been boggy ground or under shallow water in antiquity. They were found at a depth of about two metres below modern ground level, but much of this is to be accounted for by post-Roman alluvial deposition. The plates were deposited as a group, probably in a container for which no evidence survived, and would therefore have sunk down into the mud. The digger driver reported no other finds, and the regular archaeological observation had established that the immediate area was free of occupation sites of any date.

The nearest Roman finds come from an area around 250 metres to the east though the nature of occupation there is unclear. About a kilometre north-west of the present finds a Roman pit was excavated (Frere 1943) and the 19th century finds of tesselated pavements near the Saxon cemetery at Upper West Field, Shepperton (Longley and Poulton 1982, 184) must be similarly located. About 1.5km to the north, there was probably another villa (Poulton, in prep. b), and 19th century records suggest the possibility of Roman occupation in the area of Shepperton village. The evidence is far from detailed, but the general impression is that this area of the Thames valley was well settled and reasonably prosperous in the Roman period.

It might then be thought that one of the nearby Roman households had hoarded these items in a period of disorder, but, if so, they were rather dim witted. What sense could it have made to bury goods with intent to recover in boggy ground so far from the nearest settlement? Accidental loss is a bare possibility but one needs be highly imaginative to conjure up a satisfactory set of circumstances to account for its occurrence at this location. The explanation that best fits these facts is that the plates were votive offerings, for which a waterlogged site was deemed appropriate.

St Albans (Verulamium), Hertfordshire

A find of three pewter plates from Verulamium was from a very similar site context to that at Shepperton. They were stratified in bog mud beside the River Ver, and loosely associated with a large number of coins, which point to a date of AD 375–400 for deposition. The whole group of material has been suggested as votive in origin (Goodburn 1984, 65), and, indeed, there seems no reasonable alternative explanation.

Bath, Somerset

A rich variety of pewter pieces have been recovered from the Spring in the temple of Sulis Minerva at Bath, a number with inscriptions to the presiding deity (Henig et al. 1988). These do not of course constitute a hoard in the strict sense, as deposition clearly occurred on a number of occasions. Nevertheless, this material is very relevant to the discussion here in view of the obvious association with both religion and water. Of particular interest is Cunliffe's (1988, 361) suggestion that the pewter is temple plate, associated with official rituals, deposited at the end of its useful life or by special ceremony. The Romano-Celtic temple at Harlow has also produced a miniature pewter cup (Frere 1989, 303).

Stanwick, Northants

During excavations at the Stanwick villa between 1984 and 1988 a group of

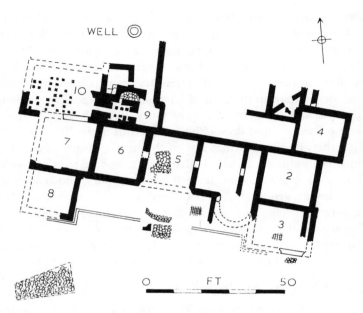

Figure 20. Brislington Villa, Avon (from Branigan).

four pewter vessels was found. Its context is interesting (Neal 1989, 165):

> the [fourth century] building to the west [had] set into its rubble
> floor . . . a quern and two pottery vessels and on the north side was
> a stone-capped drain concealing a hoard of iron objects, including
> two unequal-armed plough shares and a large wheel hub for a cart.
> The plough shares are unworn. In a pit to the north was a hoard of
> four pewter vessels and offcuts of leather indicating the manu-
> facture of shoes. The west wall of the hut was built over a well
> which was subsequently used as a rubbish and cess-pit. It contained
> coprolites of dogs.

The association of the Stanwick pewter with a watery context – the well –
and with metalwork (which has very obvious parallels with the ironwork
hoards classified as votive by Manning (1972)) and leather is significant and
will be discussed below.

Brislington Villa, Avon

The Pewter and Associated Objects. The Brislington villa, Avon (Fig. 20) was
excavated in 1899. The last discovery made during the course of these in-

vestigations was of a well, and the contents were recovered by the resilient employees of the local Sanitary Committee. At 24 feet down was found 'some tons of coarse building material, evidently the remains of the Villa', and at 28 feet a large collection of faunal remains, mostly ox skulls, came to light, along with 'other miscellaneous objects of the Roman period' (Barker 1901, 18). In clearing out the section between 28 and 32 feet down, human skulls and skeletal remains were found. Below these (ibid., 19):

> came a graduated series of seven remarkable metal vessels, with curved and ornamented handles. Most of these were fairly perfect, except that they were more or less bruised and bent, but two had been broken to pieces by the fall of heavy material upon them . . . With these objects was found the only perfect specimen of pottery that came to hand. This was a small black pitcher or jug. Another good specimen, and larger, was slightly damaged . . . and it is worthy of note that a few tesserae of the destroyed pavements were among the miscellaneous objects.

After these 'finds' came 'another extensive deposit of rough building material . . . then . . . more bones and fragments of pottery . . . and various iron objects' (ibid., 20). At the bottom of the well were found, amongst other things, bronze objects: an ornamented spoon, part of a fibula and a pin.

The Brislington Well Deposit, the Villa and the 'Barbarian Conspiracy' of AD 367: Branigan's Theory Reconsidered. The Bodies In the Well are infamous. This well deposit has been championed by Professor Branigan as evidence of the Barbarian Conspiracy of AD 367 (1972; 1977, 95 ff.) and in this he follows Haverfield, Frere and Webster. A lengthy discussion of the issue is not possible here (see Scott 1988, 221–32). The following points, however, should be noted.

1) There is very little archaeological evidence for the 'Barbarian Conspiracy' of 367, as reported by Ammianus Marcellinus. Only the north-western forts of Ravenglass and Bewcastle show signs of structural change at this date which may be attributable to destruction, though this is a moot point (J. P. Gillam pers. comm.).

2) Ammianus Marcellinus may have intended to glorify Theodosius by inventing action for him to have skilfully 'suppressed' (Todd 1981, 232).

3) The deposition/dumping of material down the Brislington well cannot be firmly dated to 367. The coin of Constantine II (found seemingly trapped on a ledge above all the deposited material? See Branigan's recon-

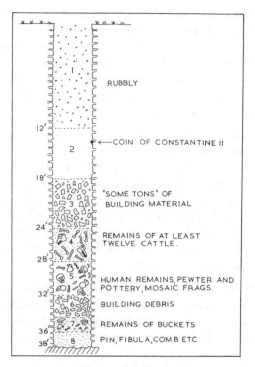

RUBBLY

COIN OF CONSTANTINE II

"SOME TONS" OF
BUILDING MATERIAL

REMAINS OF AT LEAST
TWELVE CATTLE.

HUMAN REMAINS, PEWTER AND
POTTERY, MOSAIC FRAGS.

BUILDING DEBRIS

REMAINS OF BUCKETS

PIN, FIBULA, COMB ETC

Figure 21. Brislington villa:
a reconstruction of the well deposits found in 1899 (from Branigan).

struction: here (Fig. 21) is of limited value as a dating tool.

4) The material may have gone down gradually, not during one clearing up operation. The building material in the well may have been deposited as part of a 'ritual of termination' (Merrifield 1987, 49–50; and Scott 1991) during renovations to the villa house. The frequent use of foundation deposits on villa sites (Scott 1990; 1991) indicates that the Romano-British attached ritual importance to the building process as part of the fabric of their social existence.

5) The contents of the Brislington well comprise objects often found in other more easily recognisable 'Celtic' votive contexts: complete or nearly complete pots, metal vessels, metalwork, and faunal and human remains, especially skulls (below).

The excavation report concludes of this feature and its contents (Barker 1901, 20): 'There seems every reason to conclude that this was originally the well of the Villa, but it was evidently made to serve as a rubbish pit when its use as a well was discontinued.'

Yet, if we examine the broad archaeological context, observing associations between material types, it might seem that on the contrary there are reasons to conclude that this well served a ritual, or non-rational, purpose (see below).

Appleford, Berkshire

The pewter hoard from Appleford is probably the best published of any such finds (Brown 1973). It was discovered during gravel extraction, and lay within a deep layer of soils which was recognised by the workmen as an intrusive and to them useless deposit which was thrown to one side in the pit. Some items of pewter were recovered from this and subsequently came to the attention of David Brown at the Ashmolean Museum. In consequence, the site was visited and in turn the deposit was carefully excavated. Despite the fact that it was a chance find this is therefore amongst the most informative of pewter hoards with regard to its circumstances of deposition.

The finds evidently came from the infill of a deep well or shaft cut through the gravel. Although a proportion may have been carted away with the surrounding gravel, it seems certain that a very high percentage survived for careful examination. The finds made consisted of:

1) A hoard of 24 pewter vessels, which seem to have been deposited in two piles, one of the small bowls and one of the plates.

2) A group of iron objects, consisting of an elaborate cauldron chain, a steelyard, part of a large scythe blade, a padlock, a shovel handle, a pan with folding handle, a chisel and sundry smaller items. Manning (1972, 235) has regarded this as a hoard, and in view of the parallels he quotes, and the character of the material, alternative explanations such as casual loss or rubbish disposal seem very unlikely.

3) Quern stone fragments.

4) Pottery, mostly of 4th century date, and including large portions of some pots.

5) Animal bones. A quantity were present but only a few (of *Bos* and *Cervus*) were collected, which is unfortunate in view of their potential importance (see above under *Brislington*).

6) Parts of a human skull.

7) Organic material including parts of a leather shoe and a plum or other fruit stone.

The immediate surrounding of the iron and pewter objects was a peaty soil full of rotting plant and twig remains. The human bones were all in a brown loamy earth (in parts very gravelly), with the remaining objects distributed between the two soil types. The peaty deposit had evidently formed in a waterlogged position, and it seems sensible to interpret it as a basal deposit with the loam above it. The hoarded items were therefore in a primary position in the well. This does not seem the most appropriate of hiding places if recovery was intended; on the other hand deposits of a votive character have been very commonly found in Roman well shafts (see below *Wells on Villa Sites* for references), and a votive explanation is favoured by Manning (1972) for this and the related group of ironwork hoards. Indeed, there must be some doubt whether shafts such as this ever functioned as wells; their original purpose might equally have been ritual.

The remaining finds may be compared closely with those from Brislington and are best understood by reference to the arguments advanced in that connection above. It would not be unreasonable to argue a case for regarding the pewter hoard as a votive deposit within a ritual shaft. Unlike Brislington, however, the shaft probably did not belong to a standard villa complex, as there was a complete absence of masonry in the immediate area, although there was plentiful evidence of nearby 3rd and 4th century occupation.

DISCUSSION ———

The above notes do not pretend to be an exhaustive review of the contexts in which pewter hoards have been discovered. They do, however, suggest that many pewter hoards should be regarded as having a ritual origin. Two different types of provenance seem to be involved; on the one hand deposition in riverine contexts, and on the other burial in 'well' shafts. In both cases the important factor is the association with water.

Romano-British 'Celtic' Religion and Ritual

That Celtic religion and its concomitant ritual burials and deposits continued into the Roman period in Britain has long been recognised (e.g. Ross 1968 passim; Macdonald 1977, 35–8; Laing 1979, 188), and Ross recognised that Celtic votive contexts were frequently 'watery' – wells, pits, shafts, etc. There even appears to have been an upsurge or reinvention of the Celtic tradition in fourth century Britain judging by the number of new Romano-Celtic temples which appear in the south of England at this time (Painter 1971, 157). Certain Celtic ritual activity, such as deposition of 'head objects' re-emerged strongly in the fourth century in Roman Britain. Although Ross refers to this as a 'cult' of the head, it is probably best described as part of a general *phenomenon*, and not a 'cult' (Riddel 1990). Further, it appears to be a late ritual-religious phenomenon.

Much work on the survival of Celtic religion into the Roman period has concentrated on the evidence of epigraphy and iconography which reveals how particular Roman and Celtic gods were identified with each other (e.g. Macdonald 1977, 36; Salway 1982, 669). Far less attention is paid to the ritual human and animal burials, especially pit deposits, of Roman Britain which are clearly part of the Celtic ritual tradition known from pre-Roman Britain. Laing (1979, 118) simply notes in passing that: 'Over a hundred ritual pits and wells, mostly Romano-British but some Iron Age, have been excavated in Britain.'

He adds that these pits and wells often contain the bones of dogs and ravens and 'skulls', but gives no further details. One must return to Ross's original account for the only serious attempt to review this subject (Ross 1968). Her sample of pits, shafts and wells came from a wide variety of sites, such as Roman forts (mainly Newstead), settlements, hillforts and temples, but only one villa, Brislington. She does not include pewter in her list of objects which repeatedly appear in the watery features, but her list does include a great many artefacts and natural objects which have also been found accompanying deposited pewter: animal bones; buckets; burnt stone and flints; coins; cult objects; deer antlers; metal objects; organic matter; ox skulls and bones; pins of bronze and bone; potsherds; pottery vessels, whole or almost whole; quern stones; sandals and other pieces of leather; skulls, human and animal; smooth stones; twigs, leaves, acorns, nuts, stones and seeds.

Although it has been generally accepted that Celtic 'pagan' religion and its votive practices continued into Roman period, the expected cultural limits of such Celtic survival, however, have been made explicit (Macdonald 1977, 35; our emphasis): 'Celtic beliefs are likely to have prevailed in country districts (*though not in villas*).'

The archaeological evidence, however, would appear to refute Macdonald's hypothesis. Villa occupants should not be uncritically viewed as modern-rational. Different and culture-specific 'cultural maps' are to be found in other societies, both now and in the past. Neither should they be regarded as careless wastrels, dropping, losing and failing to recover an astonishing array of artefacts and livestock from pits, wells and shafts.

Wells on Villa Sites

Wells were frequently used for non-rational purposes in Roman Britain. For example, the sixteen dogs found down a Roman well in Staines, Surrey defy any credible 'rational' explanation (Chapman and Smith 1988). A number of Roman sites, including villas, have two wells, one of which appears to be functional – i.e. not full of 'rubbish' – and one which contains a large amount of objects known to have been used elsewhere as ritual offerings. This appears to have happened at the villa of Barton Court Farm (below), and at the Roman fort of South Shields, when the original well was replaced by a second well, the first was left open and upon excavation was found to contain a number of ox skulls (Paul Bidwell pers. comm.). This ritual process is evident on many villa sites and the votive assemblages deposited in the wells and pits contain recurring – thus significant – types of objects and sometimes assemblages. Given that some of these assemblages include pewter, these wells and pits are an important link in understanding the depositional associations and contexts of pewter.

Barton Court Farm

There were two wells discovered and excavated at Barton Court Farm, Oxfordshire. One deep well, feature 832, was in use in the fourth century and probably into the fifth (Miles 1986, 14–15, 46–7). This well contained in its lower levels the best collection of ironwork found on the whole site, a large number of leather shoes, several almost complete pots, an iron-bound wooden bucket and iron hook, and 'large quantities of biological material'. It is clear that accidental loss cannot account for such a great proportion of the metalwork from the whole site having accumulated in the well. If this deposit at least was deliberate, so may other well deposits have been, particularly those whose contents tend to recur. The upper levels of this well contained 'a deliberate dump of stone, animal bones, and well preserved vegetable matter' (ibid., 15).

The second well on this site, feature 950, was situated nearer to the villa house and was housed inside a small rectangular masonry well-house. Only a small amount of 'waterlogged material' was found in this well (ibid., 32), and that this well differed in both style and its contents may indicate that the wells, though contemporary, had different uses. 950 may have been purely utilitarian, whereas 832 appears to have had a votive function.

Rudstone

At Rudstone, Humberside, the enormous well contained four stratigraphical groups of animal bones, including skulls and whole bodies, as well as pottery, the remains of buckets and chains, coins, an 'enigmatic well deposit' (Buckland 1980, 164), antlers, stonework, tesserae and wall plaster. Among the deepest stones was a block carved with the figure of a deity or *genius*. The pottery collection interestingly comprised vessels not represented elsewhere on the site (Stead 1980, 29–30, 36, 149–50).

The building debris and some of the nearly whole animal skeletons are reminiscent of the Brislington and North Wraxhall well deposits which have been considered evidence of the effects on villas of the 'Picts War' of 367. However, the deposit at Rudston was dated by Stead as being not earlier than the early fifth century (1980, 29–30).

Denton

The villa at Denton, Lincolnshire, also had a well which was found to contain building debris, and, nearer the bottom of the well, cattle bones, moss, and items of leather, including shoes. Pottery was of circa 350–400 (Greenfield 1971, 47–8, 53).

Rockbourne

There were two wells at Rockbourne, Hampshire. The 'main well', situated by the bath suite, had deposits of pottery, coins of the second to third centuries, moss, parts of a leather sandal, including its hobnails, and – reminiscent of Appleford – various fruit stones and hazel nuts. The second well appears to have replaced the first, containing fourth century 'infill of the usual debris'; and we learn that the 'quantity of animal bones was unusual' (Morley Hewitt 1971, 18, 15–16).

Rivers and Ritual

There has been much recent discussion of how 'prestige' metalwork and other items covering a chronological span from the Neolithic to the late-Saxon period (as it does at Shepperton (Fig. 22)) came to be in the rivers from which they have been recovered (e.g. Needham and Burgess 1980, 442–9; Bradley and Gordon 1988). A consensus view seems to be developing that the normal explanation must lie in ritual/religious activity, and it is interesting to note that types of objects found in rivers here are often found with burials elsewhere in Europe (Torbrügge 1972) in view of the contrast between the frequency of pewter in burials on the continent and its rarity in Britain (Beagrie 1989, 174–81).

Finds from riverine contexts are perhaps less spectacular from the

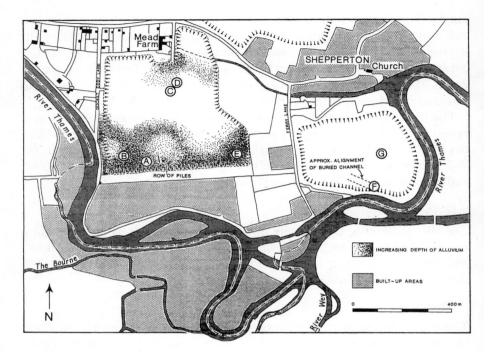

A nest of 5 pewter plates
B Iron Age and Late Saxon swords, human skull
C prehistoric sherds
D prehistoric pit
E Neolithic macehead, Late Bronze Age hafted axe, bronze cauldron, Iron Age sword and pot
F Roman sherds and whole pot, 4th/5th century wooden piles
G Roman sherds.

Figure 22. Finds from Shepperton Ranges gravel pit. The deep alluvium indicates former courses of the Thames and tributary streams.

Roman than from the prehistoric period, but finds, for example, of whole pots are not uncommon from the Thames through Surrey (Surrey County Council, Sites and Monuments Record). These must surely have found their way into the river as a result of ritual activity. Apart from the pewter hoards at Shepperton and Verulamium, several pewter hoards have been recovered from extinct river channels in Cambridgeshire (Lethbridge and O'Reilly 1933). In explaining their deposition, Lethbridge and O'Reilly (1933, 166) invoked the idea of concealed plate in the Picts War and suggested that 'It is absurd to suppose that all these hoards could have been lost by accident . . . it is possible that these pewter services were placed in chests and sunk in the rivers with a small buoy to mark the place, much as fishermen now keep lobsters alive in the sea.' This is an extreme example of reluctance to consider explaining the archaeology of Roman Britain in terms of non-rational or ritual activity.

A Context for Pewter Deposits

The above analysis of associations of deposits reveals that perhaps a more proper context for the study of a deposit of archaeological material is other deposits of archaeological material, and not an 'historically documented fact'. A useful and tenable late Roman context, independent of the non-existent 'Picts War', has been demonstrated for the pewter from Brisling-ton, Appleford and Stanwick. For instance, the use of leather shoes, skulls and other animal bones, pottery, fruit stones, coins and metal objects as votive deposits on villas is clearly important in understanding pewter deposits. The deposition of leather shoes may relate to the Romano-Celtic practice of burying hobnail boots at sites such as Bradley Hill, Catsgore and Avebury (e.g. Salway 1982, 704–5); a burial rite which was a feature in the south, west and midlands in the fourth century. Another noteworthy hoard of Roman pewter associated with shoe leather, as well as ironwork (Manning 1972, 235), pottery fragments, a coin of Constans and a spindle-whorl, was found at the base of a stone-lined well 61ft 8in deep at Thatcham, Berkshire (Collingwood 1931).

There is a great deal of material from villas which waits to be interpreted as the by-product of the non-random ritual human behaviour that it surely is. Neither is this behaviour culturally intrusive. It belongs to the Celtic tradition, and Macdonald's premise that Celtic beliefs did not prevail in the villas of Roman Britain is no longer tenable.

The pewter hoards from riverine positions lack direct association with contemporary material. Their location, however, makes the notion of hoarding with intent to recover highly unlikely, and, in a wider sense, their context is a sacred one: it is evident, for example, that certain stretches of the Thames, such as that at Shepperton, were foci of ritual activity over a very long period.

THE USE OF PEWTER —————

It has been a common assumption that pewter ware was a normal *accoutrement* of the dinner tables of villa owners in the Late Roman period. As Brown (1970, 108 – quoted with approval by Salway 1982, 636) expressed it, 'At this time it must have been usual for every reasonably stocked household to have a dresser stacked with six or a dozen or even twenty or more, assorted plates, bowls and jugs.' Such a belief is obviously closely related to the interpretation of pewter hoards as buried for safety with intent to recover. If the hoards are correctly understood as originating in ritual activity, this in itself makes the 'villa dinner tableware' notion difficult; after all, if its final usage was votive, how can we tell what its earlier function may have been? The question may, perhaps more usefully, be expressed another way: are the items in pewter hoards to be understood, like those in the comparable ironwork hoards, as everyday objects given a new function? In order to answer this it will be useful to look at some of the characteristics of the pewter ware itself.

The first point to be made is that none of the hoards recovered seem to represent anything like what we should regard as a 'dinner service'. Instead, as Brown (1973, 201) pointed out, the material in the Appleford and other hoards has comparatively few matching pieces and instead seems to represent piecemeal acquisition. This might be better explained if one supposes that the hoard has its origins in material collected at a shrine or temple. Indeed, one piece at Appleford has a *graffito* – 'Lovernianus presented the things he had bought' (Brown 1973, 193, no. 24) – which implies a religious donation. *Graffiti* on other pewter pieces seem mostly to be personal names, but these too would seem more sensibly explained in the context of votive offerings. This in turn relates to a number of otherwise puzzling features of pewter ware. Could the dinner table of a prosperous household ever have been graced by objects with their rims splitting off due to defective manufacture (e.g. Brown 1973, no. 14, described as 'very little worn as though the plate had not been used much', and no. 20); or with casting marks and other irregularities still visible (e.g. Shepperton no. E2 (Poulton in prep. a) or Appleford nos 1, 18 & 21 (Brown 1973))? Finally, it would seem that much of the pewter we have has very little sign of wear in use (Peal 1967, 28; Poulton in prep. a), something which is remarkable when one considers the ease with which this soft metal can be marked.

In sum, then, it may be suggested that some pieces seem unsuitable for the dinner table, some seem to have religious connotations (and those with Chi Rho symbols (Peal 1967, 28) should be included here), and others seem to have been little used. The nature of the hoards themselves is ritual and the great majority lack even proximity to known villas (Brown (1973, 204) was driven to suggest that the Appleford hoard had been buried for safety by occupants of the Dropshot villa, a mile distant). It could be concluded that the overwhelming majority of the pewter we have represents only items collected or used in temples or shrines, or acquired for specifically votive purposes. There is no certain evidence that any of it was used for domestic purposes, and the question must be raised whether, speaking more generally, pewter was ever so used.

In considering this question, two other aspects of Roman pewter which have been much studied need to be taken into account. The most recent discussion of metallurgical analyses of Roman pewter (Beagrie 1989, 171–5) has made a number of suggestions to account for the variable composition of Roman pewter, which is almost always a tin-lead alloy, with the tin content varying from less than 40% to greater than 95%. He rightly points to the comparative cheapness of lead as a factor: this was also true in the medieval period, when it is clear that lead was added only to hollow wares in small amounts (10–20%) (Homer 1985, 151–2) and in very small quantities (typically less than 0.5%) to flatwares (Brownsword and Pitt 1984), presumably because greater amounts would have produced items which were unsatisfactory for daily use. The point is sharply emphasised by the discovery that sepulchral chalices and patens have up to 75% lead (Brownsword and Pitt 1985: in the 19th century such discoveries were described as lead chalices and patens, as for example one found at Chertsey Abbey (Poulton 1988, 47)). Might it not be the case that the composition of the Roman pewter we have is largely determined by the use to which it was put, and that the high lead pewter was manufactured solely for ritual purposes? This in turn may explain the apparent contrast between early Roman pewter which is normally high in tin and Late Roman pewter which is predominantly high in lead, the latter reflecting the increased use of pewter for ritual purposes in the third and fourth centuries.

The second aspect to be considered is the distribution of finds of pewter and evidence for pewter manufacture. The most recent distribution map (Beagrie 1989, fig. 3) shows a concentration of finds south of the Fosse way beyond Cirencester and to the north of a line drawn between the southern shore of the Bristol Channel and Canterbury. Finds elsewhere are more thinly spread (except, perhaps, for a secondary concentration in Cornwall) and almost completely absent from large areas of Wessex, South East England, Wales and the North. If this distribution is meaningful (and the fact that it is little altered by the plethora of more recent finds from that published by Wedlake (1958) may encourage such a view) then it should, on the arguments advanced above, reflect regional patterns of ritual activity rather than any domestic use of pewter. That such was occurring may be indicated by the wider spread of pewter small finds (Beagrie 1989, fig. 3), which are likely to represent casual losses of domestic material, and by the slightly broader distribution of evidence for pewter manufacture (ibid.), which might reflect use of pewter for non-ritual purposes. Finally, it should be emphasised that its indestructability and the ease with which it can be recycled mean that pewter is highly unlikely to be discarded as domestic rubbish.

CONCLUSIONS

Wherever there is adequate evidence for the circumstances of deposition of Roman pewter an association with religious activity is indicated. It is therefore a reasonable assumption that the vast majority of the extant pieces are the result of such activity. This metal seems to have found favour in the third and fourth centuries for a variety of religious purposes, most probably because it was a relatively cheap material which could nevertheless offer the illusion of the splendour of silver plate, and as such represented both an affordable and appropriate offering to the gods. The extent to which pewter was used for domestic purposes in the Roman period is unclear, but the character of that which survives may suggest that much of it was manufactured for specifically ritual purposes or had never been used for other purposes.

Acknowledgement. We should like to thank Phil Jones for much stimulating discussion.

Bibliography

Barker, W. R. 1901 *Account of Remains of a Roman Villa Discovered at Brislington, Bristol, December 1899.* Bristol.

Barrett, J. C. and R. Bradley (eds) 1980 *Settlement & Society in the British Later Bronze Age.* Oxford; British Archaeological Reports 83.

Beagrie, N. 1989 'The Romano-British pewter industry' *Britannia* 20, 169–91.

Bird, J. and D. G. Bird (eds) 1987 *The Archaeology of Surrey to 1540.* Guildford, Surrey.

Bradley, R. and K. Gordon 1988 'Human skulls from the River Thames and their significance' *Antiquity* 62, 503–509.

Branigan, K. 1972 'The Romano-British villa at Brislington' *Proceedings of the Somerset Archaeological and Natural History Society* 116, 78–85.

Branigan, K. 1977 *The Roman Villa in South-West England*.

Brown, P. D. C. 1970 'A Roman pewter mould from St Just in Penwith Cornwall' *Cornish Archaeology* 9, 107–10.

Brown, D. 1973 'A Roman pewter hoard from Appleford, Berkshire' *Oxoniensia* 38, 184–206.

Brownsword, R. and E. E. H. Pitt 1984 'X-ray fluorescence analysis of English 13th-16th century pewter flatware' *Archaeometry*, 237–44.

Brownsword, R. and E. E. H. Pitt 1985 'Some examples of medieval domestic pewter flatware' *Medieval Archaeology* 24, 152–55.

Buckland, P. C. 1980 'Insect remains from the well' in I. M. Stead 1980.

Chapman, J. and S. Smith 1988 'Finds from a Roman well in Staines' *London Archaeol.* 6, 3–6.

Coles, J. M. and D. D. A. Simpson (eds) 1968 *Studies in Ancient Europe. Essays presented to Stuart Piggot*.

Collingwood, R. G. 1931 'Roman objects from Stanwix and Thatcham' *Antiquaries Journal* 11, 37–45.

Cunliffe, B. (ed.) 1988 *The Temple of Sulis Minerva at Bath: Vol 2. The Finds from the Sacred Spring* Oxford; Oxford University Committee for Archaeology .

Frere, S. 1943 'Romano-British finds at Littleton' *Transactions of the London and Middlesex Archaeological Society* 9, 203–4.

Frere, S. 1984 *Verulamium excavations*, 3 Oxford; Oxford University Committee for Archaeology .

Frere, S. 1989 'Roman Britain in 1988' *Britannia* 20, 303.

Garwood, P. et al. 1991 (eds) *Sacred and Profane* Oxford; Oxford University Committee for Archaeology.

Goodburn, R. 1984 'Objects of pewter' in S. Frere, 65–7.

Greenfield, E. 1971 'The Roman villa at Denton, Lincolnshire. Part II' *Lincolnshire Hist Archaeol.* 1.

Henig, M. 1988 D. Brown N. Sunter L. Allason-Jones and D. Baatz 'The small objects' in B. Cunliffe (ed.).

Homer, R. F .1985 'The medieval pewterers of London c. 1190–1457' *Transactions of the London and Middlesex Archaeological Society* 36, 137–63.

Laing, L. 1979 *Celtic Britain*. London; Methuen.

Lethbridge, T. C. and M. M. O'Reilly 1933 in 'Archaeological notes' *Proc. Cambridge Antiq. Soc.* 33, 164–7.

Longley, D. and R. Poulton 1982 'The Saxon cemetery at Upper West Field, Shepperton' *Transactions of the London and Middlesex Archaeological Society* 33, 177–85.

Macdonald, J. 1977 'Pagan religions and burial practices in Roman Britain' in R. Reece (ed.).

Manning, W. H. 1972 'Ironwork hoards in Iron Age and Roman Britain' *Britannia* 3, 224–50.

Meates, G. W. 1979 *The Roman villa at Lullingstone, Kent*.

Merrifield, R. 1987 *The Archaeology of Ritual and Magic*.

Miles, D. 1986 *Archaeology at Barton Court Farm, Abingdon, Oxon*. Council for British Archaeology Research Report 50.

Morley Hewitt, A. T. 1971 *Roman Villa, West Park, Rockbourne, Nr Fordingbridge, Hants*. Revised Edition.

Neal, D. S. 1989 'The Stanwick villa, Northants: interim report of excavations 1984-88' *Britannia* 20, 149-68.

Needham, S. P. and C. B. Burgess 1980 'The later Bronze Age in the Lower Thames valley: the metalwork evidence' in J. C. Barrett and R. Bradley (eds).

Painter, K. S. 1971 'Villas and Christianity in Roman Britain' *British Museum Quarterly (Prehistoric and Roman Studies)* 35.

Peal, C. A. 1967 'Romano-British pewter plates and dishes' *Proc. Cambridge Antiq. Soc.* 60, 19-37.

Poulton, R. 1988 *Archaeological Investigations on the site of Chertsey Abbey*. Surrey Archaeological Society Research 11.

Poulton, R. in prep. a Archaeological discoveries made in a gravel pit at Shepperton, Surrey.

Poulton, R . in prep. b Excavations and geophysical survey on an earlier and later Saxon site at Shepperton Green, Surrey.

Reece, R. (ed.) 1977 *Burial in the Roman World* Council for British Archaeology Research Report 22.

Riddel, F. 1990 Stone Heads of the North – Some Observations. Unpublished BA Dissertation, University of Newcastle upon Tyne.

Ross, A. 1968 'Shafts, pits, wells – sanctuaries of the Belgic Britons?' in J. M. Coles and D. D. A. Simpson (eds).

Salway, P. 1982 *Roman Britain* 2nd Edition.

Scott, E. 1988 Aspects of the Roman Villa as a Form of British Settlement. PhD Thesis University of Newcastle upon Tyne.

Scott, E. 1990 'A critical review of the interpretation of infant burials in Roman Britain, with particular reference to villas' *Journal of Theoretical Archaeology* 1. Oxford; Oxbow.

Scott, E. 1991 'Animal and infant burials in Romano-British villas: a revitalisation movement' in P. Garwood et al. (eds).

Stead, I. M. 1980 *Rudston Roman Villa*.

Todd, M. 1981 *Roman Britain 55 BC-AD 400*.

Torbrügge, W. 1972 'Vor-und frühgeschichtliche Flüssunde zur Ordnung und Bestimmung einer Denkmälergruppe' *Bericht Römisch-German. Komm.* 51-2, 1-146.

Wedlake, W. J. 1958 *Excavations at Camerton, Somerset*.

11

ROMAN-PERIOD ACTIVITY
AT PREHISTORIC RITUAL MONUMENTS
IN BRITAIN AND IN THE ARMORICAN PENINSULA

Kenneth Rainsbury Dark

This paper is about the archaeology of superstition, a subject often neglected, although archaeologists frequently write about religion. The paper distinguishes between ritual and superstition, and explores the Roman material evidence in detail. It is argued that the evidence for Roman period activity at prehistoric ritual monuments in Britain and Armorica is invariably reduced to anecdotal significance, obscuring important relationships. It is argued that prehistoric ritual monuments were perceived in different ways in Roman Britain and the Armorican peninsula. In Armorica they were used as religious sites throughout the Roman period and in the immediate post-Roman centuries were often Christianised; in Roman Britain they were construed in a superstitious rather than religious fashion, and formed no part of organised paganism.

INTRODUCTION

This paper is about the archaeology of superstition, a subject often neglected, although archaeologists have often written about religion. Superstition is aimed at procuring advantage or avoiding disadvantage, but not forming a broader code of living and not requiring a wider set of related beliefs. The same superstitions can, therefore, be held by believers in different religions and who follow different codes of action in every other respect. Explanation is not a necessary component of a superstitious ritual and its action requires no explanation on the part of the participant. In this respect, superstition is different from Romano-Celtic or Classical paganism, where ritual is related to belief in deities who must be appeased, honoured, or persuaded by the participant. Here, I shall examine some evidence for superstition in Roman Britain.

Romano-British religion has been the subject of much recent study (e.g. Henig 1984; Rodwell 1980a), and its principal features are well known to modern archaeologists. Yet the Roman-period material found at prehistoric (by which I mean here, pre-Iron Age) ritual sites has received scant attention from either prehistorians or Romanists. The discovery of Romano-British burials, or even allegedly altars, at such sites has been reduced to almost anecdotal significance. This neglect has continued while some scholars of later periods have felt capable of accepting continuity, into the post-Roman period, of religious veneration at prehistoric ritual sites, on the basis of a coincidence between later churches and prehistoric ritual sites, and of the uncertainly relevant evidence of late Anglo-Saxon legislation (Morris 1989, 72–74, 81–82).

In this paper I examine how some types of prehistoric ritual sites were used in Roman Britain and how we might explain this use. It may be helpful to this approach to contrast Britain with another area, and for this purpose I have chosen the Armorican peninsula, which is close geographically and was probably (in terms of levels of Romanisation) similar to Roman Britain. The Armorican peninsula also has a recently well-published relevant database.

First, a misconception common among archaeologists must be cleared up. That is, the supposition that the coincidence of later church sites and prehistoric ritual monuments, or that the evidence provided by late Anglo-Saxon texts, inform us of religious continuity from pre-Roman Britain to Roman Britain. It has been claimed that when an Anglo-Saxon, or later church, was sited inside, or on, a prehistoric ritual monument, this was to Christianise the monument because it was still venerated by pagans. It has also been claimed that late Anglo-Saxon laws prohibiting pagan practices attest the contemporary existence of these practices; so that when they forbid worship of standing stones, for example, they attest the existence of that worship at the date of writing. If one were to accept such evidence, then there would be much to support a model of continuing rural paganism from the pre-Roman Iron Age into the late Anglo-Saxon period. But this interpretation is unacceptable.

There is no archaeological or historical evidence that unambiguously informs us that any Anglo-Saxon church was sited at a place where non-Germanic paganism survived into the Anglo-Saxon period. Nor does any pre-ninth-century Anglo-Saxon penitential refer to the worship of what may be prehistoric ritual monuments, such as standing stones (Morris 1989, 62–63). It is not credible that earlier ecclesiastical legislators chose to ignore such activity, and, in this absence of ecclesiastical prohibition, Britain is unlike Gaul, where such texts are common at a much earlier date (Ferguson 1872, 24–25). Nor are there equivalent prohibitions against the worship of, or at, what may be prehistoric ritual monuments in penitentials written in Celtic Britain and Ireland (Bieler 1963). It would, therefore, seem reasonable to suppose that when these prohibitions are encountered in late Anglo-Saxon texts they derive from earlier, but presumably continental, sources, as did much of late Anglo-Saxon ecclesiastical culture (e.g. see Szarmach with Oggins 1986).

It is also necessary to note that Anglo-Saxon textual sources reveal a considerable interest in explaining the countryside, including the origins of place-names referring to the presumed pagan function of sites such as Avebury (Gelling 1978, 141–42; Burl 1979, 31, 130–32). Thus a visible, and to a (later) Anglo-Saxon, obviously pagan, place, irrespective of whether or not it was used as a religious site in the pre-Anglo-Saxon period, might have been explained as a pagan site.

It would, then, be probable that some Anglo-Saxon (or for that matter, some later medieval) churches might have been so located as to negate 'heathen *foci*' which were merely the result of Anglo-Saxon attempts to explain the surrounding landscape. The siting of such churches need tell us nothing about the pre-Christian religious use of these sites, only, perhaps, about late Anglo-Saxon (and later) attitudes to them. The Anglo-Saxon perception of the prehistoric landscape is a source for Anglo-Saxon England, not for prehistoric or Roman Britain.

Our proper sources for evaluating the possibility of the religious use of prehistoric ritual sites in Roman Britain are, therefore, Roman-period archaeological sources. It is only these sources, lacking directly relevant historical data, which may inform us of what role, if any, such pre-Iron-Age monuments had in Roman Britain, and it is to them that we may now turn.

Regrettably there is no general survey, or corpus, of Roman-period material at British prehistoric sites, and it is not my intention to attempt to provide such a corpus here. The most recent discussion of this question has been Aitchison's re-evaluation of the numismatic data, which was exclusively concerned with coins (and 'toilet-instruments') (Aitchison 1988, 275–76). Consequently, a survey, albeit brief, of the relevant data is first presented.

THE ROMANO-BRITISH EVIDENCE ————

This may be considered under categories of prehistoric ritual sites. Here, barrows, megalithic structures, and henges, are chosen as types of monument which, as stone or earthwork features, might have been readily visible in the Roman-period countryside, but which were not, in general, reused for major sites in the intervening centuries since their prehistoric ritual use.

Roman-period activity at pre-Roman Iron Age hill-forts is excluded from this discussion as it is far from clear that these sites were primarily ritual foci in their ultimate pre-Roman form. Earlier use of these sites for prehistoric ritual monuments may, therefore, have been obscured, confused, or superseded by their pre-Roman Iron Age occupation. The inclusion of pre-Roman Iron Age shrines within them should not dissuade us from this view, as these may be a ritual aspect of an otherwise domestic context. It is interesting, however, in the context of the comments below, that hill-forts were used for temples in Roman Britain, as at Maiden Castle, and so were, in this respect, unlike the sites discussed here.

Barrows

Many prehistoric barrows have produced Romano-British finds upon excavation. These finds may derive from inside, on, or adjacent to the mound and comprise two main categories, pottery and coins. Sometimes the pottery, which can occur in some quantity, is present as sherds, sometimes as complete vessels. Coins are present individually, as 'accumulations' (Aitchison 1988, 276–77), and in hoards. Chronologically, although there is a broad range, some bias towards the fourth century is visible; but this may merely reflect the greater availability of coins in fourth-century Britain, a characteristic seen also on settlement sites (Aitchison 1988, 276–77). Coin- and pottery-finds combine in coin-hoards placed in pottery vessels (ibid., 276; e.g. Kinnes and Longworth 1985, 48, 51–52, 55, 113). Pottery found at many sites encompasses a wide range of dates from the first to the fourth centuries AD, with perhaps some ceramic bias towards the fourth century, arguably lending weight to the numismatic bias. It would, however, probably be unwise to place too much significance on this as, again, it may be a reflection of no more than availability.

Burial is also, surprisingly perhaps, common. Inhumation and cremation both occur – for example at Roxton, Bedfordshire – but inhumation is, in general, more common, perhaps again suggesting a Late Roman chronological bias (Taylor and Woodward 1982, 106, 142, table 3 on 100–1; Darvill and Grinsell 1989, 58). Burials were placed on, or adjacent to, barrows. The cremations may be in urns or without urns, and characteristically burials of both types are few in number at any site, often occurring singly. It would, therefore, seem that barrows were not centres for major Romano-British cemeteries rather than for individual burial or the burial of small groups. The use of barrow sites for small groups of inhumations or for single inhumations, some with what may be associated churches of immediately post-Roman date, continued in Britain after the end of the Roman period (e.g. Edwards 1991, 131–33).

Interestingly it is not only round barrows but also, perhaps especially, long barrows that were treated in this way (Ashbee 1984, 69, 74, 152–53, 157). At Julliberries's Grave, for example, Romano-British finds included a hoard of Constantinian coins in a pot, a complete samian-ware (form-27) cup, a late fourth-century coin, an inhumation burial, and over fifty sherds of Romano-British coarse pottery, some in association with a hearth (Jessup 1937). Hearths have also been found at the periphery of a few Glamorganshire barrows (RCHM 1976, 79, 93). But the evidence from such hearths is neither obviously ritual nor obviously domestic.

Much more striking, if correctly attributed, is the evidence of altars at an alleged, and perhaps doubtful, Gloucestershire barrow, although a second possible example has been discounted on the grounds that it was an eighteenth-century gazebo (O'Neil and Grinsell 1960, 54, 104). Other than these barrows, ritual artefacts and templestructures are conspicuously absent from such sites, although the nineteenth-century discovery, adjacent to Silbury Hill, of shafts, wells and many coins could hint at an adjacent temple or complex of 'ritual shafts' there (Goddard 1913, 186).

There are two other claimed instances of Romano-British shrines at prehistoric barrows: at Haddenham the shrine stood on a barrow, but this was, as the excavator observed, also an elevated dry 'island' in a fen, so the shrine may have been positioned simply to take advantage of a small area of dry land (Evans, 1985, 88). More convincingly, at Slonk Hill, in Sussex, a pair of barrows was enclosed in a rectilinear ditched enclosure in the pre-Roman Iron Age, one of the barrows being further enclosed by a rectilinear fence or building (Rodwell 1980b, 217, fig. 10.3). But even at Slonk Hill the evidence is far from clear cut, with interpretative and chronological problems and reports of Romano-British inhumations at the site, confusing the picture (Rodwell 1980b, 216–18). If this is an instance of the use of a barrow for a Romano-British shrine, it is the only strong evidence that such locations might be specially used in this way, but it clearly is not secure enough evidence alone to be used to contradict the overall patterning visible in the data from other sites.

Megalithic Structures

Romano-British material is known from a number of megalithic sites. Stonehenge itself has produced finds of Romano-British pottery, coins and, probably Romano-British, inhumation burials (Atkinson 1956, 21, 51). Indeed, the close association between the stratigraphy of Romano-British pottery and that of 'blue-stone' chippings within the stone circle need not necessarily be fortuitous (Atkinson 1956, 92). Stone-chippings do not occur in one of the Romano-British burials on the site, suggesting that, as these chippings form a continuous layer across the site, the chippings were not present when the grave was filled in. According to Atkinson (1956, 92) the vertical and horizontal distribution of the 'blue-stone' chippings 'strikingly matched' that of Roman pottery on the site. The observation that some 'blue-stone' chippings may have been deliberately dumped in ditches (ibid., 93) tells us nothing about the origin or date of all the 'blue-stone' chippings found there, and so does not rule out the possibility of a Roman-period date for at least some. Whatever the date of the 'blue-stones's' arrival at Stonehenge, the techniques of stone finishing employed on them may indicate the use of metal tools (ibid., 137). Although it is possible that an atypical monument received atypical treatment in prehistory, perhaps it is plausible that Roman-period activity at the site included refacing the stones, rather than, as Atkinson has argued, aimed at destroying them (ibid., 2–3). The possibility that 'blue-stone' chippings derive from Roman-period reworking must re-open the question of whether the Y and Z holes are Romano-British, for deliberate deposits of such chippings were found at the bases of these holes. If so, then Stonehenge saw substantial Romano-British activity and may have received its final large-scale remodelling only in the Roman period.

Roman coins and pottery also occur at, for example, the Anglesey megaliths, although burial is not found at these sites (e.g. Smith and Lynch 1986, 79, 82, 113, 115–6, 121), and elsewhere in Britain stone circles have been the find-spots of the same sorts of miscellaneous pottery sherds and coins as found at barrows (e.g. Smith 1989, 35). Again certain Romano-British 'ritual artefacts' are not found at any of them.

Henges

The last class of prehistoric ritual site considered here is the henge. Roman coins and pottery have come from a number of these monuments, including Avebury (Smith 1965, 243).

Nevertheless, not a single Roman temple or altar demonstrably comes from a henge-site, nor (again) are 'ritual artefacts' found on them. The only possible exception is Maumberry Rings, Dorset (Bradley 1976), where the henge was changed into a Roman-period earthwork amphitheatre. Some have seen this re-use in the context of the ritual associations of amphitheatre activities, but without further evidence it may be equally likely that the henge was merely of a convenient shape to allow the construction of the amphitheatre (cf. Lambick 1988, 46–7).

INTERPRETATION

Romano-British finds and burials thus commonly occur in small quantities at prehistoric ritual monuments, but encompass a narrow range of objects (mostly coins and pottery) and features (inhumation graves, cremations, hearths). The only possible exceptions to this generalisation are all either doubtful, as at Slonk Hill, the Gloucestershire barrow with altars, and the Haddenham shrine, or otherwise exceptional as prehistoric sites, as at Stonehenge and Silbury Hill.

This range of artefacts and features stands in contrast to the rich Armorican data. Using J. André's (1961) and P. Galliou's (1989, 31, 151–53) lists of sites, it is possible to construct a table which displays this contrast more vividly than would a non-graphic presentation of it (see p. 140).

CONTRASTS BETWEEN ROMAN-PERIOD AND LATER ACTIVITY AT PREHISTORIC RITUAL MONUMENTS

With the contrast between the British and Armorican evidence set out in this way we may note that the British sites lack votive objects, reuse as temples, evidence of refurbishment, evidence of later Christianisation, and evidence of early Roman burial. The coin series at British sites is also more restricted, being primarily of the later Roman period (third to fourth century). The lack of early Roman material in Britain, but its occurrence in Gaul, might represent continuity of activity from the pre-Roman past in Gaul, but discontinuity from that past in Britain. Although artefacts were deposited in these monuments in Britain, there are no instances of amphora or glass vessels being so used, the British evidence consisting of other ceramics, coins, and other types of 'domestic' artefacts.

An interpretation of this contrast may be sought in the Roman-period attitudes to, and functions of, these monuments in Britain and Gaul, for explanation is certainly not to be found in the availability of classes of arte-

	Armorica	Britain	Correlation
coins in monument	**	**	*
coins on monument	**	**	*
coin hoards	–	*	–
fine pot in monument	**	**	*
fine pot on monument	**	**	*
coarse pot in monument	**	**	*
coarse pot on monument	**	**	*
amphora	**	–	–
tile/brick	**	–	–
glass	**	–	–
other 'domestic' objects	–	**	–
Venus figurines	**	–	–
other votive	*	–	–
altars	–	(?)	–
temple/shrine at monument	–	*	–
temple/shrine constructed out of monument	**	–	–
cremation in monument	**	–	–
cremation at monument	**	–	–
inhumation in monument	**	**	*
inhumation at monument	–	**	–
mausoleum at monument	*	–	–
Christianisation by carving	**	*	–
church on monument	**	**	*
church constructed out of monument	*	–	–

* = 1   ** = more than 1   – = not present   (?) = uncertain

factual material. Glass, amphora, and votive objects were to be found even in 'remote' highland-zone areas of Britain (e.g. Green 1978). Nor is explanation to be found in the chance patterns of discovery, or bias produced by the means of recovery; excavators of such monuments have, especially during this century, often noted the presence of Roman-period material found during their work, and both Britain and Armorica have seen much relevant fieldwork.

The most conspicuous difference between the British and Armorican evidence is the lack, in Britain, of specifically 'religious' artefacts, of refurbishment (as temples), and of Christianisation in the fifth and later centuries. The latter may, arguably, suggest pagan veneration up to that point. From this it seems reasonable to infer that prehistoric ritual monuments may have been the foci of religious activity in Gallo-Roman Armorica, but that they were not in Roman Britain.

Interestingly, the county in which there is, albeit doubtfully, an anomal-
ous instance of altars placed at a barrow site, is Gloucestershire, an area for
which Branigan has made a case for Roman-period Gallic immigration
(Branigan 1973), and where unusual religious practices – a concentration
of hill-top temples, for example – are otherwise attested. Perhaps these
altars, if they were located at a barrow in the Roman period, could be a
further expression of this Gallic dimension, but this is uncertain because
both the identification of the site as a barrow and the Gallic character of
the area can both be questioned.

EXPLAINING THE BRITISH EVIDENCE

It remains to offer an explanation for the British evidence. If it is not
'religious', what is it? The key may lie in the difference between religion
and superstition set out at the start of this paper.

In his discussion of the coin evidence from such sites, Aitchison has
briefly mentioned that we might employ early medieval Irish literary evidence in formulating an interpretation of the Roman-period conceptualisation of the monuments.

Such Irish literary evidence has frequently been employed in the search
for an understanding of pre-Christian paganism in Britain and Ireland and,
despite the late date of the texts containing it, derives in part from what
has been seen as a society chronologically, socially, and culturally close to
both rural Roman Britain and Gaul (Wait 1985, 210–34). In early medieval
Ireland the native population seems to have viewed the landscape as having
an active mythical quality in which places were associated with legends and
supernatural figures. In this highly developed ascription of meaning, seen
most clearly in relation to the ritual monuments of the prehistoric past,
monuments of the types discussed in this paper played an important role.
These were seen as the *síde*, the home of the *áes síde* (minor supernatural
figures), and as gateways to the 'otherworld' (ibid., 217–18, 226–270).

That these concepts may not have been alien to Romano-British perceptions of the landscape is suggested by the close links between Britain and
Ireland throughout the pre-Roman Iron-Age and Romano-British periods,
evidenced by archaeology, language and, possibly, literature (Stevenson
1989; O'Kelly 1989, 312, 327).

This relationship enables us to construct a model of the conceptualisation and utilisation of prehistoric ritual monuments in Roman Britain. This
would suppose that Roman Britons saw prehistoric ritual sites as dwelling

places of minor supernatural beings and especially as entrances to the otherworld. It is not necessary to assume that Romano-British and later Irish interpretations of these monuments were identical, merely, given the attested contacts between the areas, that they were similar.

Such a model enables us to reconsider the evidence from Roman Britain. A conceptualisation as entrances to the 'otherworld' might easily explain burial at such monuments, especially as adult burial was seemingly forbidden at Romano-Celtic pagan temples in Britain – even Lewis's sparse list of alleged examples probably overstates the case (Lewis 1966, 6, 13; for an example now discounted see Rahtz and Watts 1979, fig. 12 on 191, 194). The association of coins and pottery with funerary practices is also well attested in Britain (Black 1986). Alternatively, if minor supernatural beings were supposed to inhabit these places, or they were séen as leading to the otherworld, then offerings, including food offerings, might be expected. Either interpretation might account for the coins and pottery, the pottery being deposited either on its own account as a valuable item or as a container for food. In Ireland, both such votive deposits and burial are found at one excavated site, Newgrange, which we know to have been interpreted by early medieval Irishmen in this way (Aitchison 1988, 275–76; O'Kelly 1982, 42–7).

Obviously, this interpretation as burial sites closely fits the British evidence, and explains the contrast between the religious character of the Roman-period activity at the Armorican sites and the non-religious character of the British data. In order to test this model beyond its ability to fit the data which it aims to explain, we may note that such an explanation might suggest a different relationship, in each area, between such sites, their Roman-period use, and Romano-Celtic pagan religion.

Given the localised character of Romano-Celtic paganism one might expect, if the mythology associated with these sites was integrated into pagan religion, that it would also be localised in character (Jones and Mattingly 1990, 274–83). This is what we find in Armorica, with most cases occurring in the Morbihan. In Britain, conversely, there is a thin scatter of such sites throughout and beyond the Roman province. This contrast in distribution reinforces the contrast between the lack of certainly relevant religious artefacts and structures (with the exception, perhaps, of Slonk Hill) in Britain and their presence in Armorica.

If our interpretation of the Roman-period use of these sites as burial places is correct, this must suggest a very widespread popular perception of the landscape, separate from localised Romano-Celtic pagan religion. Such a perception, assigning advantage to be obtained from burial or offerings at these locations, can be considered to be superstition rather than religion. It is not integrated with a specific set of wider beliefs or a broader code of action, but relates to the advantage to be gained by ritual (burial or offerings) at specified locations.

It may also be significant that the later Roman period was, in Britain, marked by an increased variability of burial practice, interpreted by Miranda Green as deriving from anxiety about the dead reaching the 'otherworld' (Green 1986, 130–32). Such anxiety may have led to burial at places claimed as entrances to the 'otherworld' so as to facilitate the passage of the dead, explaining the apparent Late Roman bias in the British evidence. Interestingly, Green (ibid, 132–35) has also shown that ritual shafts may themselves be associated with entrance to the underworld; so perhaps explaining the evidence from Silbury Hill.

The possibly more elaborate treatment of Stonehenge remains an anomaly to this overall pattern. It may be explained as a response to the site's unique character as a monument in the landscape: certainly a source of special comment in later centuries. But, again, the most confidently attested Roman-period features at the site are burials.

If separate from pagan religion, and seen as a widespread superstitious belief about gaining easy passage to the otherworld by burial and/or offerings close to its entrances, then, obviously, on these grounds too, religious structures and artefacts would not be expected. It is significant that burial and 'religious' structures on the one hand, and artefacts on the other, do not occur together at the Armorican sites, although both are found within the total range of Armorican evidence. Adult burial would, then, have been permissible at such sites precisely because they were *not* religious foci, but places appropriate to the disposal of the dead. Indeed, the presence of adult burial strongly suggests in itself that these places were not used for religious purposes.

Consequently, we may interpret this activity as a result of widespread non-religious folk-beliefs about the landscape. Therefore, it is hardly surprising that British and Irish ecclesiastical legislation did not include denunciations of the worship of prehistoric ritual sites, for pagan religious activity at these monuments did not exist in Britain and Ireland.

CONCLUSION

It would seem that prehistoric ritual monuments were perceived in different ways in Roman Britain and in the Armorican peninsula. In Armorica they were used as religious sites throughout the Roman period and were, therefore, often Christianised in the immediately post-Roman centuries, in opposition to this continuing veneration. In Roman Britain they were construed in a superstitious rather than religious fashion, and formed no part of organised paganism.

Such an interpretation encompasses all the relevant available archaeological and historical information and, perhaps, gives us more understanding of the differing rural religious and antiquarian perceptions of Roman provincials. It also provides a potential 'middle-range' logic for recognising superstition rather than religion in the archaeological study of Roman Britain.

Bibliography

Aitchison, N. B. 1988 'Roman wealth, native ritual: coin hoards within and beyond Roman Britain' *World Archaeology* 20, 270–84 .

André, J. 1961 'Les Dolmens Morbihannais remployés à l'époque romaine' *Ogam* 74–5, 248–54 .

Ashbee, P. 1984 *The Earthern Longbarrow in Britain*, 2nd edition. Norwich.

Atkinson, R. J. C. 1956 *Stonehenge*. Harmondsworth.

Bieler, L. (ed. & transl.) 1963 *The Irish Penitentials*. Dublin.

Black, E. W. 1986 'Romano-British burial customs and religious beliefs in south-east England' *Archaeological Journal* 143, 201–39.

Bradley, R. 1976 'Maumberry Rings, Dorchester: the excavations of 1908–1913' *Archaeologia* 105, 1–97.

Branigan, K. 1973 'Gauls in Gloucestershire?' *Transactions of the Bristol and Gloucestershire Archaeological Society* 92, 82–95.

Burl, A. 1979 *Prehistoric Avebury*. New Haven, Conneticut.

Casey, P. J. (ed.) 1979 *The End of Roman Britain*. Oxford.

Darvill, T. C. and L. V. Grinsell 1989 'Gloucestershire barrows: a supplement 1961–1988' *Transactions of the Bristol and Gloucestershire Archaeological Society* 107, 58.

Edwards, N. 1991 'The Dark Ages' in J. Manley, S. Grenter and F. Gale (eds), 129–141.

Evans, C. 1985 'Tradition and the cultural landscape: an archaeology of place' *Archaeological Review from Cambridge* 4, 80–94.

Ferguson, J. 1872 *Rude Stone Monuments In All Countries: Their Age And Uses*. London.

Galliou, P. 1989 *Les tombes romaines d'Armorique*. Paris.

Gelling, M. 1978 *Signposts to the Past*. London.

Goddard, E. H. 1913 'A list of Prehistoric, Roman and Pagan Saxon Antiquities in the county of Wilts, arranged under parishes' *The Wiltshire Archaeological and Natural History Magazine* 120, 153–378 .

Green, M. J. 1978 *A Corpus of Small Cult-Objects from the Military Areas of Roman Britain*. Oxford.

Green, M. 1986 *The Gods of the Celts*. Gloucester.

Henig, M. 1984 *Religion in Roman Britain*. London.

Jessup, R. F. 1937 'Excavations at Juliberrie's Grave, Chilham, Kent' *Antiquaries Journal* 7, 122–37.

Jones, B. and D. Mattingly 1990 *An Atlas of Roman Britain*. Oxford.

Kinnes, I. A. and I. H. Longworth 1985 *Catalogue of the Excavated Prehistoric and Romano-British Material in the Greenwell Collection*. London.

Lambrick, G. 1988 *Megaliths, Monuments and Settlement in the Prehistoric Landscape*. London.

Lewis, M. J. T. 1966 *Temples in Roman Britain*. Cambridge.

Manley, J., S. Grenter and F. Gale (eds) 1991 *The Archaeology of Clwyd*. Mold.

Morris, R. 1989 *Churches In The Landscape*. London.

O'Kelly, M. J. 1982 *Newgrange: Archaeology, Art and Legend*. London.

O'Kelly, M. J. 1989 *Early Ireland: An introduction to Irish prehistory*. Cambridge.

O'Neil, H. and L. Grinsell 1960 'Gloucestershire barrows' part 1 *Transactions of the Bristol and Gloucestershire Archaeological Society* 79, 3–149.

RCHM 1976 *An Inventory of the Ancient Monuments in Glamorganshire. 1 Pre-Norman, Part 1 The Stone and Bronze Ages*, Cardiff.

Rahtz, P. and L. Watts 1979 'The end of Roman temples in the west of Britain' in P. J. Casey (ed.), 183–201.

Rodwell, W. (ed.) 1980a *Temples, Churches and Religion: Recent Research in Roman Britain* 2 vols. Oxford.

Rodwell, W. 1980b 'Temple archaeology: problems of the present and portents for the future' in W. Rodwell (ed.) 1980a, 211–41.

Smith, C. A. and F. M. Lynch 1986 *Trefignath and Din Dryfol. The Excavation of Two Megalithic Tombs in Anglesey*. Cardiff.

Smith, G. H. 1989 'Excavation work at the David Stoke Megalithic Monument, Stoke Bishop, Bristol 1983' *Transactions of the Bristol and Gloucester Archaeological Society* 107, 27–37.

Smith, I. F. (ed.) 1965 *Windmill Hill and Avebury – Excavations By Alexander Keiller*, Oxford.

Stevenson, J. 1989 'The beginnings of literacy in Ireland' *Proceedings of the Royal Irish Academy* 89, 127–65.

Szarmach, P. E. with V. D. Oggins (eds) 1986 *Sources of Anglo-Saxon Culture*. Kalamazoo.

Taylor, A. F. and P. Woodward 1982 'A Bronze Age barrow cemetery and associated settlement at Oxton, Bedfordshire' *Archaeological Journal* 142, 73–149 .

Wait, G. A. 1985 *Ritual and Religion in Iron Age Britain* 2 vols, 210–34. Oxford.

12

COMPARATIVE FRONTIER STUDIES

Patricia Southern

This paper presents a positive view of comparative frontier studies. It explores the environmental and geographical factors which govern military operations, by comparing Roman practice with later, better documented, methods of controlling territory. It concludes by examining campaigns conducted in Scotland at widely different periods.

INTRODUCTION————

In the interpretation of archaeological remains, the use of comparative evidence from different periods, which have little or nothing to do with the one under consideration, may be deemed a rather useless exercise. Readers of this persuasion will no doubt pass straight on to the next paper, with only a cursory glance at the title of this one. A conviction that comparative evidence has its uses is no real recommendation for its application; it was Goethe who pointed out that talking or writing about anything is a waste of time, since all that usually happens is that opponents of one's views go away confirmed in their opinion, while adherents adhere all the more. Everyone is entitled to an opinion, but this admirably liberal view should be tempered by the fact that opinions can differ so radically even when based on exactly the same set of data. Archaeology is not the most accurate of interpretative tools, and the auxiliary information which comparative evidence can provide ought at least to be taken into account.

ANTHROPOLOGY AS COMPARATIVE EVIDENCE————

The anthropological approach to archaeological interpretation has long been valid for prehistoric archaeologists (or more accurately, archaeologists who study prehistory). This is a form of comparative evidence which accords well with the study of societies whose only legacy is artefactual, with no contemporary documentary sources to enlighten or confuse the researcher. Hence there are books with titles such as A. Mitchell's *The Past in the Present*, published in 1880, and Ian Hodder's *The Present Past* published a century later in 1982. The latter must contain something useful, judging by the number of times it has been stolen from our departmental library. In the hundred years which separate these two works, all that has changed is the attitude to ancient and modern autochthonous peoples. Our imperialist ancestors did not hesitate to apply the label 'savages' to such peoples, and the use of such terminology in the following quotation uncomfortably jars the modern mind. These words written in 1880 should be heard by all those who hold an implicit belief in the theory of the ascent of man (Mitchell 1880, 214):

> We can scarcely hesitate to conclude that civilisations are lost as well as gained; that all existing savages possibly are, and some of them certainly are, in a state of civilisation below that which their ancestors occupied; and that there is no intrinsic tendency in human societies separately to pass ever on and ever up to something better, and higher, and nobler.

Comparative evidence from different periods of history has some validity, if only because people remain people; only the outward trappings change. It is these outward trappings which lead successive groups of scholars to reinterpret archaeological evidence in accordance with each individual's background and experience, so that historical and archaeological received opinion follows trends, and acquires a dated look with the passage of time. This is in itself a form of anthropological approach to the study of archaeology. Given a completely unreferenced selection of archaeological writings, would it be possible to date them and guess their country of origin by analysing the ideas expressed in them? Probably.

COMPARATIVE MILITARY STUDIES————

In archaeological interpretation there is no single correct solution. Several concurrent hypotheses are all equally valid in most cases, simply because in reconstructing the minutiae of human life in times past, we do not have all the necessary information from which to make any judgement. This is where a theoretical approach can benefit the study of the archaeology of the Roman Empire, provided that the word theoretical is constantly used and understood. Rigidity of interpretation is perhaps much more harmful than the less certain ground of flexibility. Archaeologists should perhaps bear in mind that, on occasion, elements of doubt can be quite healthy, indeed vital, as demonstrated by this *cri de coeur* from someone not perhaps noted for flexibility, Oliver Cromwell: 'I beseech you, in the bowels of Christ, think it possible you may be mistaken.'

I have found comparative evidence most useful in military studies. In the social sphere it is perhaps not so easliy applied, since some allowance should be made for customs and social *mores* which are not necessarily subject to a set of predictable rules. Armies, on the other hand, share the common need to protect themselves, by a limited number of possible means, while on the march or on campaign, or while permanently encamped within their fortifications. They need to supply themselves with food and equipment and to recruit new soldiers when the existing ones are killed or die or simply run away. When they watch over a newly conquered area, their dispositions are surely dictated by geography, and useful comparisons can be made on this basis, in examining how other armies, operating at other periods in similar or the same terrain, set about achieving their goals.

It is only in recent times that there have been any far reaching changes in transport. Until the nineteenth century, armies moved on foot, or rode on horseback or in wagons pulled by horses. Their problems were possibly not all that different from those faced by the Romans. As far as I am aware, there has been no change in the design of human legs, and as Marshal Saxe succinctly phrased it 'all the mystery of manoeuvres and combats is in the legs, and it is to the legs that we should apply ourselves' (Watson 1988, 55).

In the study of Roman temporary camps, it is useful to have some idea of how far troops can be expected to march in a day, while still having the wherewithal to build fortifications, however slight, at the end of that day. The departure of thousands of men from one location and their arrival at another location some distance away, is not something that can be left to chance, and information on how military authorites organised this procedure can be useful. A study of the armies of more recent historical periods is facilitated by the existence of better documentation than anything which is available for study of the Roman army. Such documentation provides practical information on how many miles of road will be taken up by numbers of marching troops, depending on how many men march abreast, the type of terrain to be crossed, and the distance to be left between the various units on the march. It is possible to estimate the time it would take for a given body of troops to cover a given amount of ground, and to take into account the variable factors which influence these calculations, which many archaeological models ignore.

This practical information can be applied to the study of lines of Roman temporary camps of roughly the same size and shape in north Britain. The usual method of study is to measure the distances between such camps, and on the basis of a theoretical day's march, to predict where the missing camps in the series will be. A brief reading of any of the many surviving diaries left by soldiers serving in armies of different periods will suffice to show that armies cannot operate in such a mathematical way, so that measuring distances can be only a very rough guide at best. Many factors influence the way in which an army marches, such as the constant presence of the enemy, or even more simply, the weather. A day's march can range from over twenty five miles to less than six. Tacitus (*Agricola* 22) mentions that during one campaigning season, the Roman army was hindered by bad weather. He is not more specific than that, but without his statement there would be not the least hint of any hindrance at all. Archaeology cannot demonstrate such imponderables. Comparative evidence can.

The study of how armies marched could throw some light on troop movements in the Roman Empire, for example from the Rhine to the Danube in times of crisis. It seems that legions were sometimes shunted along from place to place when major wars broke out, for example legionary detachments from Britain seem to have replaced Rhine troops, which in turn marched to the Danube. It is interesting to compare Marlborough's march over the same ground in 1704. From the Low Countries, he progressed steadily but rapidly and arrived at his destination with 40,000 men, with their horses and equipment in good condition, in less than a month (Chandler 1989, 129–30). The march was impressive and exceptional, but it shows what could be done, and demonstrates how rapidly Roman troops may have arrived at threatened points when wars were being waged. Another exceptional march was made by Napoleon in 1805, when he moved troops from Boulogne to Ulm before the enemy had properly mobilised. He used every available means of transport, but he moved nearly five times the number of troops in Marlborough's army, with all the attendant logistical problems of supplying that number of men

(Chandler 1966, 385).

Comparative study of logistical problems is illuminating. Practical investigations into how much a large army eats, what it eats, how such food is manufactured, where and when it is manufactured, and how it is stored and transported may not always answer similar questions raised by the study of the Roman army, but can help researchers to arrive at a closer understanding of the problem. The restrictions of seasonality on food supply scarcely apply to the inhabitants of the modern western world, but they were of paramount importance to military planning throughout history.

COMPARATIVE FRONTIER STUDIES

In the USA, comparative frontier studies have been in vogue for some time, but this approach has only recently been adopted in Roman frontier studies. There is much valuable food for thought in such an approach. Frontiers can be delineated in many forms, ranging from an open stretch of territory patrolled occasionally by a few soldiers, to a continuous running barrier such as Hadrian's Wall. If comparative studies have no other purpose, then they do at least highlight the need for a precise definition of terms.

Not only is there better documentation on the structure of more recent frontiers, and more reliable evidence for their appearance, but there is also more evidence of the purpose behind them and the way in which they worked. Much ink has been spilled on the functions of Roman frontiers, but archaeology alone cannot elucidate purely abstract concepts such as purpose and method of operation. The Russian *cherta* lines pictured in Christopher Duffy's *Siege Warfare* (1979, 205–7) look remarkably similar to the currently accepted reconstructions of the German *limes* (a convenient word which we are not supposed to use any more). A ditch accompanied by a timber palisade and a string of watchtowers is a very basic form of frontier defence, so it is perhaps not surprising that seventeenth century Russia and second century Rome should employ similar methods to protect themselves from tribesmen living beyond their own lands. The Russian lines are not known in their entirety, but much more is known about them than about the Roman system. For instance, accurate numbers of the troops involved are recorded, and it is known that defence of particular sectors of the Russian frontier was under a single united command, and that there were periods when the lines were temporarily abandoned because troops were called away to deal with crises elsewhere.

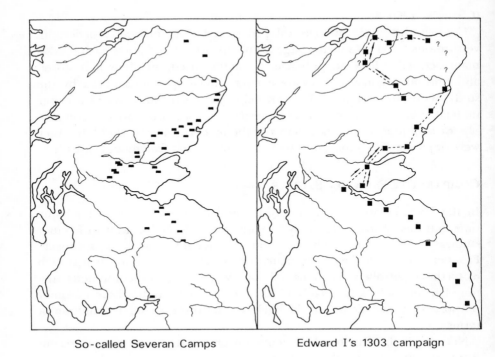

So-called Severan Camps   Edward I's 1303 campaign

Figures 23 and 24. (drawn by Graeme Stobbs).

Students of the Antonine Wall please note.

To turn to the Roman period in Scotland, it would seem that geographical considerations affect the way in which invasions of this country were planned and implemented. William I for example did not even try to subdue it totally. He reached the Tay, and after Malcolm Canmore submitted to him, or became his man, in feudal terms, William marched back south. The turning point is interesting. Agricola reached the Tay in his third campaigning season, and for a year he advanced no further, either because he was ordered not to do so by the Emperor or because he thought he needed to consolidate the territory behind him. The latter consideration is worthy of note. Agricola had a larger army than William, but it is significant that both military leaders recognised the point beyond which it was not safe to advance unless the lands behind were secure.

The Roman Emperor Severus, on the other hand, probably did advance almost immediately past the Tay into northern Scotland. It is by no means

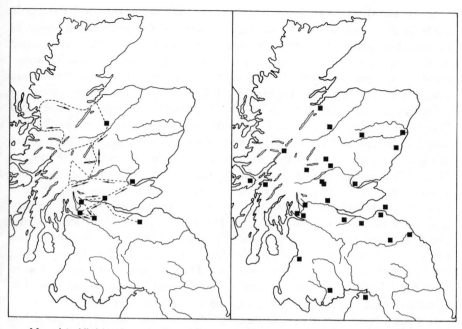

Monck's Highland campaign 1654

Garrisons who have allowance
for fire and candle 26th July 1657

Figures 25 and 26. (drawn by Graeme Stobbs).

certain that the camps which are labelled Severan do in fact belong to his campaigns, but Dio says that the Emperor penetrated northern Scotland, and he presumably built camps on the way there and back. He did not occupy the territory he overran, even though he campaigned for three seasons before his death and the abandonment of Scotland by his sons. His campaigns may be constructively compared with those of Edward I. The source material for Edward's itineraries derives from contemporary records, brought together and published by Gough (1900), with the result that we are much better informed about where Edward went than we are about Severus's movements, but nonetheless it seems that there are similarities in their choice of routes (Figures 23–24). Both monarchs skirted the edge of the Highlands without actually penetrating them, using the more hospitable eastern lands in which to move their armies, probably provisioned by sea. I should add that Edward is not new: Gordon Maxwell invented Edward in a most useful paper delivered in 1983 at Aalen (1986).

There are those who deny that the Romans ever penetrated the High-lands of Scotland, using the analogy of Severus' campaigns and those of Edward I to prove that armies found it far easier to stick to the lowland routes, and that the mountains looked forbidding, and would hinder move-ment. Given that the Carpathians and the Atlas range did not deter Roman troops, what claim can the Highlands put forward for such superiority?

Figures 25 and 26 show Monck's Highland campaign in 1654, and Cromwell's garrisons in the Highlands, revealing that it is possible to maintain troops in the mountains, and to emerge successfully after a series of rapid marches. I believe that the first century Roman forts at the mouths of the Highland glens were not simply guard posts to block exits from the valleys, nor were they part of a linear frontier, but their presence in such locations indicates that troops did go into the mountains. The essential difference between the campaigns of Monck and possibly Agricola on the one hand, and those of Severus and Edward I on the other, is that the last two never succeeded in subduing Scotland and never held it down, despite the fact that they fought battles and won. The campaigns of Monck, and of Agricola, wherever he fought, were successful and longer lasting than any-thing achieved by a march round the edges of the mountains.

If what I have said seems tenuous in the extreme, because there is no direct archaeological evidence with which to back up the theory, then at least it should have demonstrated that answers to archaeological problems are not single and immutable, and in many cases, what is visible on the ground is not, by itself, enough to construct any hypothesis.

Bibliography

Chandler, D. G. 1966 *The Campaigns of Napoleon*. Weidenfeld and Nicolson.

Chandler, D. G. 1989 *Marlborough as Military Commander*. Spellmount Ltd.

Duffy, C. 1979 *Siege Warfare: the Fortress in the Early Modern World*. London; Routledge and Kegan Paul.

Gough, H. 1900 *Itinerary of King Edward I Throughout His Reign A.D. 1272–1307*. Alexander Gardner.

Hodder, I. 1982 *The Present Past*. London; Batsford.

Maxwell, G. 1986 'Sidelight on Roman military campaigns in north Britain' *Studien zu den Militargrenzen Roms III: 12 Int. Limeskongresses, Aalen, 1983*, 60–3.

Mitchell, A. 1880 *The Past in the Present*. Douglas.

Watson, S. J. 1988 *By Command of the Emperor: a life of Marshal Berthier*. Ken Trotman.

13

SPACED-OUT SANCTUARIES:
THE RITUAL LANDSCAPE OF ROMAN GREECE

Susan Alcock

Effects of the Roman conquest of Greece have been little studied, in favour of emphasising the 'reverse imperialism' of Greece's cultural conquest of Rome. Such a perspective masks the undoubted impact felt throughout Greek society at the time of its incorporation and assimilation into a wider imperial system. This paper examines the Greek response to their altered political and economic state through the evidence of ritual geography, specifically changes in the location and ditribution of cult places in the landscape. Several patterns are discerned, each of which reveals in its own way the redistribution of social power in Greece under Roman rule.

INTRODUCTION————————

A hitherto fitting motto for Roman Greece is to be found in Horace's *Epistles*: 'captive Greece took captive her captors and brought the arts to rude Latium' (2.1.156). Studies of Greece within the Roman empire have concentrated upon the cultural gifts of Greece to Rome, the processes of 'reverse imperialism' or 'reverse acculturation'. Much of this emphasis stems from the nature of the research conducted. Of the relatively few scholars who have dealt with 'captive Greece', almost all were trained first and foremost as classicists, preferring to consider the Greeks as unique, even in their response to external conquest. Looking to other provinces, such as Roman Britain, for useful *comparanda* and scholarly inspiration was never on the agenda of such individuals. This disciplinary divide between 'classicists' and 'Romanists' has proved an insidious problem, not least because it has isolated Roman Greece (and to a lesser extent the eastern empire at large) from more wide-ranging discussions of Roman imperialism and 'Romanisation'. What cannot be forgotten is that Rome, through its military power, conquered and annexed Greece, forcibly uniting its various constituent polities to form the relatively insignificant province of Achaia. The dynamics of social change under Roman rule require attention here as for any other Roman province, with explorations of issues such as instability or continuity in landholding patterns, residential preferences, demographic trends, and civic organisation (Alcock 1989a; 1989b). In its turn, this paper considers the composition of Achaia's sacred landscape in the early imperial period.

The concept of landscape as social document is currently what might be termed a 'hot property' among Roman archaeologists (e.g. Barker and Lloyd 1991). Human geographers, anthropologists and archaeologists have long recognised the power contained within the sacred or ceremonial landscape, framing it through questions such as: where were public ceremonies performed? Where precisely were megaliths, mounds, temples or tombs? How did these locations relate to places of human settlement or naturally occurring features? How were territorial claims, both social and geographic, defined through the organisation of sacred space? Underlying these questions is the assumption that the ritual landscape is a social construct, with its patterning a result of various human decisions and strategies. In addition, if concepts of space and place are viewed through the 'perspective of experience' as Tuan puts it, then clearly landscapes are not only culturally constructed, they are historically sensitive as well (Tuan 1974). The creation of a people's perceived environment follows the shifts and changes of their fortunes. The sacred landscape will not be immune from such developments, instead affecting and reflecting its larger social and political context. Imperial incorporation might be expected to result in the reorganisation of sacred space; the ritual landscape will respond to the imperial presence.

Accompanying the Roman presence in Greece (formal annexation occurred in 27 BC after almost two centuries of military activity and political intervention), fundamental changes took place in many spheres of Greek society. If spatial order reflects and reinforces social order, and if sanctuary placement can be linked with changing relationships of power and influence, what then of the sacred landscape? How do our 'cultic maps' alter under the early empire? To reconstruct this 'landscape of the gods', a mixture of archaeology, epigraphy, and Pausanias (a second century AD traveller interested in religious activity) can be employed. Three different categories of cult – displaced cult, centralised cult and rural cult – will be identified in this discussion, and transformations within each category traced. In the end, of course, each is allied with the others, forming part of the overall symbolic system of the province as a whole, and of its individual political components. For this initial analysis, however, we will explore them individually.

DISPLACED CULTS————

Displaced cults, as the name suggests, are those which, through the process of conquest and incorporation, were deliberately shifted from one place to another. It must first be noted that Roman intervention resulted in certain significant territorial rearrangements in Achaia. Chief among these were major *synoecisms* creating Nicopolis (Victory City), a free city established near the site of Augustus' camp at Actium, and Patras, a Roman colony on the west end of the Corinthian Gulf. Large areas of western Greece, notably Aetolia and Epirus, were placed under the sway of these cities, and local populations forcibly dragooned to settle them. The regions involved were not arbitrarily selected for the treatment received; instead they represented areas of concern to the imperial authorities, not least for their history of opposition to the Roman presence. These imperial foundations have received much attention. What has been less appreciated is evidence for an accompanying symbolic reorganisation in these areas. Removal of long-established cult images, and their ceremonial installation in a new and imperially chosen location, formed one chief tactic of domination, and one with frequent cross-cultural parallels. Kalydon in Aetolia, heart of the area affected by these *synoecisms*, gave up cult images, among them a famous Artemis Laphria (Pausanias 7.18.8–13). These images reappear being worshipped in, not surprisingly, Nicopolis and Patras. Two small cities annexed to Patras by Augustus (Pharae and Triteia) also lost cult statues, as Pausanias was informed by natives still aggrieved some 150 years later (Pausanias 7.22.5, 9).

Preferences shown to imperial foundations may not seem to call for special explanation. It could be argued that such actions were merited by the ordered depopulation of places like Kalydon or the newly dependent status of communities like Triteia. But it is possible to trace episodes of cult displacement in Roman Greece somewhat further afield. From the famous sanctuary of Athena at Tegea in Arcadia, Augustus took to Rome the goddess' image and the tusks of the Kalydonian boar (Pausanias 8.46.1–5). Carrying off part of a city's legendary past to the imperial capital, where they become objects of adornment or mild curiosity, could be taken simply as imperial whim or artistic fancy until one asks why Tegea was the target. The city's former opposition to Augustus was not unusual (most of Greece supported Antony at Actium), but its status as an important and influential center in the Peloponnese was another matter. Augustus here deliberately struck at the Tegean sense of history and, above all, independence.

To the victor belongs the spoils; in general, the effect of transferring or removing Greek cult images on Roman authority has been under-estimated. The images are too easily perceived as *objets d'art*, with Roman generals cast in the roles either of boors or of connoisseurs. If instead the removal of a city's deities is viewed as a deliberate tactic of control, a more realistic understanding of displaced cult emerges. The symbolic violence of such an deed would undercut local loyalties, shattering established relationships of authority and allegiance (Gordon 1979). At worst, loss of a patron god or goddess could represent the symbolic destruction of a community. On the other hand, some centers (Nicopolis, Rome) benefited from these ritual reshufflings, just as they did from associated concentrations of population and economic resources. For good or ill, such behaviour chiefly affected areas of especial imperial interest or sensitivity. Displacement of a cult then can be summed up as an externally motivated act, designed to disrupt or override local symbolic systems in the interests of the new political order.

CENTRALISED CULTS———

The second category, centralised cults, concerns those sanctuaries located overwhelmingly within the urban centers. The early imperial period witnessed the appearance or florescence in Greece of new or newly popular gods: Isis, Serapis, Antinoos and, most especially, the emperor. All of these fall directly within this second category, but I shall concentrate here upon the imperial cult. As Simon Price discovered in Asia Minor, there is an overwhelming urban bias in the distribution of imperial cult centres (Price 1984). More than that, in Achaia they are inevitably found at the most central and prominent locations of the ancient city, most frequently on the acropolis or in the agora. As just one example, on the Athenian acropolis a temple to Roma and Augustus was set before a Parthenon rededicated to Nero. Numerous similar cases could be cited (Trummer 1980). As part of the cult celebrations at Gytheion in Laconia, a procession moved around the city, symbolically linking key urban centres of political and religious life: sanctuaries, the theater, the agora (*Supplementum Epigraphicum Graecum* 9.923).

If this predilection for placing the imperial cult where it would be difficult to miss is clear, the strength of this compulsion is demonstrated by the fact that outlying sanctuaries assimilated into the imperial cult on occasion were physically transferred to the urban centre. One particularly extravagant example is provided by the movement into the Athenian agora of elements taken from fifth century BC temples (including one complete temple dedicated to Ares) from the Attic *demes* of Acharnai, Sounion, and Thorikos (up to 40 kilometers away). These transfers are assigned to the era of Augustus or shortly thereafter (Shear 1981; Camp 1986; Dinsmoor 1982). Various explanations have been advanced for these 'itinerant temples', as they are known, but by far the most convincing argument links these structures with imperial cult activity. Glen Bowersock (1984) has correlated the Ares temple with dynastic conflict in the Greek East, particularly in the succession struggles between Gaius Caesar, who left Rome for Athens in the guise of the New Ares, and Tiberius. The 'infilling' and domination by imperial monuments of the formerly open public and political space of the agora offers its own testimony about altered civic and political conditions in Roman Greece.

Why was it apparently so essential for the imperial cult to be centrally located? It might be helpful to ask which sets of political and social relationships the cult served to negotiate. In the first instance would stand relationships between the external authorities and the provincial communities. Achaia was an unarmed province, lacking any substantial body of standing troops, and possessing a typically underdeveloped bureaucratic infrastructure. In such circumstances, the imperial cult served as a prime means to represent the power of Rome to the provincial population at large. Effective communication of this message, especially to a largely urban based population, required a prominent urban setting.

Second, a relationship was articulated between imperial authorities and local civic elites. It is not new to report that under Roman rule more oligarchic regimes were encouraged in the Greek cities, as elsewhere. The need to foster this harmony of interest led to an urban based elite ready and eager to demonstrate loyalty. While Price has demonstrated that the imperial cult was not simply an elite game, it remains undeniable that wealthy members of provincial society were the most active, and indeed highly competitive in promoting cult activities. This development can be charted from city to city in Achaia with monotonous regularity.

Finally, the imperial cult formulated new relationships within the provincial communities as well. Civic elites used the cult as one major opportunity to bolster their role in guiding or controlling the local populace. A strategic urban location not only ensured clarity about who now led the way in civic affairs, but potentially unenthusiastic elements were also more easily kept in line. Placing this particular cult 'downtown' served, among other things, to guarantee a healthy and necessary show of respect for the imperial authority.

Behind all the relationships the cult could negotiate lie some that it could not. The imperial cult held no place in the countryside, taking no part in mediating between man and natural forces or in defining the link between territory and city. Its orientation instead demanded that it dominate the space of civic decision-making and political activity. To reinforce the various roles played, the imperial cult had to be centralised.

RURAL CULTS

The third and final topic for consideration deals with the fate of rural sanctuaries. According to surface survey results, the Greek countryside in early imperial times underwent a relative abandonment, with fewer rural sites or other signs of human use detected. This development can be interpreted to suggest both increasing nucleation in the towns and an overall decline in population levels across the province. Both possibilities offer potential repercussions for the sacred landscape. Indeed, Pausanias, in the course of his travels, periodically reports temples without roofs or desolate sanctuaries. Depopulation and the economic distress of cities undoubtedly lie behind some of these losses (Jost 1985). To accept these as the only factors involved, however, is to ignore the symbolic valuation these places possessed, or rather failed to possess in times of difficulty. It also fails to explain how and why a very considerable number of sanctuaries actually survived. For every roofless temple, a dozen or more functioning rural shrines can be identified in Pausanias' account. No simple and direct correlation can be made therefore between levels of habitation in the countryside and levels of ritual activity. Pausanias and intensive survey between them evoke an early imperial rural landscape still inhabited by its daimons and its gods if not by its people.

How to account then for the maintenance of these numerous cults in the countryside? One force at work must have been the stolid archaism of

Greek life, fostered as it was by Roman cultural demands. It has been claimed that Greece at this time was 'a country learning to be a museum'; a conscious cultivation of the glorious past was clearly a common strategy among Achaian cities in their dealings with the Roman authorities (Bowersock 1965; Cartledge and Spawforth 1989). Economic and political advantage could be winkled out of the indulgent authorities if a city possessed the necessary illustrious pedigree and history. Yet continuity of rural cult cannot be assigned solely to a calculated ossification of religious life, to a desire to 'look old'.

One alternative way forward is to employ a model found useful by the French scholar Franois de Polignac in exploring the birth of the Greek city (de Polignac 1984). Among de Polignac's basic arguments is the claim that monumental extra-urban sanctuaries served as markers of cultural and territorial boundaries. Centrifugal processions from the town out to these sanctuaries helped both to define a city's territory and to foster civic unity. For the early imperial cities, with their much altered civic organisation, labouring under new external pressures and with abandoned rural hinterlands, is there any evidence that similar behaviour was perpetuated?

The continued presence of major rural sanctuaries, where urban dwellers went out to sacrifice and hold festivals, reveals that a ritual 'taking possession' of the land still formed one feature of civic cult. Several cases could be culled from Pausanias. He tells, for instance, how it was the custom of the Phigaleians (citizens of a town in Arcadia) to start their processions from the urban sanctuary of Artemis Soteira out to major civic sanctuaries in the countryside, for example to the Temple of Apollo at Bassae (8.41.4–8). He also gives us one glimpse of such a procession at Hermione in the Southern Argolid (2.35.5–6):

> The manner of it is this. The procession is headed by the priests of the gods and by all those who hold the annual magistracies; these are followed by both men and women. It is now a custom that some who are still children should honour the goddess in the procession. These are dressed in white and wear wreaths upon their heads. . . . Those who form the procession are followed by men leading from the herd a full-grown cow, fastened with ropes, and still untamed and frisky.

On one level, such activity demonstrates a continuing civic commitment to rural cult, and thus to the rural landscape during the early empire. The countryside had not become a place to exploit, then ignore. One can consider in this light the problem of the disintegration of the *polis* unit, that quintessentially Greek union of town and country. Various ancient historians have occasionally asked (and imperfectly answered) what effect Roman conquest had upon that bond. Sanctuaries now can be seen to help preserve the *polis* union, long after many of the other traditional glues (hoplite military service, widespread rural residence) had vanished. When the end of the city-state in Greece is discussed, the evidence of rural sanctuaries must play some part in how that history is written.

Rural cult survival does not present, however, a uniform pattern. Surviving cults were relatively important sanctuaries, at the upper end of the spectrum of visibility or popularity. Surface survey evidence backs up the literary sources on this point. From a small sample of survey data, it would appear that relatively minor local cults, identified through surface evidence alone, go out of use at this time (e.g. Wright et al. 1990; Runnels and Van Andel 1987). Such shrines would have been dependent upon local dwellers, an individual proprietor or perhaps a small rural community: in other words the very people who now abandon rural residence. One is left with the distinct impression that the early imperial period proved a watershed time for small sanctuaries in the countryside; it was this 'minor' level of cult activity that was hard and directly hit by other changes in the rural landscape. A similar, roughly contemporaneous loss of rural shrines was noted in Italy by Martin Frederiksen. He attributed the development to a centralisation of population and economic resources, which in turn encouraged spending and attention on town based cult (Frederiksen 1976; cf. Crawford 1981; Blagg 1985). While to a point his observations match the Greek evidence, they also show by contrast that the Achaian willingness to maintain rural sanctuaries is significant and probably a centrally taken decision. What endures in the countryside are more major 'state run' cults, sanctuaries of a suitable size and prestige.

Who makes such decisions in the cities of Greece during the early empire? If anything is clear from our sources, it is the period's increasing reliance upon euergetism, the largesse of benefactors, to keep civic institutions afloat. This extended into the sphere of religious organisation. Wealthy individuals paid for temple upkeep, held priesthoods, financed festivals, revived defunct celebrations, and restored rural sanctuaries (e.g. Oliver 1971). What can we make of this elite involvement, especially in the case of rural cults? In some cases, a direct personal motivation can be detected behind continued celebrations; prominent families are cult priests or own land nearby. More generally, however, loyalty to local interests can be observed among the civic elite groups. Support for select rural sanctuaries would have been one strategy selected by benefactors to maintain civic integrity and to boost the chances of civic survival. Those joyous processions from town to countryside also require re-evaluation. While not erasing or denigrating their role in bonding town and country, or even as a communal force uniting elements within the city, those individuals leading the way (Pausanias' priests and magistrates) must have taken on a new pre-eminence. As with the imperial cult, these rituals allowed civic luminaries to shine, marching in processions they often organised to sanctuaries they often subsidised. Celebration of rural cult, in addition to its other roles, created and supported the new social structure of the city.

CONCLUSIONS

To sum up, we can look again at the three categories of cult location:

> *Displaced cult,* the symbolic disruption of 'natural' pre-existing territorial divisions and loyalties, acted as a controlling device, occurring where Rome's hand fell most heavily or its favour most freely. *Centralised cult,* with no role to play in the countryside, mediated social and political relationships between the external authority and dependent communities, as well as within those communities. *Rural cult* helped to keep the age old bond of town and country from tension and disintegration. Civic elites played a major part in preserving such celebrations, both in order to demonstrate local loyalties and to authorise internal social strategies.

These categories express, in their different ways, changes in the distribution of social power in Greece under Roman rule. When they are reunited and viewed together, common or complementary patterns begin to emerge: the inescapable influence of the imperial authority, competition for prestige and resources among cities and among civic elites, reinforcement of new divisions within society. Observations about sacred landscapes in other Roman provinces, notably in the west, are beginning to emerge, promising a fruitful subject for cross-provincial comparisons (Blagg 1986; Wilson 1973; Picard 1983; Hingley 1985; King 1990).

The degree to which old Greece was affected by Roman conquest has for too long been severely under-estimated, with 'captive Greece' thoughtlessly celebrated as cultural victor. The sacred landscape now adds its testimony against that rather complacent perspective. Where sanctuaries are and where they are not, which endure and which do not, all reveal new forces at work within the province. Moreover, the organisation of sacred space clearly acted to create and perpetuate this new political environment with its new allegiances. Displacements, foundations, abandonments, endurance: all can be seen in the sacred landscape of early imperial Greece. As one would expect in a human construct, one sensitive to historical change.

Bibliography

Alcock, S. E. 1989a 'Archaeology and imperialism: Roman expansion and the Greek city' *Journal of Mediterranean Archaeology* 2, 87–135.

Alcock, S. E. 1989b 'Roman imperialism in the Greek landscape', *Journal of Roman Archaeology* 2, 5–34.

Barker, G. and J. Lloyd (eds) 1991 *Roman Landscapes*. Archaeological Monographs of the British School at Rome 2. London.

Blagg, T. F. C. 1985 'Cult practice and its social context in the religious sanctuaries of Latium and Southern Etruria: the sanctuary of Diana at Nemi' in C. Malone and S. Stoddart (eds) 33–50.

Blagg, T. F. C. 1986 'Roman religious sites in the British landscape' *Landscape History* 8, 15–25.

Blagg, T. F. C. and M. Millett (eds) 1990 *The Early Roman Empire in the West*. Oxford.

Bowersock, G. W. 1965 *Augustus and the Greek World*. Oxford.

Bowersock, G. W. 1984 'Augustus and the East: the problem of the succession' in F. Millar and E. Segal (eds) 169–88.

Camp, J. M. 1986 *The Athenian Agora: Excavations in the Heart of Classical Athens*. London.

Cartledge, P. and A. Spawforth 1989 *Hellenistic and Roman Sparta: A Tale of Two Cities*. London.

Crawford, M. H. 1981 'Italy and Rome' *Journal of Roman Studies* 71, 153–60.

Dinsmoor, W. B. Jr. 1982 'Anchoring two floating temples' *Hesperia* 51, 410–52.

Frederiksen, M. W. 1976 'Changes in the patterns of settlement' in P. Zanker (ed.) 34–55.

Gordon, R. L. 1979 'The real and the imaginary: production and religion in the Graeco-Roman world' *Art History* 2, 5–34.

Hingley, R. 1985 'Location, function and status: a Romano-British "religious complex" at the Noah's Ark Inn, Frilford (Oxfordshire)' *Oxford Journal of Archaeology* 4, 201–14.

Jost, M. 1985 *Sanctuaires et cultes d'Arcadie*. Ecole Française d'Athènes, Etudes Peloponnesinnes 9. Paris.

King, A. 1990 'The emergence of Romano-Celtic religion' in T. F. C. Blagg and M. Millett, 220–41.

Malone, C. and S. Stoddart (eds) 1985 *Papers in Italian Archaeology IV: Classical and Medieval Archaeology* Oxford; British Archaeological Reports (International Series 246).

Millar, F. and E. Segal (eds) 1984 *Caesar Augustus: Seven Aspects*. Oxford.

Oliver, J. H. 1971 'Epaminondas of Acraephia' *Greek, Roman and Byzantine Studies* 12, 221–37.

Picard, G. C. 1983 'Les centres civiques ruraux dans l'Italie et la Gaule romaine' in *Architecture et société de l'archaïsme Grece à la fin de la republique romaine*. Paris.

de Polignac, F. 1984 *La naissance de la cité grecque*. Paris.

Price, S. R. F. 1984 *Rituals and Power: The Roman Imperial Cult in Asia Minor*. Cambridge.

Runnels, C. N. and T. H. Van Andel 1987 'The evolution of settlement in the Southern Argolid, Greece: an economic explanation' *Hesperia* 56, 303–34.

Shear, T. L. Jr 1981 'Athens: from city-state to provincial town' *Hesperia* 50, 356–77.

Trummer, R. 1980 *Die Denkmäler des Kaiserkults in der römischen Provinz Achaia*. Dissertationen der Universität Graz 52. Graz.

Tuan, Y.-F. 1974 *Topophilia: A Study of Environmental Perception, Attitudes and Fears*. Englewood Cliffs.

Wilson, D. R. 1973 'Temples in Britain: a topographical survey' *Caesarodunum* 8, 24–44.

Wright, J., J. F. Cherry, J. L. Davis, E. Mantzourani, S. B. Sutton and R. F. Sutton Jr 1990 'The Nemea Valley archaeological project: a preliminary report' *Hesperia* 59, 579–659.

Zanker, P. (ed.) 1976 *Hellenismus in Mittelitalien*. Göttingen.

14

ROMAN PEASANTS AND RURAL ORGANISATION IN CENTRAL ITALY: AN ARCHAEOLOGICAL PERSPECTIVE

Peter van Dommelen

Roman rural landscapes have long been associated with villas, that generally were regarded as its central feature; studies of Roman landscapes were consequently often limited to a villa and its immediate vicinity. This bias in most historical and archaeological research is now increasingly being redressed, mainly by intensive archaeological surveying. The resulting large numbers of small rural sites in particular point to a much more varied Roman countryside with considerably more complex organisation. Concentrating on the rural landscape outside the villas, therefore, the peasantry and their relations with the rural elite are the central issues in a case study of a small valley in Roman northern Etruria.

INTRODUCTION: STUDYING ROMAN RURAL LANDSCAPES

Landscape archaeology is a relatively new development in Mediterranean archaeology, and until recently most archaeological attention has been directed towards the city. Traditionally, in fact, the countryside has been considered to be of hardly any interest at all, because 'the Mediterranean world is a world of town-dwellers', as Collingwood forcefully stated. As the urban bias of Classical archaeology is now increasingly being redressed, and the awareness is growing that cities are not isolated features in an otherwise 'empty' landscape, studying rural landscapes has become a valuable means of understanding wider socio-economic organisation in Antiquity (Snodgrass 1987, 67–69; Barker and Lloyd 1991).

Roman landscapes, however, have been less overlooked, as some rural aspects have been studied intensively from a historical perspective. Because of the nature of available literary sources these studies have generally been rather one-sided: agrarian organisation, as part of the ancient economy, has constituted the main theme of the historical debate and other aspects of the rural landscape have been treated as secondary to it. A certain 'urban bias' has moreover affected these studies as well, as attention has been focused on the larger *villa* sites, and consequently no coherent notion of a continuous rural landscape has been developed. Concepts such as the 'consumer-city' have furthermore regarded the countryside as a secondary counterpart to the city.

The perspective I want to adopt in this paper is an archaeological one. An important reason for doing so is constituted by the increased prominence of Mediterranean survey archaeology and its achievements during the last decade. First of all, the regional approach of survey archaeology is of course particularly appropriate for studying rural landscapes. As such, it is well suited both to improve traditional archaeological practice and to complement historical research in a fruitful way (cf. Snodgrass 1987, 99–131). Secondly, intensive archaeological surveying has not only redirected archaeological attention to rural landscapes, but has also upset some traditional views: the substantial numbers of small sites that have been discovered everywhere have unequivocally refuted the notion of an 'empty' landscape (cf. Barker 1991a, 6–7). An approach based on archaeological survey, therefore, may be able to compensate somewhat for the rather elitist perspective inherent in most literary sources (cf. Hodges 1989, 179–186). The theme I intend to pursue regards rural organisation in general rather than agrarian organisation in a more narrowly defined sense; this paper accordingly deals not only with economic aspects of rural organisation but with its social dimension as well. Taking into account small-scale settlement and organisation, I particularly intend to focus on those features of rural organisation that 'have no history' but nevertheless represent an essential part of it.

A VILLA LANDSCAPE————

Roman landscapes are traditionally considered entirely in terms of villas. Such a view has largely been based on documentary sources dealing with agriculture from a landlord's point of view and discussing how to run large estates (cf. Garnsey 1979, 1–3). Historical research has consequently treated villas as dominating and determining Roman agrarian organisation.

In its wake, extensive topographical work has resulted in more or less 'empty' landscapes dominated by relatively large villa sites (cf. Leveau 1983, 921–933).

Similarly, Roman agrarian organisation is generally regarded as being both characterised and dominated by the so-called 'villa system': large villa-based estates using slave-labour to produce specialised crops and agricultural products such as olive oil or wine. The villa buildings, usually divided into residential and working parts, constituted the central and typical feature of the villa system (Carandini and Settis 1979, 46–49). Initially, this system was presented as being rather uniform over large parts of Italy although three variations were proposed. The first, an intensive villa system producing oil and wine, was thought to be typical of the coastal areas and large alluvial plains of western central Italy; the second system, an extensive pastoralist one practicing large scale transhumance, was found mostly in the mountainous regions of central Italy, Apulia and internal Sicily, and the third villa system, geared at the intensive production of cereals, was regarded as typical of Sicily (Carandini 1979, 198–199). All three types, however, are minor variants on an essentially uniform theme of large-scale slave-run estates and as such these have been contrasted with small-scale rural settlement (Carandini 1981, 252–253).

Increasing evidence from intensive surveying of small-scale farm sites is resulting in a much more differentiated perception and representation of rural landscapes. Small and medium-sized sites are often generically referred to as smallholders' farms and are usually assumed to represent small possessions of independent free-holders. Small-scale rural settlement has not only been found to precede the villa system, but has also turned out to have coexisted with it (cf. Potter 1979, 120–139; Celuzza and Regoli 1982, 37–41). Consequently, small-scale farms have often been incorporated in the villa system as a significant but secondary element: it has been suggested that free-holders supplied temporary labour at peak-times (e.g. harvest), thus allowing the villas to maintain a smaller slave workforce and to avoid surplus labour (Corbier 1981, 428–434). Alternative interpretations play down the dominance of the slave mode of production and propose a wide variety of non-slave labour coexisting with slave-run villas (cf. Garnsey 1980; Foxhall 1990). From such a point of view the relationships between smaller rural sites and villas can be highly variable and the interpretation of small-scale rural settlement itself becomes more problematic.

The coexistence of small farms and large estates cannot be negated and it is now widely recognised that the villa system has never been the most widespread type of agrarian organisation (cf. Pucci 1985, 17). Their relative importance remains to be defined. A recent detailed examination of archaeological evidence in Italy has contributed significantly to these ends (Vallat 1987) and has led to some important refinements of current generalisations: differences in agrarian organisation between various regions sometimes depended on geomorphological characteristics of the area; in other cases historical traditions of land use proved to have had their influence. Even in one region several different villa systems or types of agrarian exploitation might coexist and result in a far more complex agrarian organisation and rural landscape (ibid., 212–213). As a result, the presupposed dominance of the villa system or slave mode of production in Roman agrarian organisation must be rejected; small farms and large estates must no longer be regarded as two different types of agrarian organisation that might coexist and even be interdependent but yet remain distinct and separate. Instead, rural settlement should be treated as one continuous settlement system made up of several elements. Variations in – for example – land use, land quality or pre-existing settlement may have given rise to specific forms of rural organisation in particular areas. More-over, new ways of agrarian organisation, such as the villa system, may com-plement rather than replace older forms (ibid., 212).

ANALYSING ROMAN RURAL SETTLEMENT————

A means for examining rural settlement systems is provided by survey archaeology and regional analysis (cf. Lloyd 1991). Intensive surveying in the lower Biferno valley (Molise, southern Italy) has resulted in a complex rural settlement pattern, in which relatively large and probably slave-run estates are not lacking; these nevertheless are far less lavish than their cen-tral Italian counterparts (Lloyd and Barker 1981, 296–301). As small farms, hamlets and villages coexisted with Roman villas, the part played by the villa system must have been limited; the close association of villas with urban centres may suggest a certain importance of cash crops (Barker 1991b, 46–51). With regard to central Italy and Roman Etruria in particular, archaeological evidence has revealed equally complex settlement patterns even within one single region: the occurrence of villas is highly variable; they show considerable variability in size and other features and are more often than not accompanied by small-scale rural settlement (Vallat 1987, 182–199). While the mere coexistence of several types of agrarian organisation and consequently of different modes of production may be monitored quite closely by archaeological survey and now in fact seems to be beyond doubt (cf. ibid., 199 and 212–213), establishing interdependence or perhaps dominance of any mode of production requires closer study and more detailed analysis.

Previous attempts to deal with the interpretation of rural settlement usually have set out by classifying the raw field survey data. An important criterion adopted has been site size but the relevance of other features such as durable or expensive building materials and fine wares was also soon realised (cf. Celuzza and Regoli 1982, 56–57). The problem of identifying various types of rural settlement has been difficult to resolve; different classes of rural settlement have been proposed but the applicability of each classification seems to be limited to each specific situation (cf. Vallat 1989, 113–114). Perhaps the only useful categorisation is the string *villa, casa* and *tugurium* (corresponding to large, medium and small farms: Potter 1979, 122) but even this generic division has only relative significance in specific local contexts, as a comparison of the 'villas' in the Biferno valley with those in South Etruria shows. As any fixed relationship between morphological features of rural sites and their function seems problematic, if not improbable (cf. Slofstra 1983, 84), sites should be interpreted in relation to the *whole* of rural settlement in an area, using various criteria including not only building materials or associated ceramics, but also location (cf. Vallat 1989, 114–116).

Understanding rural settlement, therefore, should not be focused on any site in particular, whether a villa or a cottage, but should start analysing the functioning of an entire settlement system in a regional analysis (cf. Johnson 1977). An important criterion is *site size*, as this is related to 'functional size', i.e. the number of functions exerted by a certain site. A site possessing a large number of 'functions' is usually referred to as a central place and the larger a site is, the more central it is supposed to have been (Johnson 1977, 495). The implication is that most sites are dependent on such places for one or more 'functions' in the form of services or items; the relationships between settlements might therefore be described in terms of 'dependency' and 'independency'. By ranking all sites according to site size, such relationships can be represented graphically. A second basic criterion is *site location*. The significance of this reveals itself when both criteria are applied jointly by classifying the mapped sites after the rank size graph. Although such a classification remains essentially arbitrary, the combination of both features allows the identification of some basic characteristics of the settlement system (Fig. 27).

Rural exploitation systems might similarly be distinguished, since perhaps one of the most distinctive features of the slave-based villa system is the virtual absence of any rural settlement in a considerable territory surrounding the villa site. That area is assumed to have been worked by slaves housed in the central villa (Celuzza and Regoli 1985, 51–53; cf. Carandini 1988, 121–129). This phenomenon is interpreted as 'a drastic alienation of the producers from the means of production (land)' (Carandini 1981, 250; cf. Carandini 1979, 151). A situation where, on the contrary, most of the area is occupied by numerous small sites may be interpreted as one in which the productive means are not alienated from the producers. If a surplus value is somehow extracted, this is usually achieved through imbalanced exchange between the producers and a non-producing elite: control of some critical resource – not necessarily land but possibly commodities such as imported objects or salt – enables the elite to obtain the producers' surplus in exchange for access to that scarce asset (cf. Amin 1983). The elite thus ensures their privileged economic position by control of exchange and distribution rather than production (Smith 1976, 311–312). These make up distribution networks that, in the Roman case, are organised through primitive or peasant markets that are generally associated with central places. Typically, such central places are closely related with the rural elite (ibid., 313–321; cf. Hodges 1988, 127–131). The functioning of rural settlement, therefore, may be understood in terms of these distribution networks; the latter, furthermore, exhibit spatial characteristics that have been crudely summarised in a number of descriptive models (see Smith 1976, 333–338). An analysis, therefore, of a region's settlement system and distribution networks may lead to a broad outline of regional economic organisation and overall socio-economic structures, in which these networks are firmly embedded.

PEASANT CULTIVATION AND ROMAN RURAL ORGANISATION———————

Taking the term 'rural organisation' as a reference to the socio-economic dimension of the Roman countryside, the anthropological concept of 'peasantry' seems to be particularly applicable: since Roman society was a complex state society with clear-cut social strata or 'classes', the vast majority of the rural population lived and worked in a position of economic and political subordination that neatly fits Eric Wolf's principal criteria of dependency and integration (1966, 11):

Thus, it is only when a cultivator is integrated into a society with a state – that is, when the cultivator becomes subject to the demands and sanctions of power-holders outside his social stratum – that we can appropriately speak of peasantry.

Peasantry as a concept is remarkably difficult to define, but as a first approximation peasants might be described as (Shanin 1987, 3):

> small agricultural producers, who, with the help of simple equipment and the labour of their families, produce mostly for their own consumption, direct or indirect, and for the fulfilment of obligations to the holders of political and economic power.

Although this definition admittedly covers only part of peasant variability and heterogeneity, it does stress the fundamental interwovenness of peasant economic and social organisation (cf. Shanin 1987, 3–4): particularly in agrarian, non-industrial economies social rather than purely economic motives play a significant, if not decisive part in agrarian decision making. With regard to the Roman agrarian economy, the relevance of a 'peasant economic' rationality has recently been argued for, as opposed to the primitivist point of view denying any economic rationality in agrarian production and the 'bi-sectorial' perspective combining an 'irrational' subsistence sector with capitalist-like, maximising principles (Foxhall 1990, 98–104).

From this point of view, a fundamental theme regards the relationships between two basic social groups: how did peasants relate to landlords and vice-versa? This relationship essentially has been one of economic exploitation of peasants by a landlord in which peasants could occupy several different positions, ranging from owner-occupants, tenants, share-croppers to slaves[1] (Garnsey 1980, 36–41). The efficiency of the various exploitation systems has been much discussed and from a purely economic point of view each system has its own advantages, albeit mainly for the landlord. Nevertheless, comparative evidence tends to favour tenancy and share-cropping, as, at least in non-industrial economies, large possessions can be exploited most efficiently in small units (Martínez-Alier 1983). The main differences are non-economic and consist of social or legal obligations of peasants or landlords. Again, tenancy and share-cropping offer most advantages to both peasants and landlords as such relationships must often have coincided with debt-bondage or patronage (Foxhall 1990, 101–104 and 111–112); given the extensive patronage networks existing in Roman society, a close correlation of such relationships with economic ones seems very likely (cf. Slofstra 1983, 89–95). Nevertheless, exploitative systems obviously have coexisted, resulting in complex, varied and often fluid relationships (cf. Pitt-Rivers 1971, 36–46). In this way peasant cultivators and landlords presumably have often been linked into a single system of both economic and social interdependence.

In the archaeological record economic aspects of regional rural organisation can be examined in rural settlement systems and distribution networks as described above.[2] Such an analysis, however, only regards the more generic, overall trends within a region; it may point to some relationship of dependency between certain areas or even sites, but it cannot 'identify' this particular relationship as a share-cropping agreement and that one as a case of slavery. This difficulty to interpret any *specific* relationship between sites largely arises from the fact that most of the variability of exploitative relationships is social in nature. Therefore, other features in the archaeological record must be taken into consideration as well: besides site size and location, the range and combinations of objects found at a site are particularly relevant in this respect. Thus it may be possible to argue for a more detailed interpretation of specific relationships between rural sites or areas: for example the contrast of high-quality masonry and agricultural equipment with poor, coarse pottery found in some small farm sites as well as their remote location have been proposed as arguments to identify these sites as habitations of share-croppers (Foxhall 1990, 109–111).

PEASANTS AND LANDLORDS IN ROMAN NORTHERN ETRURIA

A small coastal plain in northern Etruria (Figs 27–29), in the region nowadays referred to as the *Maremma toscana*, has provided the setting for studying a Roman rural landscape. Naturally defined by the watersheds of the lower river Pecora – sometimes quite steep hills heavily wooded with *macchia* – the area is well suited to examine regional and local peasant-landlord relationships. As the steep and high hills south of the plain extend westward into the sea to form a small promontory and thus effectively block all easy access from the south, the coastal plain can be reached most easily either from the north where the hills are separated from the sea by a narrow strip of dunes and lowland or from the east along the upstream Pecora. To the west, the coastal plain originally was delimited by a now drained lagoon, the extent of which in Roman times is known only approximately.

In the years 1980–82 an archaeological survey was carried out in the lower Pecora catchment as part of the Scarlino archaeological project of the University of Siena (Cucini 1985, 147–150). The survey was concen-

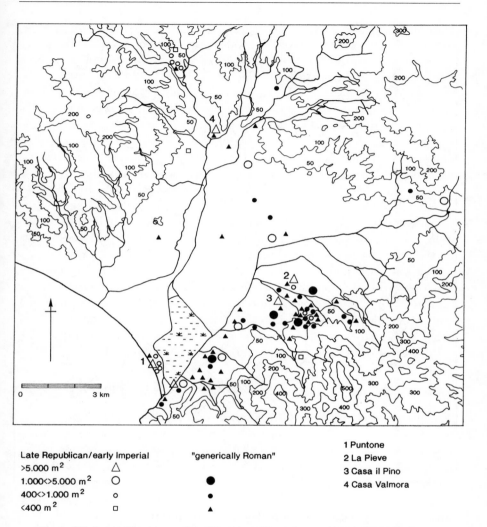

Late Republican/early Imperial   "generically Roman"

>5.000 m² △
1.000<>5.000 m² O   ●
400<>1.000 m² o   •
<400 m² □   ▲

1 Puntone
2 La Pieve
3 Casa il Pino
4 Casa Valmora

Figure 27. Lower Pecora, northern Etruria, Italy survey area: sites mapped by size (after van Dommelen, drawn by Sandra Hooper).

trated on the coastal plain, part of which was surveyed intensively, while other samples were surveyed more extensively; the intensively surveyed area, referred to as the *Scarlino area*, roughly coincides with the southern foot-hills and is more or less naturally bounded by the lagoon shore and the southern hills (Fig. 28, number 1). As far as the earlier Roman period is

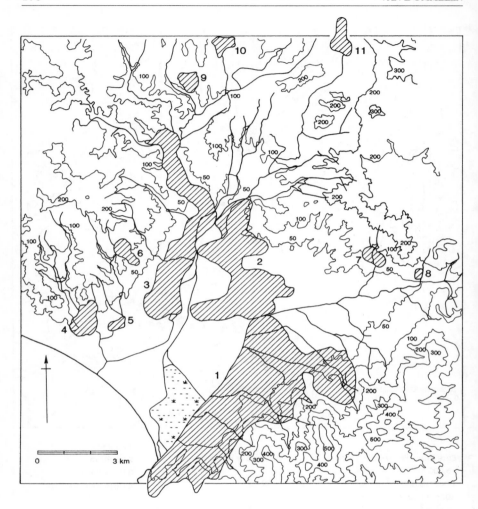

*Figure 28. Lower Pecora, northern Etruria, Italy
(after van Dommelen, drawn by Sandra Hooper).*

concerned, the Scarlino survey has registered 113 sites in the coastal plain of the Pecora valley; of these, 27 sites have been dated in the Republican phase (more or less 3rd-2nd century BC) and 26 in the late Republican/early Imperial phase (more or less 1st century BC – 1st century AD), while the remaining 60 sites could be assigned only generically to the Roman period.[3] Far from being useless, these 'generically Roman' sites

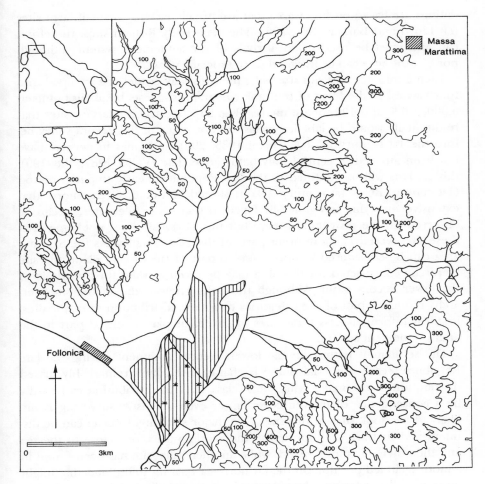

Figure 29. Lower Pecora, northern Etruria, Italy
(after van Dommelen, drawn by Sandra Hooper).

represent a significant feature of the valley's settlement system, as the rank size graph shows (Fig. 27): while the sites dated to either of the phases represent more or less the same but incomplete part of the rank size distributions, the category of generically Roman sites roughly supplements their missing lower parts. These sites, therefore, effectively represent the lower part of the settlement hierarchy, the 'small-scale rural settlement'. The difficulty of dating these sites more precisely is a reflection of this, as such datings are based on fine wares that are usually lacking in small farm sites (cf. Lloyd and Barker 1981, 296). The generically Roman sites, therefore, can and must be used in an analysis of the settlement system, although none of the sites can be assigned to any specific phase.

Taking into account site size only, the sites may crudely be grouped into four classes, as the form of the rank size-graph suggests breaking points at 5,000, 1,000 and 400 square metres (Fig. 27). Because the largest sites that traditionally would be labelled 'villas' do not occur in the Pecora valley before the 1st century BC (cf. Cucini 1985, 290), and villas in general have not been attested in central Italy before that date (Vallat 1987, 198–199), this analysis will be confined to the late Republican/early Imperial period (1st century BC – 1st century AD). It should be noted, furthermore, that extensive surveying has generally failed to register smaller sites, as can be observed on the distribution map; but this obviously does not imply that these sites were lacking in other parts of the Pecora valley. As the Scarlino area can be considered a representative part of the coastal plain, the site hierarchy constructed for this area may be taken as valid for the whole of the lower Pecora basin. Although the lacking lower end of the site hierarchy reduces a plot of site categories to a mere distribution of major sites, it still is informative, as these sites in particular play a central part in the area's settlement system.

The settlement pattern in the lower Pecora catchment during the late Republican/early Imperial phase is characterised by a remarkably biased distribution of the major 'villa' sites (class 1). This distribution can hardly be a consequence of uneven covering, as even extensive surveying is unlikely to overlook sites of this size. Two major settlement nuclei can be distinguished that are both located in the Scarlino area, one close to the sea and the other one more inland, while another 'villa' site has been found in a more secluded position on the far north-eastern foothills. Sites that might be termed 'large farms' (class 2) have been found all over the coastal plain and are generally situated at some distance from the larger sites. Only one of these can be associated with a 'villa' site. Four out of the ten 'large farm' sites, however, cannot be assigned to the late Republican/early Imperial phase with certainty nor can the possibility be excluded that some of these sites have been missed by the extensive survey. The remainder of small sites have mainly been found in the Scarlino area for the reason mentioned; they usually seem to be associated with larger sites.

The settlement cluster on the coast near modern Puntone consists of two 'villa' sites that must have been separated from each other by the lagoon outlet. The southern site is accompanied by a 'large farm' as well as by several medium-sized and small sites. The northern one, on the contrary, is closely related to extensive metallurgical activities: huge slag heaps as well as the remains of at least one furnace, all positively dated in the late Republican/early Imperial phase, illustrate the enormous quantities of iron ore that were transported from the island of Elba and smelted near Puntone. This settlement cluster must have been situated on the ancient *Via Aurelia*, a major Roman through way along the Italian west coast, and is usually interpreted as a *statio* or road station, probably the one named *Manliana*. The *Via Aurelia* must have continued its way northward either around the lagoon or, after crossing the lagoon outlet at Puntone, over the dunes of the coastal barrier (Cucini 1985, 298–300). More inland, where circumstances are most favourable for agriculture, a 'villa' site has been located at La Pieve. This site is by far the largest in the Pecora valley, having more than twice the size of other 'villa' sites. A more modest but still significant 'villa' site has been found at nearby Casa il Pino and in the immediate surroundings several smaller sites have been located. At a short distance to the south a number of medium-sized and small sites have been found to cluster on the lower hill slopes. The 'villa' site at Casa Valmora is the only one outside the Scarlino area; it may very well be accompanied by several smaller sites but presently only one has been found. The location in the north-eastern corner of the coastal plain is a strategic one, as both the northern foothills and the upper Pecora valley are dominated by this large site.

INTERPRETING A ROMAN RURAL LANDSCAPE

Late Republican/early Imperial settlement in the lower Pecora valley can be interpreted from a regional point of view in terms of central places and distribution networks (cf. Lloyd 1991, 233–236; Gualtieri and de Polignac 1991). Four central places can thus be distinguished in the study area but each with slightly different characteristics: given its location at the Via Aurelia and the likely presence of a port, as well as the metallurgical activities, the *statio* at Puntone undoubtedly represents a major first-order central place with substantial external contacts. The large villa at La Pieve must have been an equally important central place of significance to the whole of the lower Pecora basin. Although agriculture presumably had a considerable share in the villa's economy, it seems likely that most of the local agrarian activities were administered through the villa at Casa il Pino. This must have functioned as a second-order central place for most of the fertile south-eastern area. The villa at Casa Valmora similarly must have been a local central place for the upper Pecora valley and perhaps part of the northern coastal plain, although it may have been less directly subordinate to the villa at La Pieve.

In terms of economic organisation, the lower Pecora valley in late Republican and early Imperial times was operated by a so-called 'dendritic' central place at Puntone (cf. Smith 1976, 338–345), whereas internal distribution in the valley was administered by a 'solar' central place at La Pieve (cf. ibid., 345–352). Both Casa il Pino and Casa Valmora presumably were subordinate local central places. All four must have represented focal points of both economic and socio-political organisation in the lower Pecora basin where peasant surpluses were – usually unevenly – exchanged for access to land or other assets. Such exchange could take the form of either direct payment of rent or indirect contribution through a controlled periodic market (ibid., 333–338). These acts simultaneously reconfirmed and thus reproduced the peasants' subordination to the elite; these in turn stressed their dominating role at the central places and in the entire valley by ostentious display of wealth.

The proximity of a first and second-order central place in a small, relatively secluded part of the valley suggests an uneven economic development of the entire lower Pecora area. In the southern part of the coastal plain, roughly coinciding with the Scarlino area, a rigid site hierarchy developed, indicating an increasingly vertical structuring of socio-economic relations that cannot be parallelled elsewhere in the Pecora valley. Although agriculture was practised in the entire basin, the southern part seems to have benefited most. Non-agrarian economic activities on the other hand, such as metallurgy or exchange, all seem to have been limited to the Scarlino area where nearly all indications found are concentrated. Signs of wealth such as marble fragments, mosaic *tesserae* or remains of baths are also practically limited to this area, while elsewhere only modest farms have been found. The southern part of the coastal plain must have occupied an exceptional position in the lower Pecora basin. Both the uneven distribution of wealth and the regional division of labour suggest that the south of the valley was linked to the surrounding areas in the basin by a local centre-periphery relationship (Rowlands 1987, 4–5).

Although the presence of villas in the lower Pecora catchment is evident, the existence of a slave-based villa exploitation system needs more and better arguments. In this particular case, a predominantly slave-based agrarian and economic organisation seems doubtful for several reasons. Firstly, numerous medium-sized and small sites were scattered all over the Pecora valley, resulting in a densely settled landscape of which the villas represented just one aspect; the small farms must have had their own separate agricultural production. It is also significant that the villas had not *replaced* earlier dispersed settlement but seem to represent an intrusive element in the local economy (see Fig. 27; cf. Cambi and Fentress 1989, 81). Not all the villas fit the model of a mainly agricultural settlement either; as the above analysis indicates, distribution and exchange must have constituted important activities of these villas: those at Puntone in particular seem to have had little in common with a 'typical' slave-run villa (cf. Carandini 1988, 19–108). Slaves nevertheless must have played some part in these villas and the Pecora valley as a whole: the metallurgical activities in particular are likely to have been dependent on slave labour. At the villas too, slaves undoubtedly were used for agricultural and related ends; this practice, however, must have remained limited to the estates proper, since slavery never seems to have become so important or dominant as to influence the valley's agrarian economic organisation significantly (cf. Cucini 1985, 297). Therefore, instead of the means of production being alienated (cf. above), it must rather have been a surplus that was extracted from a free but dependent peasantry. The valley's settlement system suggests this was achieved both directly and indirectly, with the villas in some cases functioning as a (periodic) market-place and in others as a landlord's estate with dependent tenants. In either case, peasants must have been farming primarily for subsistence.

The above regional analysis has resulted in a 'macro-economic' review that merely indicates more general dependencies. Taking this analysis as a point of departure, the rather processualist representation of the valley's socio-economic organisation can be refined, if particular cases are examined in their specific contexts. One such a specific case is constituted by the settlement at Puntone, where the villas have been suggested to represent a peculiar case.

Interpreting the settlement cluster at Puntone as a first-order central place and a centre of metallurgical production that was agriculturally non-productive has several implications for the smaller sites near the villas. It should be noted that the immediate vicinity does not permit agriculture at any scale. The smaller sites that may be associated with Puntone all cluster in the southern end of the southern foothills, where the nearest good agricultural soils are found. These are likely to have satisfied the settlement's agricultural needs, since its inhabitants – not only the villa-elite but the labourers and slaves as well – must have been dependent on agrarian production elsewhere. It seems improbable that these small farms were inhabited by slaves, as the attention of the villa-elite was focused on other activities; these farms should therefore be interpreted as peasant farms. The archaeological remains of these farm sites are invariably poor, consisting of fragments of amphorae, coarse wares and usually roof tiles; they are most of all in sharp contrast with the lavish *pars urbana* of the two villas. The exact nature of this dependent relationship is of course difficult to establish, but the relatively large number of sites in a limited area suggests one of share-cropping, as this is the most common and effective exploitation system in such a situation (Martínez-Alier 1983). The presence of a slightly larger farm may also be significant as a collective processing place (Gill 1983, 146–148). The combination of roof tiles and coarse ceramics might also point at a share-cropping arrangement with the landlord providing the house (cf. Foxhall 1990, 109–111). The proximity of a population concentration at Puntone might even have encouraged cash-cropping on the smaller plots of land (Wolf 1966, 36; Foxhall 1990, 105–106). Share-cropping arrangements would be the best way of providing the settlement with a constant production, without the necessity of close supervision. Although share-cropping arrangements usually are complex and variable, they are likely to have been complicated even more by day labourers who are hard to trace archaeologically.

Small rural sites largely similar to the ones just discussed have been found in the northern half of the coastal plain; if their relatively remote location is taken into consideration, however, a slightly different situation seems to emerge. Archaeologically, these smaller sites are also different from the ones near Puntone because roof tiles are generally lacking: these sites should therefore represent even poorer farms. As the area closer to the river was best suited for grazing, animal husbandry presumably was more important at these farms. Agriculture could be practised on the alluvial fans immediately to the north. The area north of the river Pecora where these sites are located is relatively distant from any of the central places and direct exploitation of these farms from there seems somewhat implausible. The relationships between these small farms and presumably the large estate at La Pieve may therefore have consisted of tenancy arrangements, with rents paid in produce for example (cf. Pitt-Rivers 1971, 44–45). The peasants can also have been owner-occupants who were somehow tied to the large estates: such ties may be socio-political or commercial, the estate functioning as a periodic market (Wolf 1966, 49–59). In both cases, however, peasants were subsistence farmers dependent on a land-lord. Although ownership may guarantee some form of *economic* independence, this often can be annulled by relationships of *social* dependence, such as patronage or debt-bondage (ibid., 86–87). The effective difference between ownership and tenancy can thus be reduced, since tenancy offers certain advantages to peasants in marginal situations: a combined tenancy-patronage relationship guarantees both a fixed price and a protector (Foxhall 1990, 111–112). Such arguments probably apply to the northern half of the Pecora basin that has been argued to be peripheral to the southern part. The scanty archaeological evidence of these farms fits this interpretation also quite well, since peasants were responsible themselves for housing and agricultural equipment, although complicated arrangements of cooperation often exist (Wolf 1966, 85–86).

Yet another case of small rural sites has been found upstream the river Pecora at Campo Ruffaldino. Where the river valley narrows, five small farms are clustered closely together on a river terrace. In the valley itself farming is possible on a limited scale, and the surroundings hills allow growing olives and vines. Shepherding must also have been a profitable activity of the farms' inhabitants. These farms differ from the previous ones because of the relatively rich finds: at each site several fragments of fine wares – *sigillata italica* – and amphorae have been found as well as roof tiles. An interpretation as a small nucleated village or hamlet seems plausible; such hamlets are usually referred to as a *vicus* (cf. Garnsey 1979, 6). The relative well-being of these peasants and their outlying residence suggest a certain degree of independence: they most likely owned the small plots of land along the Pecora that they farmed essentially for subsistence. Their autonomy, however, must have been limited by the villa at Casa Valmora as the local periodic market place on which these peasants were reliant.

Conclusion: Rural Organisation without History

The specific cases just discussed constitute an illustration of the points made earlier in this paper, since the variability and, most of all, the complexity of small-scale rural settlement in the lower Pecora valley are obvious. With regard to the villa discussion, these examples confirm the conclusions reached by Vallat in his review of Italian rural organisation: villas are highly complex and variable (Vallat 1987). In the case of the Pecora valley, the principal archaeological similarity between the 'villa' sites is the presence of a *pars urbana*: in all cases the inhabitants' wealth was openly displayed, while the way in which this prosperity was achieved may have varied considerably. The Pecora case study furthermore offers a good illustration of the interdependence of villas and small-scale settlement: these relationships have been distinguished not only at a local level (e.g. at Puntone) but regionally as well. Whereas the part played by a villa in an agrarian economy can largely be studied by analysing regional archaeological distributions, understanding agrarian organisation in all its dimensions requires a more detailed examination: from a processualist point of view, small-scale rural settlement may seem to fulfil similar functions, but a consideration of specific contexts results in a more detailed and varied representation. The adoption of such a perspective in Roman studies may focus attention on the peasantry that has turned out to constitute an integral and essential feature of rural landscapes. The examples from the Pecora valley demonstrate that Roman rural organisation cannot be well understood if the peasantry is not considered (cf. Hodges 1989, 180). An approach to rural landscapes that appreciates the part played by the peasantry must be an archaeological one of necessity; it will, however, rarely be a definitive one. Even this limited case study has already demonstrated that no easy criteria can be formulated for distinguishing various kinds of small-scale rural settlement, since most variability in agrarian organisation is of a socio-economic nature and often archaeologically difficult to trace; alternative explanations may be possible. But such a discussion already represents a contribution towards constructing the peasantry's part in Roman history.

Acknowledgements. I would like to thank Dr Pieter van de Velde for his helpful comments on an earlier draft of this paper.

Notes

1. For the vague and often fluid distinction between slaves and free but otherwise dependent tenants or share-croppers (see Garnsey 1980, 34).
2. This holds in particular for regions with dispersed rural settlement as in the following case study; in case of more nucleated settlement – e.g. agro-towns – more attention should be paid to intra-site patterns within these sites.
3. All data concerning sites and the Scarlino survey in general are based on the survey publication (Cucini 1985).

Bibliography

Amin, S. 1983 'Economic and cultural dependence' in T. Asad and R. Owen (eds), 54–60.

Asad, T. and R. Owen (eds), 1983 *Sociology of 'Developing Countries'*: *the Middle East*. London.

Barker, G. 1991a 'Approaches to archaeological survey' in G. Barker and J. Lloyd (eds), 1–9.

Barker, G. 1991b 'Two Italys, one valley: an *annaliste* perspective' in J. Bintliff (ed.), 34–56.

Barker, G. and R. Hodges (eds) 1981 *Archaeology and Roman Society*. Oxford; British Archaeological Reports (International Series 102).

Barker, G. and J. Lloyd (eds) 1991 *Roman landscapes. Archaeological survey in the Mediterranean region*. London.

Bintliff, J. (ed.) 1991 *The Annales School and Archaeology*. Leicester.

Brandt, R. and J. Slofstra (eds) 1983 *Roman and Native in the Low Countries*. Oxford; British Archaeological Reports (International Series 184).

Cambi, F. and E. Fentress 1989 'Villas to castles: first millennium A.D. demography in the Albegna Valley' in K. Randsborg (ed.), 74–86.

Carandini, A. 1979 *L'anatomia della scimmia*. Rome.

Carandini, A. 1981 'Svilupp e crisi delle manifatture rurali e urbane' in A. Giardina and A. Schiavone (eds) stet., 249–260.

Carandini, A. 1988 *Schiavi in Italia*. Rome.

Carandini, A. and A. Ricci (eds) 1985 *Settefinestre. Una villa schiavista nell'Etruria romana*. Vol I. Modena.

Carandini, A. and S. Settis 1979 *Schiavi e padroni nell'Etruria romana*. Bari.

Celuzza, M. and E. Regoli 1982 'La valle d'Oro nel territorio di Cosa; Ager Cosanus e Ager Veientanus a confronto' *Dialoghi di Archeologi* 4, 31–62.

Celuzza, M. and E. Regoli 1985 'Gli insediamenti della Valle d'Oro e il fondo di Settefinestre' in A. Carandini and A. Ricci (eds), 50–61.

Corbier, M. 1981 'Proprietà e gestione della terra: grande proprietà fondiaria ed economia contadina' in A. Giardina and A. Schiavone (eds) 1981a, 427–444.

Cucini, C. 1985 'Topografia del territorio delle valli del Pecora e dell'Alma' in R. Francovich (ed.), 147–335.

Foxhall, L. 1990 'The dependent tenant: land leasing and labour in Italy and Greece' *Journal of Roman Studies* 80, 97–114.

Francovitch, R. (ed.) 1985 *Scarlino I, storia e territorio*. Florence.

Garnsey, P. 1979 'Where did Italian peasants live?' *Proceedings of the Cambridge Philological Society* 205, 1–25.

Garnsey, P. (ed.) 1980 *Non-Slave Labour in the Greco-Roman World*. Cambridge Philological Society Supplementary Volume 6. Cambridge.

Garnsey, P. 1980 'Non-slave labour in the Greco-Roman world' in P. Garnsey (ed.), 34–47.

Giardina, A. and A. Schiavone (eds) 1981a *L'Italia: insediamenti e forme economiche*. Societa romana e produzeione schiavista vol 1 Rome.

Giardina, A. and A. Schiavone (eds) 1981b *Merci, mercate e scambi nel Mediterraneo*. Societa romana e produzeione schiavista vol 2 Rome.

Gualtieri, M. and F. de Polignac 1991 'A rural landscape in western Lucania' in G. Barker and J. Lloyd (eds), 194–203.

Hodges, R. 1988 *Primitive and Peasant Markets*. Oxford.

Hodges, R. 1989 'Archaeology and the class struggle in the first millennium AD' in K. Randsborg (ed.), 62–73.

Johnson, G. 1977 'Aspects of regional analysis in archaeology' *Annual Review of Anthropolgy* 6, 479–508.

Leveau, P. 1983 'La ville antique et l'organisation de l'espace rurale: villa, ville, village' *Annales ESC* 38 (4), 920–942.

Lloyd, J. 1991 'Forms of rural settlement in the early Roman empire' in G. Barker and J. Lloyd (eds), 233–240.

Lloyd, J. and G. Barker 1981 'Rural settlement in Roman Molise: problems of archaeological survey' in G. Barker and R. Hodges (eds), 289–304.

Martínez-Alier, J. 1983 'Sharecropping: some illustrations' *Journal of Peasant Studies* 10 (2–3), 94–106.

Pailler, J.-M. (ed.) 1989 *Actualité de l'antiquité*. Toulouse.

Pitt-Rivers, J. 1971 *The People of the Sierra* (2nd edition). Chicago.

Potter, T. 1979 *The Changing Landscape of South Etruria*. London.

Pucci, G. 1985 'Schiavitù romana nelle campagne' in A. Carandini and A. Ricci (eds) vol I, 15–21.

Randsborg, K. (ed.) 1989 *The Birth of Europe. Archaeology and Social Development in the First Millennium AD* Analecta Romana Instituti Danici, Supplementum 16. Rome.

Rowlands, M. 1987 'Centre and periphery. A review of a concept' in M. Rowlands, M. Larsen and K. Kristiansen (eds), 1–11.

Rowlands, M. , M. Larsen and K. Kristiansen (eds) 1987 *Centre and Periphery in the Ancient World*. Cambridge.

Shanin, T. 1987 'Introduction: peasantry as a concept' in T. Shanin (ed.), 1–11.

Shanin, T. (ed.) 1987 *Peasants and Peasant Societies* (2nd edition). Oxford.

Slofstra, J. 1983 'An anthropological approach to the study of Romanisation processes' in R. Brandt and J. Slofstra (eds), 71–104.

Smith, C. 1976 'Exchange systems and the spatial distribution of elites: the organisation of agrarian societies' in C. Smith (ed.), 309–74.

Smith, C. (ed.) 1976 *Regional Analysis* vol II New York.

Snodgrass, A. 1987 *An Archaeology of Greece*. Berkeley.

Vallat, J.-P. 1987 'Les structures agraires de l'Italie ré publicaine' *Annales ESC* 42 (1), 181–218.

Vallat, J.-P. 1989 'De la prospection à la synthèse d'histoire rurale' in J.-M. Pailler (ed.), 101–127.

Wolf, E. 1966 *Peasants*. Englewood Cliffs.